The Politics of Age

AF794005

Jørn Henrik Petersen
Klaus Petersen
(eds.)

The Politics of Age

Basic Pension Systems in a Comparative and Historical Perspective

PETER LANG
Frankfurt am Main · Berlin · Bern · Bruxelles · New York · Oxford · Wien

Bibliographic Information published by the Deutsche Nationalbibliothek
The Deutsche Nationalbibliothek lists this publication in the Deutsche Nationalbibliografie; detailed bibliographic data is available in the internet at <http://www.d-nb.de>.

Gratefully acknowledging the financial support of The Ministry of Social Welfare, Denmark.

Cover design:
Atelier Platen, Friedberg.

ISBN 978-3-631-58191-9

© Peter Lang GmbH
Internationaler Verlag der Wissenschaften
Frankfurt am Main 2009
All rights reserved.

All parts of this publication are protected by copyright. Any utilisation outside the strict limits of the copyright law, without the permission of the publisher, is forbidden and liable to prosecution. This applies in particular to reproductions, translations, microfilming, and storage and processing in electronic retrieval systems.

www.peterlang.de

Preface

On 1 April 2007, 50 years had passed since the Danish People's Pension saw the light of day. To commemorate the occasion, the Centre for Welfare State Research at the University of Southern Denmark, in collaboration with the Ministry of Social Welfare (then the Ministry of Social Affairs), organised an international conference with the title: 'Institutions, Knowledge and Change – the Danish Pension System in International Comparison'.

The conference was held on 2-4 April 2007 at the University of Southern Denmark, with the participation of Danish and international pensions experts from the universities, representatives from the central administration and from the pensions branch. A selection of the contributions then presented has subsequently been adapted to furnish material for this book.

We would like to thank those taking part in the conference for their willingness to discuss and for their comments – not least those who, in one way or another, played an active role: Associate Professor Karen M. Andersson (University of Nijmegen), Professor Robin Blackburn (University of Essex and New School University), Dr. Niels Finn Christiansen (University of Copenhagen), Professor Christopher Green-Pedersen (University of Århus), Associate Professor Michael Baggesen Klitgaard (University of Southern Denmark), Professor Stein Kuhnle (Hertie School of Governance, Berlin), Professor Niels Kærgaard (University of Copenhagen), Professor Asbjørn Sonne Nørgaard (University of Southern Denmark), Research Director Niels Ploug (SFI, The Danish National Centre for Social Research), Associate Professor Caroline de la Porte (University of Southern Denmark) and Professor Else Øyen (University of Bergen).

Our thanks also to Heidi Vad Jønsson and John Irons for their contribution in the editing and linguistic improvement of the publication.

A special word of thanks goes to the then minister of social affairs, Eva Kjær Hansen, who participated in a festive opening of the conference.

Last but not least, our grateful thanks to the Ministry of Social Welfare and the research programme 'Reforms of the Welfare State' (Department of Political

Science, University of Southern Denmark) which, by their financial support, made the conference and this publication possible.

Centre for Welfare State Research,
University of Southern Denmark
June 2008

Jørn Henrik Petersen & Klaus Petersen

Table of contents

Introduction

Jørn Henrik Petersen & Klaus Petersen

Forty years after '1968' the fat's in the fire again. Back then in the late 1960s, a generation of young people attacked the established society, the ruling structures and the prevailing norms. Today, the established systems and the political and administrative rulers are once more under pressure, but this time it has nothing to do with reforming the universities, Marxist slogans or free love, but with security in old age. The pension systems established since the beginning of the 20th century are being restructured – and this does not always take place without some furore.

Since the early 1990s, the streets of European cities have occasionally been characterised by protests from angry and dissatisfied present-day and future pensioners. While the youth revolution of the 1960s only involved a small, albeit vociferous section of a generation, the pensioners' protests have a far broader social base: For the vast majority of citizens, no matter what country they live in and what pension model they therefore 'live under', publicly controlled pensions play an important role for their livelihood in old age. So it is not surprising that protests regarding changes, adaptations and cuts to the public pension system have proved to be political dynamite.

This is most evident in such countries as Italy and France, where the protests have been extremely intense, and where the reform capacity of the governments has shown itself to be relatively limited. Protests about planned pension reforms have repeatedly paralysed large sections of French society since the early 1990s, for example. In Central Europe, discussions about pension reforms have contributed to changes of government in both Germany and Austria. In the former socialist states of Eastern Europe, pension reforms have been part of the movement towards a market economy and membership of the EU. In the traditional top-of-the-class countries, such as market-based Great Britain, Sweden with its 1994 pensions reform as the ideal for 'care on time' and Denmark, which is emphasised as an ideal with its 'multi-pillared' pensions model, pension reforms have been politically 'cost-intensive'. Even such political action men as Arnold Schwarzenegger in California and Vladimir Putin in Russia have had to struggle with protests against pension reforms.

Politicians are seldom keen on implementing controversial or disagreeable reforms – and pension reforms are definitely among the most dangerous of that category. They affect large sections of the public budgets, interfere with the life situation of many people in both the short and the long term, and many strong political and economic interests are linked to the pension systems.

So even if such international institutions and think tanks as OECD, the World Bank and the EU have been virtually falling over each other in pointing out the necessity of reforms – and even if the problems linked to the declining birth rate, early retirement and fiscal sustainability have, at least to some extent, been and still are predictable – the concept of the 'pension bombshell' has not only referred to the increasing financial pressure on the pension system but also been a warning as to the possible political fall-out in implementing a reform.

That pensions are a highly politicised and controversial subject will be evident from the contributions in this book. However, the contemporary challenges can only be understood when also including a more historical perspective of how these systems were established and reformed. Whereas the most recent publications on pension systems deal exclusively with recent and contemporary challenges, this book offers a more detailed account of the historical development underlying the contemporary situation. Two important insights are achieved by this approach: Firstly, that there is a close connection between the historical development of the pension systems and the way in which they have actually been challenged by economic, demographic and politico-ideological changes. Secondly, that the often highly stereotype understanding of the individual pension systems in comparative welfare research becomes much more complex on a closer historical analysis. This raises new questions about equalities and differences. History matters – also when it comes to pensions policy.

History matters

Pension systems do not come from nowhere or completely at random. At a given point in time, the political, legal, economic, socio-structural and socio-cultural relations provide a framework which – combined with the international context, the views and ideas of prominent players and experts, the influence of organisations, etc. – determines the challenges facing the politicians. But no matter how the framework conditions are structured, they must be mediated by a political process: Policy matters! At the same time, there is a link between the opportunities that exist at a particular point in time and the decisions that politicians have previously taken: History matters!

Sometimes external relations change, so that they are almost an imperative to political actions (cf. for example the discussion on Ageing Europe and the need for pension reforms), but it is still the politicians who have to 'translate the imperative' into institutional changes. The understanding or 'translation' of the politicians is what determines the political actions. At other times, external relations can mean that even the political system is changed. This was the case, for example, when industrialisation meant the emergence of a working class as a recruitment base for supporting social democratic policies. And this was crucial in the establishment of the national pension systems around 1900. And at yet other times, the possibilities that exist for politicians can be limited by the external conditions. No matter which of these applies, politics and politicians play a decisive role.

If new institutions are introduced, or if changes are undertaken in existing institutions, this simultaneously influences the population's perception of society and may lead to a change in the population's behaviour and norms, including their view of the legitimacy of the institutions. This then reflects on politics, since it involve changes in political behaviour – and this in itself means that the political scope changes. So all this is a dynamic process of interaction that links decisions in the present to future potential for political action. This applies not least to the pension systems, which by their very nature involve decisions with a very long time-horizon – both backwards and forwards.

At the same time, there is a dynamic interaction that creates a link between present-day decisions and those that have been taken in the past. Analyses of processes of change show that we are often dealing with a considerable paradigmatic continuity – so-called path dependency. An institution of a particular type, once developed – e.g. a pension system – places restrictions on what future decision-makers can implement. The chosen institution becomes locked-in, because the force inherent in and underlying a decision once taken makes the implementation of other possibilities less likely in the future. Research has demonstrated this, not least when it comes to pension systems.[1] A pension system has a long time-horizon and involves considerable contributory or taxation payments. When citizens have lived for a number of years with such binding and rights-creating actions within the framework of a particular pension model, change to the scheme in question become exceptionally difficult. In this connection, research often speaks of cumulative feedback mechanisms. This means that the costs involved in shifting from one path to another one increase through time. The chosen pension scheme becomes locked-in in a path dependency that makes more fundamental changes difficult. If a number of different schemes are established at the same time, using the same template or pattern, an 'institutional density' develops, with the existence and form of the one scheme underpinning the other.

1 See, for example, Jørn Henrik Petersen, *Den danske lovgivning om alderdomsforsørgelse 1891-1933, Fra skøn til ret*, (Odense, 2007).

Path dependency thus means more things at one and the same time. Firstly, concrete changes strongly depend on events that have taken place at an earlier stage in a cohesive historical sequence of events. Events that therefore enter 'too late' do not make a decisive impact, even though they could have been of great importance if they had taken place at an earlier point in time. Secondly, the 'process' must have a starting point. This means that there must be a 'start' that cannot be 'explained' or linked to a sequence of events that lies even further back in time. And thirdly, inertia must occur that locks in the pattern of development, so that to an increasing extent it becomes difficult or impossible to carry out changes to the overall principles which are embedded in the structure of a given institution. When starting, there must be an 'open' choice process, whereas subsequent development is increasingly characterised by more bound choices – until 'something' weakens or eliminates the mechanisms that locked in the policy initially chosen. If this happens, the way is open for a change of a more fundamental nature.

Locking-in can be due to a number of things. One possibility is that the players – i.e. in principle the politicians – can see that the gains from changing outweigh the costs – a utilitarian justification for reproducing the system that has already been chosen once. Another possibility is that the chosen institution is seen as serving a particular function in the overall societal system – a functional explanation. A third possibility is that power relations mean locking-in, while a fourth possibility is that the chosen structure of, in this case, the pension system is conceived as being morally 'just'.

This naturally also means that changes can originate from the same four relations. Social learning (sometimes from a transnational perspective) can change the perception of players regarding gains and costs involved in respectively maintaining and changing the given institution. More 'effective' solutions can appear on the agenda, or social learning can indicate future advantages that can offset the short-term costs an actual change will involve. From a functional point of view, exogenous shock may occur or be expected which causes the chosen pension system to appear to be less functional in the overall societal pattern. That also opens up the way to a change. Or changes can be due to the fact that power elites to date are weakened, while new 'rulers' gain ground, as was the case, for example, in Eastern Europe after the fall of the Wall. New 'moral values' can of course also bring about changes.

Whatever applies, the point is that former decisions have a tendency, for one reason or another, to develop cumulative processes that lock in the original decision.

All in all, this means that there is not any pre-assumption that more radical changes will be implemented through time of a pension system that has once been approved. Many details can be altered. Many parameters can be ascribed new values. New instruments can be introduced, but the overall set of values – the paradigm that is embedded in the once-chosen system – remain unchanged. A paradigm shift or reforms are not everyday occurrences. They take a lot of doing.

For this reason, it also makes good sense to describe the basic pension system of various countries as a kind of ideal or prototypes – but at the same time it should be noted that in the vast majority of countries we are dealing with a more differentiated pension system. There are not many countries that do not have a more or less developed three-pillar system: a publicly organised, legally prescribed, normally pay-as-you-go financed and benefit-defined pension system, a publicly or privately organised compulsory pension system that is normally actuarial and contribution-defined, and a private, non-compulsory system based on market-economic conditions. Even though it makes sense to speak of a 'Danish', a 'continental European' and an 'Anglo-saxon' pension model, in most countries one finds all three systems existing side by side, although with different emphasis placed on the individual components of the overall system. That point is clearly demonstrated by the individual contributions to this book.

This book has a special focus on so-called basic pensions which includes both Nordic and European countries and offers a historical as well as a contemporary perspective. Furthermore, the book offers detailed accounts of small European states such as Denmark, Sweden and Hungary that are often excluded from larger comparative studies, even though these countries, historically speaking, have served as pioneer countries in international social political development.

The chapters of the book focus on basic public pensions. Firstly, the historical development and political discussion of basic public pensions is addressed for countries where such pension systems were introduced (such as Denmark, Sweden, Hungary, Britain) and for countries that did not initially introduce basic public pensions (such as Germany). Secondly, the focus is turned towards attempts to reform and transform basic pension systems. The core question is about institutional lock-in effects (path dependency) and reform capability. In some countries there has been a strong degree of path dependency, where attempts to introduce a paradigmatic change have proved almost impossible – at least until the 1980s. In other countries there have been gradual or paradigmatic changes. Several of the chapters study this process of institutional continuity and change and the role of political decisions and external pressures in the development of basic pension systems. In this way the individual chapters discuss the conditions that explain political decisions about changing or not changing a pension system.

The content of the book

Contributions to the book focus on understanding the historical development of the national pension systems, the main focus being on basic public pensions. Most contributions thus trace the pension system of a country over a given period of time.

This applies to Winfried Schmähl's examination of the German pension debate and the role ideas about a basic pension have played in it. Schmähl demonstrates that such thoughts are far from being alien to the German debate but have been there all the time, from the early, so-called Bismarckian reforms of the 1880s right up until the reform discussions typical of Germany today. Apart from providing an analysis of the German pension system from the non-winning perspective, the contribution also provides insight into the changing means of the concept 'basic pensions'.

In her chapter, Dorottya Szikra provides an overall view of the development of the pension system in Hungary. In many ways this is a more dramatic history than in the other countries, characterised by a number of striking changes to the political system. It is remarkable even so that the German-inspired system that was established in the interwar years was so firmly anchored that it came to form the foundation of a state-socialist pension system in the post-war period. It was not until after the fall of the Wall that the system really came under pressure from more market-based solutions.

In his chapter on 'The benefit formula in Danish old age pensions', Jørn Henrik Petersen is critical of viewing the Danish People's Pension as a basic income support programme providing flat-rate benefits to all. By studying the completely concrete measurement criteria from the first pension reform of 1891 up to the most recent years, he shows that the development can be described as a continuous pattern in which universalism and targeting have gone hand in hand as the dominant element of Danish pension politics. In their joint work, Jørn Henrik Petersen and Klaus Petersen turn their attention to the political dynamics behind the introduction of the so-called People's Pension in 1957. Precisely this pension reform is often singled out as marking the breakthrough of the modern welfare state in Denmark, and their contribution shows how the reform combined historical continuity with a Social-Democratic and social-liberal desire for reform, the original nature of which, after two decades of political discussion, was one of a broad political compromise – one that also included the parties of the Right.

Broadly speaking, pensions have exclusively been studied on the basis of what in their own self-understanding can be described as 'gender-neutral' perspectives. But in her contribution, Pat Thane analyses the British pension system from a gender perspective, showing that women have almost systematically been worse off than men. The present problem of poverty among elderly British women is thus not something new. The composite British pension system, with a relatively low state pension and a strong emphasis on labour-market and private pension savings, means that women are unable to ensure their old age to the same extent as men.

The above-mentioned contributions deal to a greater or lesser extent with the pension reform discussions of the 1990s and 2000s. A central theme is to what extent the pension systems will continue to show historical stability, or whether they are in the process of changing. In his contribution, Karl Hinrichs provides an overall view of the development of the national pension systems both in and outside Europe. He finds that the dynamics of pension reform in Europe has obviously increased in recent years. The above-mentioned path dependency has apparently decreased, among other things because of the influence of a new paradigm in pension politics. The result of this process is not quite clear as yet, but generally speaking points in the direction of more composite multi-pillared pension systems. Einar Overbye follows this up with the message that 'Pensions can be cut', which has clearly been shown by the successful implementation of pension reforms over the past two decades. Based on studies of the Swedish pension reform of 1994 and other reforms, Overbye discusses what conditions promote the possibility of carrying out a successful reform and in this connection points to the framing of public opinion.

Recent pension reforms are also the theme of the last two contributions to the book, where Torben M. Andersen and Urban Lundberg discuss them from two widely differing perspectives. In his contribution, Torben M. Andersen adopts an economic view, indicating on the basis of economic models what is needed to ensure the Danish and Swedish pension systems in relation to the ageing population – a challenge that most European pension systems are facing. The perspective is adaptation and economic stability. In Urban Lundberg's contribution, the discussion is reversed. Based on detailed studies of the Swedish pension reform of 1994, he discusses whether the prerequisite for successful pension reforms is that politicians to a greater or lesser extent short-circuit the democratic decision-making process in both the short and the long term.

The contributions are not completely parallel in the structure of their discussions; even so, there are occasionally various points of contact that have to do with more overall, general themes related to pensions and pension reforms. It is obvious that countries influence each other – as when, for example, the Swedish reform of 1994 is often cited as a typical example of a successful reform process – and it is obvious that the themes and issues recur across the national systems and contexts.

From one crossing-point to another?

One of the patterns that recurs in both the national and the more general contributions has to do with periodisation. It is not possible to summarise all cases and examples in one firm chronology. National variations and the importance of the historical context are too great for this. But, despite everything, certain general tendencies or patterns are apparent which, to a greater or lesser extent, seem to exert a broad influence. One can, for example, point to the emergence of a transnational era in pension systems in the 1950s, when it was a question of the role of the state, with a second phase of change taking place around the turn of the century, when it became a question of adapting to a new economic, demographic and politico-ideological reality.

The explanation of such patterns is probably quite simply that even though the pension systems are bound to their national contexts, they have not been constructed in an enclosed national space. Already when the first modern legislation on the state organisation of providing for the elderly was introduced in the last decades of the 19th century, countries peered over each other's shoulders. This took place via the transfer of ideas and discussions as well as via the establishing of transnational epistemic communities.[2] A parallel reading of the contributions to this book clearly illustrates this. The German model – the so-called Bismarckian model – thus became the ideal in a number of Central European countries such as Hungary. Even where countries chose to go in completely different directions, this took place in an explicit dialogue with the already established German old age pension. This was the case, for example, in Denmark.[3] Generally speaking, the time around the beginning of the 20th century was a fruitful period for pensions. Germany was on the scene in 1889, Denmark in 1891, France in 1895, Italy in 1898, Belgium in 1900, Britain and Ireland in 1908 – and in the countries that first joined in after 1910 there was a phase of intense discussions about how a future scheme to provide for the elderly ought to be organised. Without going into details concerning the history of European pensions, one can discern two important periods in the post-war age when reforms were discussed both inside and across national borders – and in a number of cases these reforms were actually implemented.

2 See Daniel T. Rodgers, *Atlantic Crossings. Social Politics in a Progressive Age*, (Cambridge, 1998); Klaus Petersen, 'Constructing Nordic Welfare? Nordic Social Political Cooperation 1919-1955', Niels Finn Christiansen ea. (eds.), *The Nordic Model of Welfare. A Historical Reappraisal*, (Copenhagen, 2006).

3 Jørn Henrik Petersen, *Den danske alderdomsforsørgelseslovgivnings udvikling I*, (Odense, 1985).

The 1950s in particular can be seen as a period when there were intense discussions in many countries of a future pension system, and when basic alterations to the systems were made. At the time, this had to do with adjustments, adaptations and alterations in the wake of the end of the Second World War. The welfare state, in the modern sense of the term, was gradually being put on the agenda,[4] and countries had to think about how, based on their historical traditions and wishes for a more systematised future pension system, they ought to organise things.

This applies, for example, to Denmark and Germany, where the theme 'basic pensions' was a subject of debate throughout the 1950s, even though different solutions were arrived at for political and historical-institutional reasons. This is dealt with in more detail in chapters of this book by Jørn Henrik Petersen, Klaus Petersen and Winfried Schmähl.

On the basis of the pension reforms carried out in the 1950s and 1960s, researchers from the 1980s carried on a discussion of typologisation of welfare states. Best known is Gøsta Esping-Andersen's 'Three Worlds of Welfare Capitalism' from 1990: the liberal, the conservative and the social-democratic (Nordic) welfare models. In this and competing welfare typologies pensions normally play the determining role. However, it is worth noting – as many of the contributions make clear – that despite categorisations and ideal types, the pension systems virtually without exception rested on more than a single pillar. State-organised pensions, private pension savings and labour-market-related schemes existed side by side through history. What distinguished countries from each other and was capable of changing through time was the balance between the three pillars. Several contributions justify a finer grading of the sometimes highly one-dimensional understandings of the national pension systems – e.g. the Danish pension system as being universalistic and flat-rate – so as to have a better point of departure for understanding and analysing reform dynamics.

While researchers started to categorise the welfare states and pension systems as they had been until then, a new era seemed once more to dawn towards the end of the 20th century. Developments in the 1980s and 1990s must be seen as a period when possible changes were put on the agenda – but were also most definitely met with considerable scepticism and opposition. Once again, one can say that the underlying reason was changes to the external context, this time caused by an expected demographic development in the direction of an ageing society. With a constantly increasing population above the pension ages that applied until

4 Klaus Petersen, 'Velfærdsstaten i dansk politisk retorik', *Tidsskrift for velferdsforskning*, 4 (2001); Gerhard Ritter, *Der Sozialstaat. Entwicklung im internationalen Vergleich*, (München, 1991).

then, an expected increase in life-span and a dwindling fertility, it was possible to envisage a tense relationship between the generations, something that possibly invited thinking about more fundamental changes both to the content of the individual pillar and regarding the emphasis that ought to be placed on the individual pillar in a future pension system. This is also obvious from the contributions to this book. A systematic discussion of these tendencies is to be found in Karl Hinrichs' contribution and it is also touched on in a number of the national contributions (not least that of Winfried Schmähl on Germany and that of Dorottya Szikra on pension reforms in Hungary). There was a polyphony of explanations behind this: demography and financial pressure, new ideological paradigms, political changes of power, transnational players that adopted different forms of expression in the various countries. In certain countries such as Hungary this led to a shift in the system, while the other countries juggled with more or less successful adaptations of the pension systems. In that connection, it is remarkable that the Nordic model has been restored to its former glory. Precisely Denmark and Sweden are often cited internationally as examples of successful future-orientations of the financial stability of the pension system. This is dealt with in several contributions.

We hope that the contributions in this book will be of interest to both researchers and others who are interested in the development and dynamics of pension systems. One should be cautious about drawing firm conclusions on the basis of historical development, but conversely it would also seem to represent the height of folly to discuss future pension systems without a clear understanding of their historical backgrounds and the dynamics linked to those backgrounds. In this book we have attempted to link past with present in and across the individual contributions, so that together they can make a contribution to the discussion about old age pensions in both research and politics.

The Coalition of the Willing and the Breakthrough of the Welfare State – the Political History of the Danish People's Pension

Klaus Petersen & Jørn Henrik Petersen

In the autumn of 1956, a long-standing political debate on reforming the Danish old age pension system came to an end. The Bill on the People's Pension (to be realised from 1 April 1957) was passed. The history of the Danish welfare state is full of laws passed and reforms adopted but the 1956 pension reform sticks out as something special. The people's pension is more than a strong public- and tax-financed pillar in the Danish pension system. It is an important symbol of the Danish welfare state and has to a large degree become an integral part of our national identity.

The 1956 reform has been described by contemporary observers as well as later historians as the breakthrough of the universal, tax-financed welfare state[1] – and that is *to some extent* correct.[2] But at the same time it was a reform very much in tune with the pension policies institutionalised over the previous five or six decades. The reform has also been celebrated both as an illustration of the key role played by the Social Democratic party[3] in developing the welfare state and as the opposite: an example of how liberal and social-liberal thinking has played a significant role.[4] Both interpretations are *to some extent* correct. But in depth studies of the policy process shows that these understandings do not fully grasp the complicated interplay between the political parties and the historical context.

A more profound understanding of the political history of the Danish people's pension has to take its point of departure in a historical-institutional perspective and recognise that the social political positions of the political parties (as well as other key agents) cannot be reduced to static, stereotype understandings of a So-

1 Cf. Henrik Pers, *Velfærdsstatens gennembrud i Danmark. Den politiske debat omkring folkepensionens gennemførelse*, (Copenhagen, 1981).

2 Jørn Henrik Petersen & Klaus Petersen, 'Folkepensionsreformen 1956', Jørn Henrik Petersen & Klaus Petersen, *13 reformer af den danske velfærdsstat*, (Odense, 2005), pp. 97-116.

3 See Klaus Petersen, *Legitimität und Krise. Die politische Geschichte des dänischen Wohlfahrtsstaates 1945-1973*, (Berlin, 1998), pp. 137-49; Søren Kolstrup, *Velfærdsstatens rødder. Fra kommunesocialisme til folkepension*, (Copenhagen, 1996), pp. 389-392.

4 See Peter Baldwin, *The Politics of Social Solidarity. Class Bases of the European Welfare State 1870-1970*, (Cambridge, 1990); Jacob Christensen, *Socialpolitiske strategier 1945-1972*, (Odense, 1998), pp. 55-66.

cial Democratic or a Liberal solution to the pension issue. As stated by the Danish Prime Minister Anker Jørgensen during an internal debate in the Social Democratic Party: 'Pension policy is a complicated matter in which no solutions are obviously right.'[5] Ideology and class interests certainly have played a role but as argued by the Swedish historian Klas Åmark they do not offer any precise answers when choosing between social political measures – and in addition class interests are interpreted through institutions and discourses and are influenced by the political landscape and tactical manoeuvring.[6] Our argument here is that the process leading to the 1956 pension reform can only be understood in terms of the interaction between institutions, political agents and ideas. Rather than a general 'social science-style' explanation, we argue for a more complex historical-type explanation.

This chapter will discuss the political process leading to the introduction of the 1956 pension reform in Denmark. How was the idea of a people's pension put on the political agenda? What were the positions of the political parties, interest groups and other important political agents? How did these positions change through the post-war discussions on the future of the pension system? What were the political strategies and deals made when finally enacting the reform in 1956? We shall start out with a look back in history.

The Historical Heritage

The first piece of modern social political legislation in Denmark was the 1891 old age pension introduced after more than two decades of political discussions and expert commissions.[7] It was a national basic pension with universal coverage in the sense that the local authorities were to grant pensions to all morally upright and needy citizens over the age of 60, with half of their expenses reimbursed by the state. It is perhaps characteristic for Denmark that the major part of the financing came from a tax on beer. Benefits were needs tested and the local authorities also decided on the size of the benefits. Consequently, due to local po-

5 Minutes from the meeting of executive committee of the Social Democratic Party 11. May 1977 (Archives of the Danish Labour Movement, Collection of the Social Democratic Party, box 942-943).

6 See Klas Åmark, 'Inkomsttryghet i Norge och Sverige. Klass, arbetarrörelse och välfärdspolitik 1930-1970', *Arkiv för studier i arbetarrörelsens historia*, 77-78, (1999), p. 49. Se also Klaus Petersen, 'Fordelingspolitik, samfundsøkonomi og spørgsmålet om tillægspension 1963-1990', *Historisk Tidsskrift*, (2002), pp. 126-168.

7 Cf. Jørn Henrik Petersen, *Den danske alderdomsforsørgelseslovgivnings udvikling vol. 1*, (Odense, 1985).

litical and socioeconomic constellations, benefits differed from place to place.[8] The deserving elderly were singled out from the Poor Law as were, in the following years, the sick, persons hit by accidents, the (self-insured) unemployed and the disabled.[9] The 1891 reform made it possible for an increasing number of persons to receive a public old age pension, but it was discretionary by nature. Even though the number of persons in 1916, compared to 1891, had doubled, statutory old age pensions included only a minority of the population above the age of 60.[10]

Choosing a tax-financed system, with discretionary and needs tested benefits for all deserving citizens, Denmark followed a path different from the one chosen by Germany in 1989. The German model was rejected for several reasons.[11] Firstly, leading Danish economists insisted that, from an economic point of view, the difference between taxation and compulsory contributions was theoretical and ideological. Secondly, a tax-financed system avoided the problem of the long build-up period of a funded system. Thirdly, the tax-based Danish model of 1891 was easy to administer and did not lead to excessive bureaucratisation. Finally, it was broadly accepted that many people would not be able – for example during periods of unemployment and sickness – to pay the contributions necessary to finance an insurance-based pension scheme. This group would demand either the state or the municipalities to take responsibility anyway.

The 1891 Danish pension reform act was the result of moderate members of the Conservative Party and the agrarian dominated Liberal Party agreeing on 'practical' solutions to a social problem. The influence of the small Social Democratic Party was, at most, indirect, as the socialist 'threat' was important in

---

8 Søren Kolstrup, *Velfærdsstatens rødder. Fra kommunesocialisme til folkepension*, (Copenhagen, 1996), pp. 231-250; *Danmarks sociale lovgivning*, Vol. I, (Copenhagen, 1918), pp. 134-135.

9 The first law on sickness insurance was legislated in 1892, on workers accidents in 1898 and on unemployment in 1907. All reforms were based on the idea of help to self-help. See Niels Finn Christiansen & Klaus Petersen, 'The Dynamics of Social Solidarity. The Danish Welfare State 1900-2000', *Scandinavian Journal of History*, 26:3, (2001), pp. 178-79. The act on Invalidity pensions was passed in 1921.

10 *Danmarks sociale lovgivning,* Vol. I, (Copenhagen, 1918), pp. 153-54. In 1893 15.5 per cent of the population above the age of 60 did receive an old age pension, in 1911 21.3 per cent. The share of women receiving a public pension was about double that of men. See also Jørn Henrik Petersen, *Den danske lovgivning om alderdomsforsørgelse II 1891-1933,* (Odense, 2006), pp. 443-462.

11 See Jørn Henrik Petersen, *Den danske alderdomsforsørgelseslovgivnings udvikling vol. 1*, (Odense, 1985), pp. 119-132; Peter Baldwin, *The Politics of Social Solidarity. Class Bases of the European Welfare State 1870-1970*, (Cambridge, 1990), pp. 65-82. See also Jørn Henrik Petersen, 'The Danish 1891 Act on Old Age Relief: A Response to Agrarian Demand and pressure', *Journal of Social Policy*, 19, (1990), pp. 69-91.

getting the agrarians and the conservatives to come to terms. Furthermore, Social Democratic opinions on old age pensions pointed in a totally different direction. In 1888, the party had demanded that provision for the elderly should be offered in the form of 'cosy and well arranged public institutions'.[12] In parliament, the Social Democrats voted against the 1891 reform arguing that the help offered the elderly would be insufficient.

The Conservatives as well as the Liberal Party saw the 1891 reform as a temporary solution until their long-term goal of compulsory old age insurance was made possible.[13] The two bourgeois parties wanted to introduce the principle of 'helping people to help themselves' also in the field of old age pensions. But at the same time the political capacity to realise fundamental changes in the public pension system was lacking and from the 1920s until the 1950s political demands for a fundamental change of pension system were gradually abandoned. As argued by the Minister of the Interior in 1922, when introducing the Act on old age provision:

> 'It does not serve any interest to revive the old debate on people's insurance versus non-contributory provision in case of old age. The previous thirty years history in our country makes it natural to continue the development based on the principles originally adopted irrespective of one's opinion concerning what might have been the most desirable solution in the first place'.[14]

In this way the liberal Minister anticipated the arguments of institutional minded political scientists 60–70 years later on path dependency and 'lock-in effects'. An interpretation that has become the dominant narrative on Danish pension policy: There have been reforms and changes but they all mirrored a move along the path chosen in 1891.[15] Most important was the reform in 1922 that

---

12 Jørn Henrik Petersen, *Den danske alderdomsforsørgelseslovgivnings udvikling vol. 1*, (Odense, 1985), pp. 21-22.

13 Jørn Henrik Petersen & Klaus Petersen, 'Shake, Rattle and Roll! From Charity to Social Rights in the Danish Welfare State 1890-1933', Steven King & John Stewart (eds.), *Welfare Peripheries. The Development of Welfare States in Nineteenth and Twentieth Century Europe*, (Bern, 2007), pp. 149-180.

14 Quote original in Danish from *Rigsdagstidende 1921-22, Folketingets Forhandlinger*, col. 4126. For a more detailed analysis of the discussions in the 1920s and 1930s, see Jørn Henrik Petersen, *Den danske lovgivning om alderdomsforsørgelse II 1891-1933*, (Odense, 2006).

15 For this line of argument see Jørn Henrik Petersen, *Den danske lovgivning om alderdomsforsørgelse II 1891-1933*, (Odense, 2006); Klaus Petersen & Klas Åmark, 'Old Age Pensions in the Nordic Countries, 1880-2000', Niels Finn Christiansen ea. (eds.), *The Nordic Model of Welfare. A Historical Reappraisal*, (Copenhagen, 2006), p. 183.

gave up discretion and introduced a benefit formula[16], often referred to as the introduction of social rights in the Danish pension system, and the 1956 reform which will be discussed in the following. Paths, however, are constructed backwards and not forwards; consequently, we have to be careful not to overstress path dependence and the political consensus. This was not a fact taken for granted in 1891 (when the reform was presented as a temporary solution), nor was it after the reform of 1922 or in the post war era.

At several moments in history the existing Danish pension tradition has been challenged politically and there have been political conflicts on pension issues. It seems reasonable to argue that the Social Democrats and the Social Liberals have been the primary advocates of (tax-financed) 'free provision' with the bourgeois parties arguing in favour of (more) insurance-like systems. The 'battle' was fought in a number of parliamentary debates, in expert commissions, in public debate, by the agents involved with political parties and even by fractions within these. Experts were mainly professors of economics with more or less explicit links to political parties. The most important interest organisation was that of old age pensioners. Since 1945 public opinion has been highlighted by continuous opinion polls. However that may be, it seems reasonable to assert that even though the bourgeois parties have challenged the predominant paradigm this has mainly been an ideological manoeuvre since in practice they have to a large extent involved themselves in promoting innovations and reorganisations in accordance with the paradigm of 'free provision'.

In the following we will limit ourselves to describing the most important moments in the policy process leading from the post-war discussions around 1945 to the pension reform of 1956.

Post-1945 discussion regarding the old age pension

As soon as the German occupation of Denmark had ended in May 1945, the political parties started to reposition themselves within the political landscape.[17] However, the political propositions for the now liberated Denmark launched by the parties during the summer 1945 did not mirror any spectacular pension reforms. Only the *Social Liberal Party* (Det radikale Venstre), which was influenced by the leading Danish social political expert professor Frederik Zeuthen, argued, cautiously, in favour of a 'general people's pension' – at least as a vision

16 See Jørn Henrik Petersen's contribution to this volume.
17 See Klaus Petersen, *Legitimität und Krise. Die politische Geschichte des dänischen Wohlfahrtsstaates 1945-1973*, (Berlin, 1998), pp. 34-74.

for the future.[18] The party strongly opposed movements towards a 'comprehensive insurance system'. The *Social Democrats* saw old age pensions as 'a natural act of justice towards those citizens who have contributed to society by a life's useful work'.[19] A number of immediate improvements were mentioned in the Social Democratic 1945-programme and it was emphasised that the old age pension had to cover all 'with a need', but a general people's pension paid irrespective of need was explicitly rejected. The rejection of the idea – even as a future objective – might be explained by a fundamental objective to target the pensions, but also by a fear that a people's pension might give rise to contributory payments and by anxiety about criticism from the Communist Party, because a people's pension in the short term was to the advantage of the middle classes.

According to the *Conservative* 1945-programme, a general people's pension ought to be discussed without prejudice, but from the commentaries it is seen that the Conservatives identified people's pension with an insurance scheme to be implemented in one way or another.[20] The *Liberals* (Venstre) also underlined the party's desire to improve living conditions for the elderly but emphasised that such improvements ought not to discourage personal saving.[21] The liberal strategy aimed at an extension of old age pension by an overarching voluntary or compulsory insurance scheme. It was admitted, however, that even if it had been desirable to have initiated provision in old age on an insurance basis in the first place – this opportunity was missed.

In this way the four dominant parties had taken their stance. The two bourgeois parties, the Liberals and the Conservatives, were more or less in favour of (unspecified) insurance based schemes (supplementing or altering the existing system) whereas the Social Democratic-Social Liberal bloc was opposing movements towards insurance. Even though the two latter parties did not agree on a positive goal their resistance towards insurance brought them together in the longer run.[22]

In many respects the post-war positions of the parties represented a déjà-vu of the attitudes of the 1920s and the 1930s with insurance models in one form or

---

18 *Efterkrigstidens Samfund*, published by the parliamentary group of Social Liberal Party 1945.

19 *Fremtidens Danmark*, party programme adopted by the Social Democratic Party in August 1945.

20 *Det konservative Folkepartis program. Med kommentarer*. Party programme adopted by the Conservative Party 1945.

21 *Venstre og efterkrigstiden,* Political statement by the Danish Liberal Party August 1945.

22 The *Communist Party* that played some political role in the first years after the occupation was not clear as regards principles but did initiate a policy of always promising more than its opponents.

another opposed to the existing tax financed provision in old age. Outside the parliamentary arena the discussion on reforms within the pension system were followed closely by experts as well as future and present recipients of old age pensions. Since the late 1930s the latter had been well organised and in many ways the monthly publication of the National Association of Old Age Recipients (*Aldersrente-Bladet*) mirrored the national political debate. The role of the organised pensioners was not so much that of initiators of new plans or ideas, but in the long run the Association organising about 80.000 old age recipients became important in insisting that the politicians fulfilled their promises.

In the early post-war years, Danish politicians were generally hesitant to introduce any new comprehensive social legislation. Their objectives were to reestablish Danish society after the German occupation politically as well as economically. Whereas the first objective was realised quite easily when the so-called old parties (the Liberals, the Conservatives, the Social Liberals and the Social Democrats) regained their dominant position after the elections in 1945 and 1947, the economic situation was characterised by low growth, dollar-shortage and financial political instability.[23] Until the late 1950s, the economic problems remained the main political concern which means that the discussions on the pension system took place within an economically pessimistic frame.

In the short term, the four old parties were united in their wish to improve the conditions of the pensioners, but they did not agree on how this was to be implemented – and at what pace. The conflict was about liberalisation of the offsetting system that on the one hand extended the group of recipients and on the other hand targeted benefits.

The Social Democrats were pressing especially for improvements for the less well-off pensioners through targeted one-off payments.[24] These were legislated on a number of occasions in the 1940s and 1950s. In a more comprehensive proposal from 1946 the Social Democrats advocated a reform package including improvement of the basic pension as well as targeted personal additions, equal pensions for men and women and a liberalization of the off-setting mechanism for incomes from personal work.

The Liberal minority government (supported by the Conservatives) tried to gain momentum by proposing an alternative reform package with a less redistributive profile. The government suggested that basic pensions should be increased, that the off-setting mechanism be liberalised also in case of income from

23 Hanne Rasmussen & Mogens Rüdiger, *Danmark efter 1945*, (Copenhagen, 1990), pp. 74-106.

24 Se Klaus Petersen, *Legitimität und Krise. Die politische Geschichte des dänischen Wohlfahrtsstaates 1945-1973*, (Berlin, 1998), pp. 78-87, 127-150 for a more detailed account of the debate in the late 1940s and early 1950s.

savings and fortune, that the differentiation of benefits between towns and municipalities be reduced, and that the degree of discretion of local authorities be diminished by the adoption of more specific regulations of the personal additions. Improvements in benefits were partly to be financed by an increase in the age of entitlement from 60 to 65 years of age. The rise of the age of entitlement meant that the government's proposal was less costly and therefore made room for strengthening the 'basic' and flat rate elements in the pension system. The latter has to be understood as part of the discussion on introducing insurance elements. A basic, flat-rated pension would make overarching insurance arrangements easier to implement. It was said that the idea of 'free provision' (the taxed financed basic pension) had been given enough room and that time was ready for introducing a supplementary insurance scheme as a second tier in the Danish pension system.[25]

The Social Liberals were firmly placed in the middle of the two proposals but ended up supporting the government, which as part of a compromise accepted the principle of equal pensions for men and women. The Social Democrats were especially discontent with what they saw as a Social Liberal sell-out or even betrayal compared to the party's position in the summer of 1945.[26] The Social Democratic proposal, however, had gained broad public support from influential players such as the Association of the Municipalities Social Committees as well as the organisation of pensioners, which represented a steady growing number of old age pension recipients. What is also interesting is that in the realm of this political debate the idea of a 'general people's pension' seems – as opposed to the bourgeois ideas – to be constructed on an insurance scheme. But, as one commentator noticed the concept of a people's pension was at this time very vague (he labelled it a 'floating concept').[27]

The 1947 election paved the way for a Social Democratic government as well as for social democratic ideas on public old age pensions. Not very surprisingly, the Social Democrats now wanted to target improvements especially for the economically less well-off pensioners. The government proposed a moderate increase in the general pension level but most of the improvements were given as increases of the income tested personal additions.[28] In this way, the social profile of the bourgeois 1947 reform was partly offset[29], but the generational profile was

25 See *Aldersrente-Bladet,* 7 (1946).

26 *Aldersrente-Bladet,* 8 (1946).

27 C. Nielsen, 'Aldersrente eller livrente', *Aldersrente-Bladet,* 1 (1945).

28 Klaus Petersen, *Legitimität und Krise. Die politische Geschichte des dänischen Wohlfahrtsstaates 1945-1973,* (Berlin, 1998), p. 81.

29 See Henning Friis, 'Socialpolitikken i Danmark belyst ved udviklingen i de sociale udgifter', *Socialt Tidsskrift,* 1-2 (1954), pp. 1-27.

kept intact as the age of retirement was to stay 65 years of age. The Social Democrats pursued a strategy of gradual improvements within the existing scheme mainly to make it more targeted by benefitting the low income groups. This can not be interpreted as an ideological resistance to the idea of a 'general people's pension' but it has to be remembered that the pension agenda in the late 1940s was open in the sense that both the Conservatives and the Liberals were advocating insurance-based supplements or alternatives.[30] The Social Democratic Party had to face the risk that discussing a genuine reform would open a Pandora's Box of unwarranted solutions, including insurance.

On their side, the bourgeois parties were in a dilemma. They preferred a general overhaul of the entire pension system as an alternative to the budding by gradual improvements and one-off payments.[31] Extensions of the group of recipients, obviously, were to the advantage of their electorate, but on the other hand they made a move towards a genuine insurance scheme less likely. Whereas the Conservatives and the small Single Tax Party (Retsforbundet) insisted on the ideologically preferred solution it seems as if the Liberals adopted a more pragmatic position.

The three pension models – the existing system with a more or less targeted profile, a genuine insurance model or an insurance-based second tier pension – were debated on several occasions during the late 1940s and early 1950s. Furthermore, the Social Liberals had since 1945 advocated for a people's pension without offering any detailed description of its content. The Danish pension system is often described as characterised by consensus and a very high degree of continuity in which decisions taken in 1891 have constituted a dominant paradigm for the subsequent development. But at the same time we also have to notice that on several occasions continuity was only preferred to change by a small margin. The early 1950s was a window of opportunity for those who wanted more or less radical changes to the existing pension system.

While principles were toned down and extraordinary additions were frequent the day-to-day politics discussions of principles were placed with a Commission established in February 1948.[32] The nomination of the commission can be seen as a concession from the Social Democratic government to the non-socialist opposition or at least as the establishment of a ceasefire. But at the same time the commission enabled the Social Democrats to pursue the policy of extraordinary addi-

30 This line of thinking can be followed in internal Social Democratic reports and debates from the 1940s and onwards.

31 Klaus Petersen, *Legitimität und Krise. Die politische Geschichte des dänischen Wohlfahrtsstaates 1945-1973*, (Berlin, 1998), p. 139.

32 Klaus Petersen, *Legitimität und Krise. Die politische Geschichte des dänischen Wohlfahrtsstaates 1945-1973*, (Berlin, 1998), pp. 82-83.

tions. For the proponents of a genuine reform and the introduction of insurance schemes the nomination of the commission was dangerous, because its work actually postponed major changes and tended to favour a piece-meal development by day-to-day political decisions each of which made it even more difficult to implement major reforms.

The Pension Commission of 1948

The commission – which included both politicians and experts – started its work in 1948 and did not publish its report until 1955.[33] The assignment of the commission was to investigate possibilities of an insurance-based pension system and to discuss basic questions such as financing, benefit levels and distribution. Since the Social Democrats appointed the chairman they were to some degree able to control the discussions within the commission. When a preliminary report leaked to the press in November 1949, it was obvious that the commission almost from the outset had rejected the idea of a genuine People's Insurance.[34]

The main message of the leaked report was that a transition towards an insurance arrangement did not offer security to a larger extent than did the present scheme, and that benefits offered by an insurance model would not be value-fixed (unless they were guaranteed by the state). Furthermore, the administration of a compulsory insurance would be more expensive than was the existing pension system, and a change of systems would impose a heavy burden on the working population during the transition period (the so-called 'double payer' problem). In this discussion of advantages and disadvantages of an insurance arrangement there is no doubt that particularly the expert members of the commission emphasised the disadvantages and in this way played an important role in dismissing the idea of an insurance-based pension system.

The Commission's analytical work unfolding the experts' basic scepticism with regard to insurance-like schemes was completed in 1951.[35] The commission, however, continued its work until 1955, but following the leak of the preliminary report the political process took place also outside of the commission. In many ways the commission lost its role as an independent player in the political game

---

33 Jacob Christensen, *Socialpolitiske strategier 1945-1972*, (Odense, 1998), pp. 44-54.

34 Klaus Petersen, *Legitimität und Krise. Die politische Geschichte des dänischen Wohlfahrtsstaates 1945-1973*, (Berlin, 1998), p. 83; *Betænkning vedr. en forsikringsmæssig overbygning på aldersrenten. Afgivet af det nedsatte aldersrenteudvalg*, (Copenhagen, 1949).

35 Jacob Christensen, *Socialpolitiske strategier 1945-1972*, (Odense, 1998), pp. 46-47.

and was reduced to be more like a forum for political negotiations controlled by the political parties.

Social Democratic-Social Liberal take-off

The 1950s are often overshadowed by the more dynamic 1960s during which decade Danish society underwent a genuine social revolution, economic growth boomed and the welfare state gloomed.[36] The 1950s, nevertheless, is a very important chapter in the history of the Danish welfare state. It was early in this decade that the ideological underpinnings of the welfare state were spelled out especially by Social Democrats and rationalising experts and intellectuals.[37] It was also the period of the Cold War and the epoch of Nordic discussions on a possible 'third way' between American-style capitalism and Soviet communism. It was in these years that the concept 'welfare state' was coined and the idea of a people's pension was put on the political agenda.[38]

The national election in 1950 resulted in a Liberal-Conservative coalition government which remained in power until 1953. Within the Social Democratic Party this made possible a reformulation of the party's political strategy and an ideological movement from a more traditional socialist (reformist) ideology towards a pragmatic and growth-orientated political course.[39] Put in a simplified manner the ideological goal was the welfare state offering social security and a basis for individual self-realisation. Full employment, modernisation and growth were meant to finance it all. Universalism and inclusion were to secure the necessary political support. The change of political strategy was paralleled by a closer

---

36 Cf. Klaus Petersen, *Legitimität und Krise. Die politische Geschichte des dänischen Wohlfahrtsstaates 1945-1973*, (Berlin, 1998), pp. 159-176; Knud J.V. Jespersen, *A History of Denmark*, (Basingstoke, 2004), pp. 172-180.

37 Klaus Petersen, 'Om formuleringen af velfærdsstaten som et politisk projekt. Et bidrag til den moderne velfærdsstats historie', *Arbejderhistorie*, 4 (1996), pp. 62-78.

38 For those with semantic interests it is quite interesting that the vivid public discussion on the concept 'welfare state' 1954-1957 actually was triggered by the discussion on a People's Pension. See Klaus Petersen, 'Velfærdsstaten i dansk politisk retorik', *Tidsskrift for velferdsforskning*, 4 (2001), pp. 16-28.

39 This is more or less the argument in Gøsta Esping-Andersen, *Politics against Markets. The Social Democratic Road to Power*, (Princeton, 1985). For a more detailed discussion about the formulation of this strategy see Klaus Petersen, 'Om formuleringen af velfærdsstaten som et politisk projekt. Et bidrag til den moderne velfærdsstats historie' *Arbejderhistorie*, 4 (1996) and Klaus Petersen, *Legitimität und Krise. Die politische Geschichte des dänischen Wohlfahrtsstaates 1945-1973*, (Berlin, 1998), pp. 107-114.

parliamentary alliance between Social Democracy and the Social Liberals. One of the important results of this was the adoption of a universal people's pension.

The Social Democrats had established an internal working-party on pensions reporting in May 1952.[40] The report emphasised two points. The first had to do with the differences in pension rights between civil servant and other old-age pensioners regarding criteria of eligibility and benefit levels. The second pin-pointed that a targeted pension system had to rely on a strict control of the individuals that was incompatible with individual dignity. The report, therefore, opted for a gradual liberalisation of the offsetting procedure leading towards a universal system with benefits paid to all irrespective of income and fortune. The idea was to reduce the existing old-age pension (*aldersrente*) parallel with the rise of the universal people's pension. The idea was over a period of thirty years to raise benefits from 48 per cent towards 65 per cent of the average breadwinner income. Financing had to rely on the pay-as-you-go procedure and all efforts to change the burden of financing by introducing 'premiums' were dismissed. Voluntary additions based on insurance were no business of the state. Furthermore, geographical differentiation was to be gradually equalised, and as a tribute to demographic and financially concerns the age of entitlement was to be raised to 62 for women and 67 years of age for men. With this proposal the Social Democrats had embraced the idea of a basic public pension.

The change of the Social Democratic Party's position compared to the 1945 standing was motivated by several factors, two of which were the dominant ones. Firstly, there was concern about possible motions from the bourgeois parties leading towards an insurance-based alternative. Secondly, the proposal would cover the whole population within one system and could, therefore, be seen as a strategic move. It would not only increase pension levels among the party's traditional voters but it would also attract new groups of white-collar workers as well as making it possible to create an alliance with the Social Liberals. It is not clear, however, how strong the proposal was anchored within the party. There are some signs of a traditionalist opposition which argued that money could be spent better than by offering public pensions also for those the better off. Later decisions of reintroducing targeted elements in the pension formula make this argument plausible.[41]

---

40 *Betænkning om Folkepension*, (København, 1955).

41 See Klaus Petersen, *Legitimität und Krise. Die politische Geschichte des dänischen Wohlfahrtsstaates 1945-1973*, (Berlin, 1998), pp. 137-150; Søren Kolstrup, *Velfærdsstatens rødder. Fra kommunesocialisme til folkepension*, (Copenhagen, 1996), p. 414.

The Social Liberals responded positively and a joint working-party was set up.[42] From this moment, the cooperation between the Social Democrats and Social Liberals became the prime mover towards a reform. The alliance meant that a majority in parliament (also including the Communist Party) was in favour of introducing some kind of a basic public pension and the debate was framed in a completely new way as ideological rhetoric was exchanged for pragmatic and strategic considerations. From the outset, it was clear that the majority wanted a broad political compromise which included at least one of the bourgeois parties. The Liberals and the Conservative Party on their side started a process – which also implied internal disagreement within the two parties – towards a beginning acceptance of the idea of a basic public pension. But important questions – on financing (income taxes or contributions), on the possibility of a insurance-based compulsory supplementary pension scheme, on liberalisation of off-setting mechanisms v. targeting/exclusion of those better off and on the process of moving from one pension scheme to another – still remained.

1953 was a special year in Danish political history because a constitutional reform demanded two sequential elections.[43] The Social Democratic Party launched the demand for a universal people's pension prior to the 1953 national election and the theme played an important role in the electoral campaign claiming that a people's pension offered 'security' to the Danish population.[44] In both the April and September election campaigns the Social Democrats successfully presented themselves as the guarantee for the realisation of a people's pension. The universal people's pension became a key issue on the political agenda, and the 1953 elections mark a point of no return in the political history of the Danish people's pension. The bourgeois government stayed in office after the April election only because the Social Liberal party wanted the constitutional reform fully adopted. In September the Conservatives and Liberals tried to remove the pension issue from the electoral agenda by issuing a statement that they also wanted a people's pension, but their initiative came too late and their plan was too airy. After the September election the Social Democrats formed the new cabinet with the support of the Social Liberals. Now the time seemed ripe for a people's pension reform.

---

42 Jacob Christensen, *Socialpolitiske strategier 1945-1972*, (Odense, 1998), p. 48.

43 Hanne Rasmussen & Mogens Rüdiger, *Danmark efter 1945*, (Copenhagen, 1990), pp. 100-103.

44 See the electoral folder from April 1953 *Security by People's Pension.* It is quite interesting how key concepts from cold war discussions such as 'security' and 'freedom' in the Danish and Nordic context also became associated with welfare arrangements.

However, the Social Democratic party's leadership was hesitant about fulfilling its election pledge. The new government was actually satisfied that no report had yet come from the 1948 Commission. Large groups inside the party and the labour movement were critical towards offering the same old age pension to both 'ship owners and unskilled workers'. Furthermore, the party leadership feared the financial consequences of such a large-scale reform.[45] But public opinion and especially pressure from the Social Liberal party made it impossible for the Social Democrats to turn back. The election had left the impression that the population was in favour of improvements of the old-age pension system. This understanding was further strengthened by a Gallup poll published around the New Year.[46] It showed that 69 per cent of the respondents preferred more money spent on old-age – dropping to only 53 per cent when people were reminded, that they would have to pay higher taxes. The idea of a people's pension was on the agenda, but the content of the concept was still blurred. During the following years the Social Democratic-Social Liberal alliance had to define this empty signifier and turn it into an actual reform-proposal. It was not as easy as one might imagine.

The political debate 1953-1955

The 1948 commission was still the formal arena for the political negotiations and in the spring of 1954, the chairman called for definite proposals from the parties.[47] When the parties presented their individual views and models, it proved impossible to reach an agreement. The chairman of the commission, however, tried to establish a compromise, but the final result of the commission's work published in 1955 was a report stating the different proposals and ideas of the parties.[48] The Social Democrats repeated their 1952 proposal (see above). The Social Liberals presented a plan for the gradual build up over five years of a genuine basic pension with flat-rate benefits which would partly substitute the existing income-related old age pension. This was, actually, a version of the Social Democratic proposal with a much shorter time horizon (six years v. 30 years). The two large non-socialist parties regretted that the ideologically preferred solu-

45 Søren Kolstrup, *Velfærdsstatens rødder. Fra kommunesocialisme til folkepension*, (Copenhagen, 1996), p. 412.

46 Danish Gallup Institute, *'Der bør bruges flere penge til aldersrenten'*, artikel No. 37 (December 1953).

47 Klaus Petersen, *Legitimität und Krise. Die politische Geschichte des dänischen Wohlfahrtsstaates 1945-1973*, (Berlin, 1998), pp. 142-43; Jacob Christensen, *Socialpolitiske strategier 1945-1972*, (Odense, 1998), pp. 50-53.

48 See *Betænkning om Folkepension,* (Copenhagen, 1955).

tion had to be given up but presented two different solutions to cope with the issue. The Liberal Party suggested to start developing a supplementary pension equal to 8 per cent of the average income and to be financed by a special contributory payment. The pension level could gradually be increased parallel with a reduction of the benefit level of the existing old age pension. In this manner a basic people's pension could be developed over time. The Conservative member of the commission wanted a larger proportion of the population to contribute more directly to the finance of their own pensions and focussed on criticising the proposals of the other players. The Communist Party argued in favour of a general increase of benefit levels within the existing systems to be financed by an employer contribution. The Single-Tax Party opted for a more targeted system, and the outside expert Professor Jørgen S. Dich argued in favour of a voluntary supplementary pension on a premium reserve-basis which could be implemented by collective agreements on the labour market. No wonder that the chairman of the commission found it difficult to reach a compromise between the seven proposals. To make the situation even more complicated he himself presented a proposal pointing in a completely different direction as it was to be implemented within the existing system.

The results of the commission's work must be characterised as negative in the sense that its most important function was to dismiss or at least discredit plans about insurance based systems. The mandate had asked the commission to investigate procedures for the introduction of insurance either as a fundamental change towards a comprehensive insurance-based pension system or in the form of introducing an insurance-based overarching second-tier pension scheme. The report argued that the build up time of such arrangements was very long, that for the actual working generation a shift would cause a double burden because this generation had to pay for its own future pension (by contributory payments) and for the pensions of the contemporary pensioners (by tax payments), that benefits could not be value-fixed within a insurance-based system and, finally, that a transformation would imply building up huge pension funds which could cause both economic and political problems.

The dynamics of the reform process was to be found outside the commission among experts, the Social Democratic-Social Liberal alliance and especially in the electorate among whom opinion polls and not the least the organised recipients of old age pensions on numerous occasions urged the politicians to remember the need to improve the old age pensions along the line of a people's pension. Some even talked about broken promises to the elderly.[49]

49 See for example *Aldersrente-Bladet,* No. 4 and 5 dl, (1955).

But at the same time as the commission foundered, an important new step was taken. In the spring of 1955, Social Democratic Prime Minister H.C. Hansen put pressure on the joint working party between the Social Democratic Party and the Social Liberal Party[50] and in June 1955 the working party presented a plan for the introduction of a people's pension arrangement valid for six years (as a possible start) and implying a people's pension to be paid irrespective of income and fortune.[51] Compared to the proposals of the two parties forwarded to the commission (see above) it was more similar to the Social Liberal proposal than to the Social Democratic as it was based on a six years transition time and lacked considerations about linking benefits to the income level of the working population. However, it also implied concessions to the views of the bourgeois parties and did not present itself in an unambiguous manner. The new universal and flat-rate pension scheme was to exist alongside the old scheme with higher benefits and offsetting mechanisms. The benefit was to be increased in three steps and to be partly financed from a so-called people's pension contribution. This financing measure served the purpose of satisfying the desire of the bourgeois parties. The geographical differentiation was – much to the irritation of the Association of the Old Age Recipients – maintained and the age of entitlement was to be raised. It was a complex proposal, offering a little to most interested parties. In this sense it was a good starting point for the following political horse-trading in which the Social Democratic-Social Liberal alliance had a privileged position because it controlled a parliamentary majority.

This Social Democratic-Social Liberal endeavour to enforce a debate was still not without reservations within the Social Democratic camp. During his opening speech to the parliament in October 1955, even the Social Democratic Prime Minister voiced concern about the economic consequences.[52] He announced that the government intended to put forward a motion on a 'gradually developing people's pension', but he added that the timing must depend on the economic situation of the country, and that full financial coverage must be ensured. Therefore, it is surprising that a motion was presented in parliament in November 1955

---

50 'Minutes from government meeting April 19th 1955' in archives of the Social Democratic Party (Archives of the Labour Movement Copenhagen). In the periodical *Socialdemokratiske Noter*, No. 8-9 (1955), it is mentioned that the group included high ranking party members like Minister of Social Affairs Johan Strøm, Minister of Finance Viggo Kampmann and the social liberal economist Professor Kjeld Philip.

51 *Betænkning om Folkepension,* (Copenhagen 1955), pp. 196-97; *Socialdemokratiske Noter,* 8-9 (1955), pp. 477-78.

52 *Folketingstidende 1955-56, Folketingets Forhandlinger*, cols. 15-16. The Prime Minister had also voiced these concerns at a government meeting in the spring of 1955: See 'Minutes from Government Meeting 25 May', Archives of the Social Democratic Part (Archives of the Labour Movement, Copenhagen).

– only one month after the opening speech. The reasons are manifold. First of all, the Social Democrats were lashed to the mast and had committed themselves to introduce a people's pension. Secondly, public opinion as well as the Association of Old Age Recipients were pushing for a solution – and 1957 was an election year. Lastly, the Social Liberals were putting pressure on the government to adopt the common proposal.

Peoples Pension and the Welfare State – A Digression

In order to understand the symbolic importance of the people's pension we will have to step outside the jungle of pension policies and techniques. It is often said that the devil is in the detail, but in the mid 1950s he was also placed in the broad public debate. Two aspects in particular are noteworthy. The first one is that even though the political parties as well as the public opinion had set a course for compromise from around 1955 (if not earlier), there were still voices arguing in favour of more insurance. In this chorus we find conservative politicians as well as prominent economists, bourgeois newspapers and business interests. Secondly, the discussions on a pension reform initiated a much broader public debate on the welfare state in Danish media 1954–57.[53] Considerations on how to provide income security in old age were generalized to larger principal questions about the role of the state and the responsibility of the individual. In this way people's pension was much more than just a pension reform; it became the symbol of the welfare state.

The Battle in Parliament

In November 1955, Minister of Social Affairs Johan Strøm introduced two Bills on the future pension system.[54] The first amended the existing Act on People's Insurance[55], which was to continue to rely on a mechanism of offsetting against

53 See Klaus Petersen, 'Velfærdsstaten i dansk politisk retorik.' *Tidsskrift for velferdsforskning*, 4 (2001).

54 See *Folketingstidende 1955-56, Section A*, cols. 671 and 693.

55 This was the official title of the Act on Old Age Pensions. Actually it had nothing to do with insurance. The title goes back to the discussion of the late 1920s and the early 1930s on insurance versus tax financed old age pensioning. By the social reform of 1933, the act on old age pensions had been baptised the Act on People's Insurance. The fig leaf of this manoeuvring actually intended to bring the discussion on insur-

other incomes. The second was a Bill on the People's Pension (*Folkepension*) which was to be introduced in three steps by 1963, to cover all citizens over 67 years of age (except civil servants who had a pension system of their own) and to be financed by a special contribution. As expected, the proposals were very close to the model presented by the Social Democrats and Social Liberals five months earlier. The bills were meant to be a point of departure for further negotiations. The plans, however, were not that well received in Parliament.[56] Neither the Liberal nor the Conservative spokesman was positive. The Liberals argued that the financial burden would become too heavy and wanted that the increase in social expenditures had to be covered by savings on the state budget. The Conservatives were more sceptical, arguing against the state taking over responsibility for provision in old age for the whole population and pointing towards the weakening of incentives for personal savings.

Even though the two bourgeois parties were gradually and slowly moving towards accepting universalism and a public basic pension – the Liberals faster than the Conservatives[57] – there were still ideological hardliners within the two parties arguing in favour of insurance. In addition the debate on a people's pension had become also a discussion on the basic principles of the emerging welfare state: Was it to be selective or was it to be universal? The latter was also a topic within the Social Democratic ranks but while the Conservatives and Liberals were concerned with costs of universal reforms, Social Democrats were discussing the re-distributional effects of moving from targeting towards universalism.

The prospects of reconciliation did not look bright. The statements of the Liberal spokesman were unclear, and his Conservative colleague seemed more interested in pointing out problems than in solving them. Even within the Social Democratic Party there existed scepticism towards the financial and re-distributional effects of implementing a people's pension. But in spring of 1956 Denmark witnessed turmoil on the labour market with mass strikes and a government intervention in the collective bargaining. The result was that the Social Democratic government was blamed and the Communists gained momentum

---

ance to an end was a condition that to be entitled to an old age pension the applicant had to be a member of the sickness insurance funds.

56 Klaus Petersen, *Legitimität und Krise. Die politische Geschichte des dänischen Wohlfahrtsstaates 1945-1973*, (Berlin, 1998), pp. 144-45; Jørn Henrik Petersen & Klaus Petersen, 'Folkepensionsreformen 1956', Jørn Henrik Petersen & Klaus Petersen, *13 reformer af den danske velfærdsstat,* (Odense, 2005), pp. 110-113.

57 This can partly be explained in ideological terms and partly because the Conservatives saw themselves as representatives of the civil servants who were not to be covered by the people's pension.

within the Labour Movement.[58] In the middle of the Cold War this was looked upon with great concern and anti-Communist considerations certainly influenced the timing of the government proposal for a people's pension.

During spring 1956 the pressure from the Social Democrats and the Social Liberals was intensified.[59] The Social Democrats needed a 'positive' reform as a response to the uproar in the wake of the government's intervention in the negotiations concerning the labour market. The Social Liberals still wanted a solution, and the Social Democrats had to make use of the support from the Social Liberals while it was still there. During the first reading of the government proposal in parliament the two bourgeois parties changed strategy and raised a number of requirements to be fulfilled before they could support the proposal.[60] This included the introduction of so-called indexed savings contracts where the state guaranteed the value of individual pension savings. This can be described as a very lightweight version of a voluntary insurance model. Furthermore, the two parties insisted that the government was to balance the cost of the proposals by savings elsewhere in the state budget. Even though the Minister of Finance accepted these demands, the Conservatives and Liberals were still unwilling to clarify their positions due to inner-party opposition to the party leadership. This was especially the case in the Conservative camp.

During the parliamentary readings the two bills were fused into a single proposal in which the flat-rated basic pension became the minimum floor amount to which all the elderly were entitled and with a targeted old age pension built on top of that.[61] This can be described as universalism with a twist, excluding those better off from the lions' share of the public old age provision. This construction – taken as a whole – was named the people's pension. It is confusing that this term in Danish pension history has been (and is) used for several and very different pension proposals. But the steady use of the concept points towards the symbolic importance of the concept itself.

This more simplistic (and symbolic) proposal became the vehicle for renewed negotiations between the parties. The dialogue took place behind closed doors

---

58 See Niels Jul Nielsen, *Mellem storpolitik og værkstedsgulv. Den danske arbejder – før, under og efter den kolde krig*, (Copenhagen, 2004), pp. 256-263.

59 This was stated also by the Minister of Social Affairs – see 'Minutes from government meeting 16 April 1956', in archives of the Social Democratic Party (Archives of the Labour Movement, Copenhagen).

60 Klaus Petersen, *Legitimität und Krise. Die politische Geschichte des dänischen Wohlfahrtsstaates 1945-1973*, (Berlin, 1998), p. 144. Within the Conservative party there was strong disagreement over both pension policies and strategies in the negotiations.

61 This was an idea originally presented in November 1955 by a former civil servant from the Ministry of Social Affairs. See Jørn Henrik Petersen's contribution to this volume.

and some minor concessions were given. As a concession to the rural Liberal electorate a further equalisation of the geographical differentiation was accepted. The Conservatives were pleased by the introduction of the option to receive a higher pension benefit if the individual remained in the labour market and postponed his or her application for people's pension.[62]

At the end of the road

Finally, after years of political discussion marked by ideological and strategical considerations a people's pension was adopted in October 1956.[63] It included an income tested basic amount and a so-called 'minimum amount' which was universal and flat-rated. The age of entitlement was to be raised to 62 years of age for women and 67 for men (for the 'minimum amount' it was 67 for both sexes). It was partly to be financed by a 'people's pension contribution' equal to one per cent of taxable income (to be regulated). As a concession to the Conservatives, so-called Savings Contracts in which the state guaranteed the future value of individual pension savings were adopted.

This was *not exactly what anyone had wanted* or proposed – it was the result of a political compromise offering something for everybody and a broad coalition of 'the willing' including the Social Liberals, the Social Democrats, the Liberals and the Conservatives.[64] It was *not exactly new* as it to a large degree built on the existing pension system, and the new universal flat-rated basic pension was only the minor part of the system. It became, nevertheless, of great symbolic importance as a symbol of Danish social policy and as the epitome of the modern welfare state. Furthermore, the people's pension was *not exactly universalism* understood as a uniform embracement of one social political principle. It was universalism with a Danish twist, excluding those better off from the major part of the public pension.[65]

---

62 Klaus Petersen, *Legitimität und Krise. Die politische Geschichte des dänischen Wohlfahrtsstaates 1945-1973*, (Berlin, 1998), pp. 147-49.

63 For a more detailed discussion see Jørn Henrik Petersen's contribution to this volume.

64 A small fraction of the latter party restrained from voting in favour of a people's pension reflecting the inner-party tensions.

65 It is noteworthy that again in 1964 when a new reform was to make the people's pension genuine flat-rate and offering a pension to all citizens regardless of sex, prior income or savings the Social Democrats insisted on keeping an small income tested pension supplement and during the 1970s the relative importance of this supplement was raised, see Jørn Henrik Petersen's contribution to this volume.

It is difficult too judge who were the 'winners' and the 'losers' of the long chain of events. This is all the more difficult because the parties were motivated by tactical and pragmatic considerations. Frequently their statements were unclear or ambiguous and they certainly changed over time. There is no doubt that the trigger of the process was the politicisation of the issue provoked by the Social Democrats, in particular during the electoral campaign in 1953. The leadership of the party had probably understood the importance of a pension scheme covering the entire population as a basis for further social improvements as well as a power strategy. This mirrors what later has been called the bribery of the middle class as a means of avoiding 'welfare for the poor' becoming 'poor welfare', as the British professor Richard M. Titmuss once put it. It cannot be excluded that even a deliberate long-term strategy aimed at developing a superannuation scheme along the line of the Swedish System introduced in 1957 was an underlying factor. Even though the Social Democrats originally had proposed something partly different and on several occasions had strong reservations both about universalism and the financial sustainability of introducing a people's pension, the party emerged as winner in the long run.

In the summer of 1945, the small Social Liberal Party was the first to argue in favour of a basic flat-rate pension paid to all citizens. For the Social Democrats the alliance with the Social Liberal was a decisive part of the party's power strategy – and the alliance spearheaded most social reforms of the 1950s and 1960s. The Social Liberals successfully maintained pressure on the Social Democrats without which results might have turned out differently. In that respect the Social Liberals stand out as the 'most winning' political party – a fact that Social Liberals have not hesitated to point out.[66]

In the final phases, however, the small party lost some momentum and had to accept that several concessions were given and that the universal flat-rate element in the pension system became the smaller one. Furthermore, a small party like the Social Liberals seems to lack the 'narrative power' found in a mass movement like the Social Democratic one.

The Liberals and the Conservative obtained a number of concessions during the negotiations prior to the enactment. Both parties were reluctant towards reconciliation, but the circumstances of the day compelled them to enter an agreement. Their motive for reconciliation was probably as voiced by the Liberal MP Axel Christensen who at a public meeting stated: ' ... the newspaper editors might write whatever they want, and professors can oppose the idea of people's

---

66 See for example the leading Social Liberal politician Jørgen Jørgensen who in his memoires claims credit for the whole idea about a people's pension. Jørgen Jørgensen, *Jørgen Jørgensens Erindringer*, (Copenhagen, 1970), p. 151.

pension, and I personally am also concerned about the idea, but there is nothing to do, the people demand the people's pension ...'[67]

Even though the reform in 1956 (in effect from 1957) was only a first step and the development of the people's pension was continued in the following decades, there was a strong sense in the 1950s that this was a symbol of something bigger: the foundation of a modern welfare state. Irrespective of their principal views regarding the desirability of the enactment of the people's pension most newspapers agreed that it represented the most remarkable social reform of the post-war period – one that would have far-reaching effects not only with respect to provision for old age but for the general economic development as well. Triggered by the debate on the people's pension, a comprehensive public debate about the principles of a welfare state started from early 1950s to 1957. Twenty years later, the Conservative MP Poul Møller, the architect behind the party's strategy in the 1950s, looked back on the importance of the 1956 reform and concluded: 'In principle there was no longer any possibility to fight for or against the welfare state. It was a reality. The Liberal Party and the Conservatives now had to find their alternative vision of society less costly for taxpayers than the socialist welfare state within the framework of the welfare state ideology.'[68] In this way the people's pension became from the outset something more than 'just another reform' – it became the symbol of the Danish welfare state.

67 *Roskilde Dagblad,* (11th July, 1956).
68 Poul Møller, *Gennembrudsår. Dansk politik i 1950'erne*, (Copenhagen, 1977), p. 99.

From Bismarck to the New Pension Orthodoxy: The Historical Development of the Pension System in Hungary

Dorottya Szikra

Introduction

With the fall of state socialism, and more recently, with the accession of eight Central and Eastern European Countries to the European Union, increasing attention is being devoted to the analysis of post-socialist welfare development. One of the central questions is whether the extended European Union has a common welfare development. To what extent are Central and Eastern European and 'old' EU countries similar and different in their welfare arrangements? If they are different, can these differences be explained by their common state-socialist past?[1]

This chapter is divided into three parts. The first deals with the pre-Second World War development, the second with the state socialist period, and the final part with the new capitalist democracy. On the basis of this history of pension insurance in Hungary, I argue that there are both similarities and differences between the development of Western capitalist democracies and countries that experienced state-socialist rule. This development originates much earlier than the state-socialist rule; it starts around the turn of the century. We show that development between the two World Wars has particular importance in building up a centralised Bismarckian social insurance system, one that became strong enough to form the bases of state-socialist welfare arrangements. Despite attempts to make a radical shift of the pension-paradigm after the fall of state-socialism, some of the most important patterns of Bismarckian old-age insurance remained in place.

---

1 An analysis of welfare development was made by Béla Tomka and Dorottya Szikra recently. Béla Tomka, 'The Politics of Institutionalized Volatility. Lessons from East Central European Welfare Reforms', Michael Cain, Nida Gelazis & Tomasz Inglot (ed.), *Fighting Poverty and Reforming Social Security. What Can Post-Soviet States Learn from the New Democracies of Central Europe?*, (Washington, 2006); Dorottya Szikra,'Family and Child Support in a Postcommunist Society: Origins of the Mixed Hungarian Welfare Capitalism', Michael Cain, Nida Gelazis & Tomasz Inglot (ed.), *Fighting Poverty and Reforming Social Security. What Can Post-Soviet States Learn from the New Democracies of Central Europe?*, (Washington, 2006).

From the Austro-Hungarian Monarchy to the Second World War

The period before the Second World War can be divided into two parts. The first is the era of the Austro-Hungarian Monarchy, from its outset in 1867 to its end in 1920 when, after the First World War, the territory of Hungary was substantially reduced, creating a new, independent country with more or less the size as today. This is the period when the first compulsory social insurance legislation was established. The second period, from 1920 until the Second World War, can be characterised by the widening of the scope of social insurance, and most importantly the introduction of the first compulsory pension scheme for workers.

I. 1. The Austro-Hungarian Monarchy

Although it is not very much known, and even less analysed, Hungary was one of the first countries in the world to introduce compulsory social insurance.[2] As the table below shows, Eastern European countries – and within that, Hungary – were pioneers in the introduction of compulsory social insurance schemes, when compared to Western countries.[3]

There are three types of reasons for the early introduction of compulsory social insurance in Hungary: economic, cultural and political. The economic interest of the state lay in the promotion of new industries to compete with Austrian and Czech production after the Compromise of 1867, when the Austro-Hungarian Monarchy was set up.[4] Cultural dissemination also pushed the Hungarian government to follow Austria and Germany in social insurance legislation. 'Following' in this case meant copying the German and Austrian sickness insurance acts almost word for word.[5] It took years before the Hungarian administration and expertise became strong enough to pursue its own distinct path, though still remaining within the framework of Bismarckian social insurance. It is important to note

2 The very few exeptions include: Béla Tomka, *Welfare East and West. Hungarian Social Security in an International Comparison 1918–1990*, (Berlin, 2004); Dorottya Szikra, 'The Thorny Path to Implementation. Bismarckian Social Insurance in Hungary in the late 19th Century', *European Journal of Social Security,* 6 (2004), No 3,2.

3 I am aware of the problems with both calculating averages of years of introduction and creating sharp distinctions between 'Eastern' and 'Western' European countries. Still, I find this comparison useful, not least for the purpose of overcoming existing prejudices between sharp distinctions between 'East' and 'West'.

4 The Compromise of 1867 created a united duty-zone of the countries belonging to the Austro-Hungarian Empire.This 'union' was similar to the European Union today.

5 Magyar Országos Levéltár (Hungarian National Archives.), K231. 99. csomó.

Table 1. Introduction of Compulsory Social Insurance Schemes in 12 Western European and 11 Eastern European** Countries*

Type of insurance	First Act	Western European average	Eastern European average	Introduction in Hungary
Injuries	1884	1914	1904	1907
Sickness	1883	1923	1910	1891
Old-age	1889	1922	1919	1928
Unemployment	1911	1922	1922; 1991	1991

* *Austria, Belgium, Denmark, Finland, France, Netherlands, Great-Britain, Germany, Norway, Italy, Sweden and Switzerland.*

** *Bulgaria, Czech-Republic, Hungary, Poland, Romania, Slovakia, Russia, Slovenia, Latvia, Lithuania and Ukraine.*

Source: Authors own calculations according to Flora Alber (1982); Darvas (2000).

that experts of the Ministry for Industrial Affairs investigated possibilities of other social insurance models too. They found, for instance, that in Great Britain, a system which 'builds on free, atomic association' exists where the 'passivity of the state is striking'. However, as they argued, Hungary could not follow this route because the number of self-help associations and voluntary insurance companies was very low. The Scandinavian countries were not considered by Hungarian investigators in this early period, only after the First World War. It seems that the roots of the three basic types of welfare development – liberal, conservative and social democratic – can already be found in the primary social insurance legislation of the early 1890s. Hungary has a clear place in this typology by its choice of the Bismarckian, 'conservative' model, partly for cultural reasons.[6]

At the same time, important political reasons also made the Bismarckian solution popular among state bureaucrats. The rise of the working class movement and close connections with their Austrian and German fellows made the government fear widespread strikes and violent demonstrations. Creating a compulsory insurance system, and at the same time stopping the self-help insurance associations of industrial workers seemed to be a good solution to suppress the movements of the working class and trying to increase their loyalty to the state.

Loyalty to the state was also a central consideration when setting up the very first compulsory pension insurance act in 1912 for civil servants (Act LXL), providing generous old-age, widows' and orphans' pension for state-employees. The act, which is longer and much more detailed than any other social insurance act of the period, creates strict distinctions between employees of the ministries and

6 Gøsta Esping-Andersen,, *The Three Worlds of Welfare Capitalism*, (Princeton, 1990) and Richard Titmuss, *Essays on the Welfare State*, (London, 1958).

central state apparatus and employees of 'lower' levels of state administration, like school-teachers, administrators in local governments or members of the police force.[7]

In the same year, a voluntary pension insurance act was also created for agricultural workers. In this scheme, all agricultural workers could participate with a quite low contribution, and, in return, receive a very low pension after ten years of contribution. The fragmented nature of the pension system is well illustrated by the comparison of possible pensions received according to the two pension acts in 1912. For instance, the maximum amount of yearly pension for agricultural workers was set at 240 Koronas/year, and this was about the third of the *minimum* amount that was to be paid for a civil servant. Civil servants also received a contribution towards their housing costs which amounted to about a fifth of their old-age pensions. It is thus clear that the intention of the legislator was to create a very high level of welfare for the 'servants' of the state, so that they would remain loyal to it throughout their lives.

Table 2. Comparing contributions and pensions according to the pension schemes created in Hungary in 1912

	Voluntary Pension Scheme for Agricultural Workers	**Compulsory Pension Scheme for Civil Servants**
Yearly Contribution (in Koronas)	10 Koronas	1–1.5% of salary: appr. 60 Koronas
Minimum years of contribution	10 years	5 years
Pensions received/year (minimum – maximum)	60 – 240	40% of salary; 800 – 16,000

Because of the voluntary nature of, and the low amounts paid into, the agrarian pension scheme, very few agrarian workers chose to be insured. Also, feudalistic relations prevailed: a very high number of agricultural workers were exposed to the goodwill of their landlords, were illiterate and thus probably did not even get the information about this option. Although insurance against sickness and injuries became compulsory for all industrial workers in 1891 and 1907, it

7 For instance, the act distinguishes no less than 22 sub-categories of civil servants according to payment in the case of old-age insurance, with big differences in the pensions to be received. 1912. évi LXV. törvénycikk az állami alkalmazottak, valamint azok özvegyeinek és árváinak ellátásáról. (Act on the provision for civil servants and their widows and orphans.) *http://www.1000ev.hu/index.php?a=3&param=7190.*

was only implemented strictly in large factories.[8] Old age insurance of industrial workers only came into force after the First World War.

After the Monarchy: Hungary between the two World Wars

Hungary lost the First World War on the side of Germany. Connected to this, right after the War, two revolutions took place.[9] The first, a civil revolution in 1918, aimed at the introduction of parliamentary democracy in the country, out of which a more radical, communist revolution evolved in 1919. This latter revolution included violent attacks against the ruling elite and aimed at the radical change of the political and social system. The 1919 revolution was bloodily suppressed after just a few months.

The First World War and the revolutions had an important effect on the development of the social insurance system.[10] The War produced masses of veterans, widows and orphans that had to be taken care of. Compared to the number of families affected, protection against old-age, widowhood and orphanage came rather late, only in 1928. This is also true in international comparison, as is shown by table 1. Hungary thus lost its formerly leading position in introducing compulsory social insurance schemes. The reason for this lies mainly in the effect of the 1919 revolution.

After the suppression of the revolution, conservative, right-wing governments succeeded each other until 1945. At the same time, social democratic, communist and liberal ideology became discredited. There was a mass emigration of liberal, communist and social democratic intellectuals, as well as feminists, to Austria, the US and the UK. The illegal situation of the Hungarian Communist Party and the fight for survival of the Hungarian Social Democratic Party forced the latter to make political compromises. In 1921, an agreement was reached between the Social Democratic Party and the government[11] which entailed the right of the Social Democratic Party to take part in the elections, and the re-introduction of the

8 In small villages employees with only a few workers were not investigated and forced to pay contributions for their workers.

9 Andrew C. Janos & William Slottman (eds.), *Revolution in perspective: essays on the Hungarian Soviet Republic of 1919*, (Berkeley,1971).

10 The effect of wars on the social insurance systems is probably best spelled out in the book by Theda Skocpol, *Protecting Soldiers and Mothers: the Political Origins of Social Policy in the United States*, (Cambridge, 1992).

11 This is called the 'Bethlen-Peyer Pact' after the names of the Prime Minister and the Leader of the Social Democratic Party.

rights for association.[12] On the other hand, the Social Democratic Party had to limit its criticism of some of the most important issues, such as foreign policies, and also make every effort to contain the political organisation of the trade unions. In this much criticised compromise, the government promised to introduce old-age, widows' and orphans' insurance but, in return, social democrats had to withdraw their claim to re-introduce unemployment insurance.[13]

In 1920, according to the Treaty after the end of the War, Hungary was punished by having two-thirds of its territories taken away.[14] Thus the end of the Austro-Hungarian Monarchy and the creation of the independent nation-state of Hungary were linked, from the outset, to the national trauma of territories lost, with millions of Hungarians remaining outside the 'mother country'. The industrial cities of these territories were linked to the now 'small' Hungary by a network of railway lines. By cutting these lines and by losing major industrial centres, Hungary lost part of its economic potential. Industrialisation slowed down and it was not until the 1930s when, with major state involvement, that development could speed up again. Hungary thus remained an overwhelmingly agricultural country until the Second World War, with a slowly increasing industrial population. As compulsory social insurance was not extended to agricultural workers during the entire period, this also meant a rather low coverage of the population.

Table 3. Population according to occupation in Hungary, 1920–1941 (%)

	1920	**1930**	**1941**
Agriculture	55.7%	51.8%	48.7%
Industry	30.1%	32.3%	34.9%
Other	14.2%	15.9%	16.4%
Together	100.0%	100.0%	100.0%
Population	*7,891 100*	*9,688 300*	*9,320 000*

Source: Berend T., Iván and Ránki, György. A magyar gazdaság száz éve [A Hundred Years of Hungarian Economy]. Budapest: Kossuth, Közgazdasági és Jogi Kiadó, 1972, p.184.

12 Though with occasional hardship, the Hungarian Social Democratic Party could exist until the invasion of the country by the German troops in 1944.

13 Unemployment insurance was not introduced during the entire period.

14 This is called the Treaty of Trianon, after the name of the place near Paris, where the Allied Parties signed the treaty.

As a counter-reaction to the revolutions and the loss of territories, politics and public discourse became increasingly nationalistic and anti-Semitic.[15] Still, the Act on Pension, Disability, Widows' and Orphans' Insurance, finally accepted in 1928 (Act XL) was a partial success for the Social Democratic Party, now represented in Parliament. It was their leader, Karoly Peyer, who in 1923 proposed that Parliament should enact the social insurance for workers and employees for old age and disability following the pact with the Prime Minister in 1921[16]. At the same time, the Social Democrats could not be satisfied with the final bill, as they were in favour of a public pension scheme (a 'Volksversicherung'), financed from direct taxes and covering all employees, including the neediest agricultural workers.

Neither of their wishes were fulfilled. The pension insurance act left agricultural workers out of the scheme altogether.[17] This was no surprise as one year earlier, the Hungarian Parliament had not accepted their inclusion into the new sickness and accident insurance act either.[18] With the feudalistic land-structure, most of the agricultural workers were still dependent on the land-owners, and thus lacked a minimum of financial autonomy. Their sporadic uprisings could be violently suppressed. At the same time, the majority of the MPs were landowners, and thus against any kind of extension of social rights to the agricultural workers.

To finance pensions from taxes was not taken into consideration by the conservative leaders of the country. Indeed, their intention was to maintain the existing social structure. The conservative, Bismarckian nature of the Act can be grasped in its detailed fragmentation of workers into no less than seven categories according to salaries. Also, white-collar workers were to pay a little more (5% contribution) and enjoyed more favourable conditions than blue collar workers (4% contribution). Differences – such as providing orphans payment until the age of 15 for the children of workers, but until the age of 18 for white collar workers – showed the intention of the legislator to strengthen structural differences.

---

15 In 1920, blaming 'the Jews' for losing the war, the first anti-Semitic law of 20th Century Europe was passed, limiting the number of Jewish students to be accepted at universities.

16 Károly Peyer, *Az öregségi és rokkantsági biztosítás*. [The old age and disability pension.] Szakszervezeti Mozgalom, VII. Népszava Könyvkereskedés Kiadása, (Budapest,1929), p.11.

17 1928. évi XL. törvénycikk az öregség, rokkantság, özvegység és árvaság esetére szóló kötelező biztosításról. [Act on the compulsory insurance against old-age, disability, widowhood and orphanage]. Source: *http://www.1000ev.hu/index.php?a=3&param=7759* (10th October, 2007).

18 Agricultural workers only became insured against sickness with the same conditions as industrial workers in the year 1975 under state socialism.

The Act created a fund for accumulating contributions that were to be paid by employers and employees equally.[19] According to the traditions of early Hungarian social insurance, workers and employers formed a self-government with equal representation. With the unification of the earlier fragmented system, the National Insurance Institution was created, headed by an 'independent expert' who was appointed by the Minister of Welfare.[20] He had the right to veto the decisions of the self-government, thereby limiting the democratic institution of social insurance.[21]

Experts on social insurance investigated international experiences of old-age insurance, and finally agreed upon the main rules of the act. The age of retirement became 65. As this was higher than the life expectancy of industrial workers, Béla Kovrig, the designer of the act had to explain the decision: He stated that contributions and salaries should be raised substantially if the age of retirement were to be lowered, and this, as he put it, was not realistic.[22] The period of collecting contributions was a minimum of 10 years in case of old-age insurance, and 5 years in the case of widows', orphans' and disability insurance. There were limitations in widows' insurance in the case of blue collar workers: Payments could only be made in case the widow was over 65, or was disabled.[23] The widows of white collar workers, like office workers, clerks and works-managers could get the payment without any such limitations. Old-age pensions were made up from two parts: the so-called 'basic payment', a flat rate sum (120 Pengo/year)[24], and a contribution-based payment between 19-24% of all the contributions. Widows received 50% of the pensions of their spouses; orphans received 30%.

Already at the time of designing the scheme it was clear that the payment after 10 years – and even after 20 years – was not sufficient to cover living costs. To explain why this could not be changed, Béla Kovrig referred to the British ca-

---

19 The actual payment had to be made by the employee together with health and accident insurance.

20 The Ministry of Welfare was created in 1917.

21 The self-government only acted as 'an assistance' for the decisions of the director according to the social democrats. In Károly Peyer, *Az öregségi és rokkantsági biztosítás.* [The old age and disability pension.] Szakszervezeti Mozgalom, VII. Népszava Könyvkereskedés Kiadása, (Budapest, 1929), p. 5.

22 Béla Kovrig, Ferenc Frisch & Imre Dréhr, *Öregségi és rokkantsági biztosítás. A Lex Vass II. előkészítése.* [Insurance for old age and disability. The preparation of Lex Vass II.] (Budapest, 1928), p. 8.

23 According to the act, disability meant if the worker could not gain employment for the third of his/her previous payment because of the drop of his/her health status.

24 Meanwhile Koronas were changed to Pengos.

se, quoting Chamberlain's remark in the House of Commons on May 15th, 1925: '... no public insurance can have the task of replacing personal savings'.[25]

The level of coverage of the population remained rather low, not much more than 10% of the economically active population, and around 5% of the total population. If we compare these data with table 3, we should note that many of those who should have been insured (the total industrial population) did not actually get insured against old age. Thus a gap between the *de jure* and the *de facto* insured population remained large. Moreover, this meant a gradual increase in the difference between Hungary and the Western European countries.

Table 4. Percentage of population compulsorily insured against old age in Hungary and in Western Europe (%)

Year	Total population		Economically active population	
	Western Europe	Hungary	Western Europe	Hungary
1930	36.66	4.84	60.22	10.51
1940	42.85	7.67	67.50	16.13

Source: Author's calculation according to Flora Alber (1982), p. 76, and 'A Magyar társadalombiztosítás ötven éve' (1943), p. 44.

The pension fund accumulated a substantial amount by the mid 1930s that was partly used for substituting the shortages in the sickness fund created by the economic crisis.[26] The first payments were made from 1939. Most of the funds' resources were invested in estates and state papers. Under the siege of the country by the German troops in 1944, 40% of these buildings were ruined, and a few years later, when hyper-inflation swept the country, the value of the state-papers diminished. Thus, no matter the colour of the post-war government, the pension system had to be built up from scratch.

25 Béla Kovrig, Ferenc Frisch & Imre Dréhr, *Öregségi és rokkantsági biztosítás. A Lex Vass II. előkészítése.* [Insurance for old age and disability. The preparation of Lex Vass II.] (Budapest, 1928), p. 12.

26 Because of the lack of unemployment, insurance workers often went on sickness leave for a longer period when fired. This was especially common in the years of the world economic crisis of the 1930s. Thus sickness insurance was used for the lack of unemployment insurance, and old-age insurance was used to substitute the week resources of the sickness fund.

II. The state socialist pension system

Between 1945 and 1949, Hungary experienced a short democratic period with a left-wing coalition when not only a widespread land-reform was carried out but an attempt was made to introduce comprehensive social policy measures as well.[27] There were extensive debates about ways to re-build the pension system, international development was closely followed[28], and a special (short-lived) journal was launched where professionals could discuss related issues.[29] After the Soviet-type, anti-democratic regime came to power in 1949 public debates on social policy were stopped. From then on, social policy was merged into economic policies, which, as it was declared, were to solve poverty and other social problems automatically.[30]

The common wisdom is that state socialist countries secured their citizens not only against the traditional set of risks, like bad health, old age and unemployment 'but [secured] also the right to a job, low prices for basic food, housing, transport and energy, free or subsidized access to education and culture and a relatively egalitarian income distribution'.[31] Although this is true, there are several reasons why state socialist welfare development (and within that the pension system) needs to be subjected to a critical scrutiny:

Firstly, there have been several periods within state socialism that differed substantially with regard to welfare provisions. Three periods can be distinguished in Hungary: (a) The 1950s, with severe poverty and banned political rights for masses alongside monopolised welfare provisions for party leaders. (b)

---

27 An Institute of Social Policy was set up, and local governments were supposed to build on local social policy expertise.

28 For instance, the emblematic Beveridge Report was translated into Hungarian already during the war, and published twice in the 1940s, with detailed comments of notable Hungarian social policy analysts. Mihelics Vid, *A Beveridge Terv.* [The Beveridge Plan], (Budapest, 1943).

29 These were: 'Szociális Szakszolgálat' (Social Service) until the end of 1948; 'Szociálpolitika' (Social Policy) from 1949, issued under the name of 'Társadalombiztosítás és Munkavédelem' from Oct. to Dec. 1950. Zsuzsa Ferge, *Fejezetek a magyar szegénypolitika történetéből*, (Budapest, 1986), p. 270.

30 The overlap between economic policies and social policies, and planned economy became 'fashionable' much earlier, already in the 1930s with Keynesian economic policies. They have come to wide acceptance all over Europe during the 1940s, especially, but not only, in totalitarian dictatorships. In this sense there has been continuity between pre-War and post-War policies.

31 Katharina Müller, Andreas Ryll & Jürgen Wagener, 'Introduction. Transforming Social Security: Pensions in Central and Eastern Europe', Müller, K., Ryll, A. & Wagener, J. (eds.),, *Transformation of Social Security: Pensions in Central-Eastern Europe*, (Heidelberg & New York, 1999).

The period after the 1956 Revolution, and especially the mid 1960s to the mid 1970s, remarkable for generous social insurance provision and family policies, with still banned political and civil rights. (c) From the late 1970s until the end of the 1980s, a period when the level of welfare rights could only be kept up with financial difficulties that eventually contributed to the fall of the regime in 1989. At the same time, some civil rights were provided: Certain associations could be formed, some of them with aims that included the changing of the distribution of welfare.

Secondly, the complete lack of political and (until the mid 1980s) civil rights, violent actions and imprisonment of people not complying with the system make it impossible to talk about a 'welfare society'.[32] If we take the classical work of T. H. Marshall[33] as a point of departure, we can say that extensive and growing sets of welfare rights were provided *in return for* the lack of civil and political rights from the mid 1960s, with the aim of pacifying the population. Also, the creation and the reforms of welfare institutions were not debated by the public and in parliament, and so democratic control of the welfare system was non-existent.[34]

Thirdly, the undemocratic political system presented social provisions as 'gifts' provided by the political leaders of the country. Thus, although in some periods extensive welfare provisions were created, these never appeared as the 'rights' of citizens; the fact that the 'state' was financing these provisions from contributions of citizens was concealed.

Fourthly, although employment was a right, it was also an obligation. People not having 'proper', full-time employment were punished, quite often with imprisonment.[35] The welfare system was used to reach the economic and political aims in respect of employment.

And fifthly, welfare provisions were systematically used to favour or to 'punish' certain social classes and groups. Typical of this was the long-lasting neglect and negative discrimination of agrarian workers.

---

32 This is the term used by Haney for the 1950s and early 1960s. In Lynne Haney, *Inventing the Needy: Gender and the Politics of Welfare in Hungary*, (Berkley, 2002).

33 Thomas Humphrey Marshall, *Citizenship and social class and other essays*, (Cambridge, 1950).

34 Because of this it is more difficult to conduct research on social insurance in state-socialist (elsewhere with a hyphen) countries than in capitalist societies. Parliamentary records are either missing or useless. The most important sources are archives and interviews.

35 There was a legal sentence called 'publicly dangerous work-avoidance' used rather often against free-lance artists and intelligensia.

Coverage and administration under state socialism

Coverage by social insurance remained linked to employment. With the growth of employment, including female employment, a steadily increasing number of people became eligible for pensions. Moreover, social insurance was one of the most important means to drive people into 'socialist employment'. For instance, although agricultural workers became compulsorily insured, important differences remained in the eligibility criteria of industrial and agricultural workers as well as within the group of agricultural workers.[36] The most important aim of this differentiation was to push people into the state-run industrial sector.

Table 5. The number of pensioners and the percentage of pensioners within the total population in Hungary between 1950 and 1982

Year	Pensioners (thousand)	% of pensioners in the total population
1950	538.9	5.8
1955	573.7	5.8
1960	809.5	8.0
1965	1.156	11.4
1970	1.453	14.0
1975	1.802	17.0
1980	2.082	19.4
1982	2.176	20.3

Source: Jurth, Rudolf (1987): A társadalombiztosítási ellátások alakulása 1950–1982 között. (The development of social insurance between 1950 and 1982.) In. Szociálpolitkai Értesítő. MTA Szociológiai Kutató Intézet. Budapest, 1987, p. 146.

Meanwhile, from 1950 onwards, social insurance was taken over by the trade unions in Hungary. This long-awaited and now-fulfilled wish of the working class movement meant in reality that the central governing body of the trade union [SZOT] became the administrative agency supervising the daily organisation of the social insurance system, including controlling contributions, payments and health care services. According to sociologist Júlia Szalai, trade union leaders received the control of social insurance in return for being loyal to the ruling party: 'Without receiving the administrative control over social insurance the 'accommodating role' of the trade unions could hardly have been maintained'. After los-

36 For instance, those not being members of a state-cooperative were insured under less favourable conditions.

ing their political role, trade unions got the power to control the most important welfare institution.[37]

The main causes of the growth in social insurance coverage between the 1950s and the 1980s were the continuously increasing employment rate, the extension of rights to new social groups, demographic factors (ageing), and last but not least, early retirement schemes and easy access to disability pensions from the mid 1970s. Whereas in 1950 a sole 5.8 % of the population (a little more than half a million people) received pensions, in 1982 one-fifth of the population belonged to the group of pensioners (more than two million people).

Order Nr. 30 in 1951[38] included agricultural workers in the compulsory pension system, although with different eligibility criteria. Orders Nr. 28 in 1954 and Nr. 40 in 1958 introduced a two-pillar system: A 'basic pension' was created on the level of 50% of the insured person's previous income, and this was topped by an earnings-related scheme for those having 25 years of insured employment. The level of minimum-pension was also set.[39] 'The 'less socialist' nature of co-operatives was reflected in disadvantageous entitlements and lower payments' according to Szalai.[40] Finally, the first comprehensive social insurance act in Hungarian history was launched in 1975 (Act II. 1975), which ended the discrimination of agricultural workers.[41] It did so by gradually diminishing the differences: for instance, the previously higher pension age of agricultural workers was gradually lowered to the level of that of industrial employees. This Act declared social insurance to be the 'task of the state' and listed all the groups of society to be covered. The level of contributions was set and it was declared that the lacking amount was reimbursed by the state.[42] The Act included all the important risks covered by social insurance: sickness, disabilities, old-age, widows'

37 Júlia Szalai, 'A társadalombiztosítás érdekviszonyairól. Történeti vázlat a hazai társadalombiztosítás funkcióinak változásairól', [The Changing Interests of the Social Insurance System], *Szociológiai Szemle*, 2 (1992), p. 29.

38 Most of the legislation was enacted through so-called 'orders with the binding force of law' to avoid parliamentary debates.

39 Sándorné Szabó,'Nyugdíjrendszerünk 1929-től 1997-ig'. [Our pension system from 1929 to 1997.] *Körkép reform után. Tanulmányok a nyugdíjrendszerről.* [Essays on the pension system]. (Budapest, 2000), p. 41.

40 Júlia Szalai,: 'A társadalombiztosítás érdekviszonyairól. Történeti vázlat a hazai társadalombiztosítás funkcióinak változásairól'. [The Changing Interests of the Social Insurance System], *Szociológiai Szemle*, 2 (1992), p. 30.

41 The trade union made it explicit in 1969 that it wished to create a unified system for agricultural and industrial workers, including the (very small number of) self-employed and owners of small ventures.

42 1975. II. törvény a társadalombiztosításról. [1975, Act II on Social Insurance] *http://www.1000ev.hu/index.php?a=3&param=8505.*

and orphans' insurance, pregnancy and maternity leave – and also family allowance.[43]

Level of pensions and spending

The level of pensions did not exceed a quarter of the average salary in the 1950s. In this early period, most of the wealth produced by the rapidly growing number of employees was re-invested into heavy industry.[44] Thus, despite a growing GNP, the population only gained limited access to basic goods in the early period of state socialism.[45] Many of those previously insured lost their eligibility or received a much lower amount due to new regulations, which deliberately sanctioned previously privileged social classes.[46] Low living standards, no access to basic services, coupled with the monopolisation of welfare by the ruling elite, contributed to the outbreak of the 1956 Revolution.

After 1957, the real value of pensions steadily increased. There was an especially sharp increase during the mid 1970s. As the sociologist Zsuzsa Ferge points out, inequalities between income groups decreased from 1962 to 1982, and 'the development of the pension system played an important role in this [...] The lowest incomes and the pensions increased more than the average income, and more people became eligible to at least some kind of provision.'[47] Authors agree that the extensive growth of the welfare system in the 1960s was connected to an implicit social contract after the 1956 revolution. In 1967, child-care allowance was introduced for three years, pension rights were extended to all strata of the society.

At the same time, raising pensions was always a political decision: the Party decided which groups should be benefited or 'compensated'. This was discussed with the central trade union [SZOT] and, when the decision had been taken, the

43 The Act was a ground-breaking one as regards health-care services: by making health-care universally available for all Hungarian citizens, agricultural workers became eligible for the service on the same terms as industrial workers for the first time in history.

44 Although not openly declared, the country was preparing for the 'Third World War'.

45 On the growth of the GNP and the estimated share of social spending see Béla Tomka, *Welfare East and West. Hungarian Social Security in an International Comparison 1918–1990*, (Berlin, 2004).

46 Interview by the author with Tenner, Gyuláné, in April, 2007.

47 Zszsa Ferge, *Fejezetek a magyar szegény politika történetéből* (Budapest, 1986), p. 180.

pension funds' administrative institution developed the right formulas to reach the goal of the Party.[48]

Table 6. Level of average pensions compared to average earnings; Real value of pensions, 1950–1982

Year	% of average earnings	Real value, 1950=100
1950	21.5	100
1955	24.9	122
1960	32.4	215
1965	32.7	238
1970	35.7	300
1975	43.4	435
1980	52.9	573
1982	54.9	600

Source: Jurth, Rudolf (1987): A társadalombiztosítási ellátások alakulása 1950–1982 között. (The development of social insurance between 1950 and 1982), in. Szociálpolitkai Értesítő. MTA Szociológiai Kutató Intézet. Budapest, 1987, p. 146.

While in the 1950s and early 1960s services and goods in kind were the primary resources of the (re-) distribution of wealth, payments in cash became more important from the 1970s. Their share grew from 48% in 1970 to over 60% by 1980.[49] The level of pensions and the increasing number of recipients increased the social insurance budget six fold from 1960 to 1975.

The share of pensions within the GNP was less than 2% in 1950, in excess of 4% in 1965 and almost 10% by 1982. Both the contributions of employers and employees were raised several times during the 1980s, and the system reached its 'maturity' with virtual full coverage of the working population in the mid 1980s.[50]

48 Interview with Györgyné Tenner, Former leader of the Department of International Relations within the Central Administrative Institution of Pensions, April, 2007. The other way to increase pensions and related benefits was to do so when the price of milk and/or the price of electricity was raised, but this was not always done in the same way: sometimes compensation lagged far behind inflation.

49 Júlia Szalai, 'A társadalombiztosítás érdekviszonyairól. Történeti vázlat a hazai társadalombiztosítás funkcióinak változásairól', [The Changing Interests of the Social Insurance System], *Szociológiai Szemle*, 2 (1992), p. 31.

50 Rudolf Jurth, 'A társadalombiztosítási ellátások alakulása 1950–1982 között', [The development of social insurance between 1950 and 1982] *Szociálpolitkai Értesítő*, (Budapest, 1987), p. 132.

In comparison with other areas of social insurance, we can see that the share of pensions was lower than health-insurance and health-care for a long time (3.13% of the GNP for pensions and 4.04% for health insurance) and became equal by 1970 (both at 4.68%). After shifting health-care costs to the treasury, pensions became the highest spender within social insurance. Pensions accounted for 6.9% of the GDP in 1980 and 8.8% by 1990.[51]

Following several changes in the 1980s, the calculation of pensions made the system very complex. Pension increases were inadequate and sporadic, so 'medium-sized and higher pensions were steadily eroded, at first only relative to wages, but later in real terms, relative to prices'.[52] At the same time, the political leaders became aware of the fact that the level of welfare spending – until then only dictated by political wishes – could not be maintained. This is why Hungary applied for membership in the International Monetary Fund in 1981, and became member in the next year. Alongside this, after protracted (and not public) debates between the leadership of SZOT and the Party, administration was taken away from the unions and put in the hands of the Council of Ministers in 1984.

The reform process of the 1990s

In 1989, the Reform Committee appointed by the government developed the concept of a three-tiered pension system. In this plan the first pillar was a flat-rate basic pension based on citizenship rights; the second a strengthened income-related pillar; the third a voluntary additional pension based on small insurance funds. Most importantly, social insurance was made independent from the central revenue in 1989. This was an attempt to stop direct political influence over social insurance alongside with the introduction of democratic institutions in the country.

A Pension Insurance Fund and a Health Insurance Fund were created in 1993, run by self-governing elected bodies.[53] In the same year, private pension- and health-insurance funds were allowed to be set up, and a wide range of tax-

51 Mária Augusztinovics ea., 'The Hungarian Pension System Before and After the 1998 Reform. Strengthening Social Security in Central and Eastern Europe through Research and Technical Cooperation', *RER/OO/MO/FRA.* (Budapest, November 2001), p. 7.

52 Mária Augusztinovics, ea., 'The Hungarian Pension System Before and After the 1998 Reform. Strengthening Social Security in Central and Eastern Europe through Research and Technical Cooperation', *RER/OO/MO/FRA.* (Budapest, November 2001) p. 7.

53 This was an idea taken from the history of pre-war social insurance in Hungary.

exemptions were introduced to foster individual savings in these funds.[54] The first years of the self-government of the national health-insurance fund were full of corruption scandals, which led to both funds being viewed as ineffective. Thus in 1998 they were dissolved by the conservative government, with the state secretary of the Ministry of Welfare becoming responsible for the working of the two insurance funds.

In times at economic crisis early retirement and disability pensions were important ways for people to avoid deep poverty. This resulted in the growth of the dependency ratio from 51.4% in 1989 to 83.9% in 1996.[55] Pension expenditure increased to 10% of the GDP by 1994.

Several attempts were made to stop these processes. The retirement age was gradually raised to 62 years by 2000 for men and 2009 for women. At the same time, the actual ages of retirement constantly remain lower because of the widely used possibility of early retirement. Pensions became indexed to wages and not prices and this made the real value of pensions drop. At the same time, the problems of the complexity of the system became even worse than before. As the economist Maria Augusztinovics put it:

> 'One of the worst results of these practices was arbitrary discrimination. Different cohorts of retirees received entirely different treatment [...] Two persons with an identical work history (in terms of length of service, estimated 'pensionable' income, etc.) could receive quite different pensions in the same month, depending on when they happened to have retired.'[56]

The failure of the self-government of the insurance funds together with the non-transparency of the system added to the dissatisfaction of citizens and the government as well. So in the mid 1990s, various reform concepts were developed. That of the Pension Fund and the Ministry of Welfare was quite moderate, with plans to introduce a flat-rate basic pension scheme, strengthen the incomes-related insurance pillar and a (already existing) voluntary private pillar. The other plan was developed by the Ministry of Finance with the help of experts of the World Bank. This plan was to bring a 'paradigm change' into the pension system

54 Currently, at least one third of the active population are members of some kind of voluntary mutual benefit fund, based on their current contributions, in *National Strategic Report on Social Protection and Social Inclusion* (2006–2008).

55 Dependency ratio calculated as the ratio of the number of pensioners to the number of contributors – Mária Augusztinovics ea., 'The Hungarian Pension System Before and After the 1998 Reform. Strengthening Social Security in Central and Eastern Europe through Research and Technical Cooperation', *RER/OO/MO/FRA.* (Budapest, November 2001), p. 9.

56 Ibid., p. 10.

according to the World Banks newly published findings on 'averting the old-age crisis'.[57] It advocated the break of the solidarity between cohorts and strengthening the reliance on individual savings and thus 'independency'. Another important aim – complying with the neo-liberal economic agenda – was to foster capital investment in the country.[58]

The plans of the Ministry of Finance got much wider publicity. For instance, advertisements were ordered by the Ministry to suggest that the dependence of the elderly on today's generation (the pay-as-you-go system itself) was to come to an end.[59] At the same time, the exact plans of the proposed privatisation were not made explicit and available.[60] The detailed concept of the Ministry of Welfare and the Pension Fund never reached the wide public.[61]

We can view the above described propaganda as part of the more general discourse on 'welfare dependency' in the region. According to the (still popular) reasoning, a 'Homo-Sovieticus' developed under state-socialism[62] who was generally dependent on the state. After the fall of state-socialism, people should be 'educated' to 'rely on their own resources' and 'enjoy the possibilities of choice'. Introducing market-relations into the welfare system is one of the best tools for achieving this aim.[63]

At the same time, financial incentives – if not corruption – might have been present, influencing the outcome of the pension-debate. Orenstein suggests that some MPs might have had an interest in multinational insurance companies,

---

57 World Bank Policy Research Report: *Averting the Old Age Crisis*, (Oxford, 1994).

58 This was very much the same as advocated and introduced in South America, as discussed by Müller in detail. Katharina Müller, *The Political Economy of Pension Reform in Central-Eastern Europe*, (Northampton, 1999).

59 In one of the adverts a young couple, playing with a kid is asked: 'Do you want to be dependent on her?'

60 The author of this paper was a member of the civil initiative for the publicity of pension reform, and as such, claimed a publicly available blueprint of the reform agenda from the Ministry of Finance in 1996. Although, after long discussions, the civil initiative received the document, it said on the front page 'top secret, not to be distributed', which clearly illustrated that real public debate was not in the interest of the government.

61 Zsuzsa Ferge, 'The Politics of the Hungarian Pension Reform', Katharina Müller ea. (eds.), *Transformaiton of Social Security: Pensions in Central-Eastern Europe*, (Heidelberg – New York, 1999).

62 See Zsuzsa Ferge, 'Is there a specific East Central European welfare culture?', Wim van Oorschot, Michael Opielka & Birgit Pfau-Effinger (eds.), *Culture and Welfare State, Values of Social Policy from a Comparative Perspective*, (Cheltenham, 2007)

63 This debate is currently going on about the reform of the health care system, with exactly the same reasoning about the merits of privatisation as ten years before. At the same time, there is positive change in the publicity of the debate.

which might explain why there was not such a lively debate in Parliament as the issue would have suggested.[64] For sure, experts of these private companies were openly present in the Ministry of Finance as advisors.

The 1997 Pension Insurance Act and its consequences

The pension reform resulted in 1997 in four acts, dealing with the state-run and the private system separately.[65] The most important feature of the new system is that everyone had to remain the member of the public system, although people could opt for choosing a mix of the public and the private schemes. Those choosing the mixed system have to pay the majority of their contributions (7% in 1998, 8% in 2007) to a private pension fund and only 1% (0.5% in 2007) to the public system. Payments of the employers still go into the PAYG system. The contributions of the employees were to be raised by one percent every year, reaching 9% by 2000. At the same time, the contributions of the employers were to be reduced by one percent, to 22% until 2000. This meant, of course, a gradual (additional) decrease in the incomes of the public Pension Fund, and a provisioned increase in the private fund.

Furthermore, young people entering the labour market do not have a choice, but have to opt for the mixed system, 'implying that in the long term the mixed system would become universal'.[66] The mixed system currently covers over 60% of the whole ensured population. According to opinion polls, young employees were the most in favour of the new system, much more open to market-based solutions and more indifferent about the actual outcome of the new pension system than older generations.[67] As well as this, possible investments by pension funds were made limited, and a Guarantee Fund set up.

---

64 Mitchell Orenstein, *Political and Institutional Impacts on Pension Reform in the Transition Countries,* (Manuscript, 1998). Quoted by Katharina Müller, 'A magyar nyugdíjreform politikai gazdaságtana.' [The Political Economy of the Hungarian Pension Reform], M. Augusztinovics (ed.) *Körkép reform után. Tanulmányok a nyugdíjrendszerről,* [Essays on the pension system], (Budapest, 2000).

65 Act LXXX 1997 on the contributions; Act LXXXI regulating the public PAYG system; Act LXXXII deals with the mandatory private pension funds. An additional act (LXXXIII) relates to the health care system.

66 Mária Augusztinovics ea., 'The Hungarian Pension System Before and After the 1998 Reform. Strengthening Social Security in Central and Eastern Europe through Research and Technical Cooperation', *RER/OO/MO/FRA.* (Budapest, November 2001), p. 13.

67 TÁRKI, *Changes of Attitudes to Pensions and to the Pension Reform.* Report No. 1/5 for the Ministry of Finance, Manuscript, (Budapest, 1996).

Ironically, the pension reform hardly affected the problems of the PAYG system.[68] Most importantly, the problematic 'rules of eligibility and measures concerning old-age entry pensions ... have been sustained with a few minor exceptions'.[69] The only significant change was that of the introduction of new rules of indexation, gradually transferred to a mixed calculation of the growth of wages and prices (Swiss-indexation). All the important changes have been postponed until 2013, when elements of solidarity will be replaced by a purely actuarial pension formula.

The designers of the mandatory private pillar are celebrating the reform as a success-story. It is often maintained that the pension reform has been the 'only real reform of the welfare system' since the fall of state socialism. It is true that many more people than originally expected chose to opt for the private pillar. At the same time, it became clear by 2007 that thousands of people – especially aged 49 or more – who had opted for the mixed system ended up being worse than they would have been in the old public system. The reason for this is twofold: Firstly, widespread propaganda for privatisation and negative experiences with the public pension scheme made people believe that anything could be better than staying in the public pillar. Secondly, these decisions were usually not taken individually but by the employer. Once an employer had decided to contract a private insurance company, it made all the employees enter the same pension fund. Because it is the responsibility of the employer to pay the contribution, some employees did not even realise the importance of the change.[70] According to the most recent calculations, the level of pensions in the mixed system will be substantially lower that originally envisaged. They might even be lower than what is to be provided by the national PAYG system.[71] At the same time, there is no return from the mixed system to the PAYG system.

The question of gender-equality is not solved in the new, mixed system. Although the act on the mandatory private funds says that they have to apply the 'unisex' life-table, insurance companies, who might ultimately pay the pension of the retiree, are not obliged to apply these rules. The difference in the life-course

68 This is all the more strange, since the idea of the pension reform came from the widespread agreement on the very need of the betterment of this system.

69 Mária Augusztinovics ea., *The Hungarian Pension System Before and After the 1998 Reform. Strengthening Social Security in Central and Eastern Europe through Research and Technical Cooperation, RER/OO/MO/FRA,* (Budapest, November, 2001), p. 13.

70 This is similar to what happened in Poland, where masses of people were administratively transferred to the private system.

71 Gábor Orbán & Dániel Palotai, 'Gazdaságpolitikai és demográfiai kihívások a magyar nyugdíjrendszerben' [Economic and Demographic Challenges of the Hungarian Pension system], *Közgazdasági Szemle,* LIII. (2006), pp. 583-603.

of male and female employees is levelled-up in the public system, but this certainly will not be the case in the private funds.

Also, the pension acts declared that the costs of transition would be borne by the treasury. As the entrees into the private system were much more than expected, there is an increasing lack of resources in the old PAYG system, which adds to the eroding of the system and the budget deficit of the Hungarian state. The amount to be paid by the state-budget to the pension fund is about one-quarter of all its costs (473 billion Forints in 2006).[72] More than half of this amount (which is constantly rising) comes from the 'lost' contributions because of the compulsory entry of the young labour force into the private pillar. Thus the national cost of the privatisation of the pension system is paid for by the tax-payers, something that was never spelled out during the reforms.

The most important problem remains the very high inactivity rate, which, for persons aged 15-64 38.6% in 2005, was one of the highest in the EU. According to the National Report on Social Inclusion, 41.6% of the inactive population aged 15-64 received a pension or a pension-type benefit.[73] People with low educational levels comprise the major group of the unemployed and inactive population.

In 2006, the average level of pensions was around 60-65% of the net average income (the lower figure applies to widow's pensions and the higher one to old-age pensions). Currently, the pension system includes both the actuarially fair earnings and life-course formula, and elements of solidarity – both being historically present in the pension system. Solidarity is spelled out in the minimum pensions (although at a very low level) and the calculation of years in employment. From 2013, elements of solidarity are to cease and the PAYG pension system is to be converted into a simple earnings-related pension scheme, where all the total year's earnings are to be multiplied by 1.65. The minimum pension is also to be diminished.

According to recent calculations by Augusztinovics and Köllő, if nothing changed in the planned pension formula to be applied from 2013, the level of

---

72 Mária Augusztinovics, 'Mit reformáljon a nyugdíjreform?' [What should be reformed by the pension-reform?] *Népszabadság*, (16th September, 2006).

73 28.3% studied in full-time education, 10.6% received various child-care benefits, 4.4% received unemployment benefit, and 0.8% studied in non-full-time education. The rate of those inactive for other reasons was 14.3%, in, *Situation analysis to chapter 1 of the National Strategy Report on Social Protection and Social Inclusion, 2006-2008.*

pensions would be drastically lower for future generations.[74] Whereas today 80% of previous income is paid for someone with 40 years of contributions, the figure will only be 65% from 2013. For those with fewer active years the level will be significantly lower. About 250–300.000 people will receive less than half of the net average income. Because of the low activity rates, there will be about 250-500,000 people who are unable to fulfil the entry criteria of the PAYG pension system: the compulsory 20 years of insurance. This will create a social problem that can hardly be dealt with by the current social assistance schemes of the country.

Conclusions

Müller argues that with the reform process the Hungarian state broke with the Bismarckian-Beverigean heritage and opted for a neo-liberal new 'pension orthodoxy'.[75] While it is true that there has been a conscious break of the generational contract and the solidarity within the nation, it must be emphasised that throughout the history of the Hungarian pension system there has been no point when governments seriously considered opting for the Scandinavian or Beverigean type of universal basic pension system. Although there have been experts and (mostly left-wing) politicians from the 1920s who strongly wished for the introduction of a tax-based universal pension-system, internal and external power-relations always swept these ideas aside as something that 'could not yet be realised' in this country, so that the system always remained within the framework of Bismarckian insurance.

Flora and Alber are right when they argue that absolutist monarchies, like the Austro-Hungarian Empire, were more likely to introduce social insurance legislation at an early stage of development.[76] It was also of central importance for the Hungarian state to secure its legitimacy in an absolutist monarchy. What is especially interesting is the relative continuity of the Bismarckian-type pension system under state socialism. Although important changes occurred, such as the ex-

74 Mária Augusztinovics & János Köllő, 'Munkapiaci pálya és nyugdíj, 1970-2020'. [Life-course on the labour market and pensions, 1970-2020], *Közgazdasági Szemle*, LIV. évf., (June 2007), pp. 529-559.

75 Katharina Müller, *The Political Economy of Pension Reform in Central-Eastern Europe*, (Chetelham, 1999).

76 Peter Flora & Jens Alber, 'Modernization, Democratization, and the Development of Welfare States in Western Europe', Peter Flora & Arnold J. Heidenheimer (eds.), *The Development of Welfare States in Europe and America*, (New Brunswick, 1981), pp. 37-80.

tension of coverage to the previously non-insured agricultural workers, many of the features remained stable. The most important of these was employment-based and earnings-related insurance, which remained differentiated according to the type of employment and occupational sector. We have argued in this chapter that the state-socialist regime used the social insurance system for achieving its political aims. There were important reasons for keeping a segregated system until 1975. But even after that, the rules that seemingly changed in an *ad hoc* manner were actually conscious political decisions to 'punish' or to 'compensate' certain social groups, or, later, to try to maintain the national balance of payments.

The fall of state socialism and the economic crisis of the early 1990s happened in a neo-liberal international context. This apparently coinciding (but probably interlinked) situation made the welfare systems of the Central-Eastern European countries vulnerable. In Hungary, two ways were seen to be the future of welfare arrangements: The first, claimed by mainstream economists such as János Kornai, indicated that Hungary had to stop the 'premature' welfare state hindering the growth of the liberal economic system; at the same time, social policy experts such as Zsuzsa Ferge claimed that even state socialist arrangements left large groups without welfare, and that the situation had dramatically worsened after the fall of socialism – thus even more public welfare provision, (although organised more effectively) was needed. In the case of the Hungarian pension reform, the first argument gained partial success. The century-old Bismarckian social insurance was kept in place but substantially weakened.

List of Most Important Legislation on Pension Insurance in Hungary

1912. évi VIII. törvénycikk az Országos Gazdasági Munkás- és Cselédsegélypénztárról szóló 1900: XVI. tc. és 1902: XIV. tc. kiegészitéséről. [Act on the amendments of the Acts on the Agricultural Workers' Insurance Fund.]. Source: *http://www.1000ev.hu/*

1912. évi LXV. törvénycikk az állami alkalmazottak, valamint azok özvegyeinek és árváinak ellátásáról. [Act on the provision for civil servants and their widows and orphans.] Source: *http://www.1000ev.hu/*

1928. évi XL. törvénycikk az öregség, rokkantság, özvegység és árvaság esetére szóló kötelező biztosításról. [Act on the compulsory insurance against old-age, disability, widowhood and orphanage.] Source: *http://www.1000ev.hu/index.php?a=3&param=7759*

1954. évi 28. sz. törvényerejű rendelet a dolgozók társadalombiztosítási nyugdíjáról. [Order Nr. 28, 1954. on the pension insurance of workers.]

1958. évi 40. sz. törvényerejű rendelet a dolgozók társadalombiztosítási nyugdíjáról. [Order Nr. 40, 1958. on the pension insurance of workers.]
1975. II. törvény a társadalombiztosításról. [Act on Social Insurance] *http://www.1000ev.hu/index.php?a=3&param=8505*
1997. évi LXXX. törvény a társadalombiztosítás ellátásaira és a magánnyugdíjra jogosultakról, valamint e szolgáltatások fedezetéről. [Act on the beneficiaries of the pension system] Source. *http://www.1000ev.hu/*
1997. évi LXXXI. Törvény a társadalombiztosítási nyugellátásról [Act regulating the public PAYG system] In. *http://www.1000ev.hu/*
1997. évi LXXXII. törvénya magánnyugdíjról és a magánnyugdíjpénztárakról. [Act on the private pension funds.] In. *http://www.1000ev.hu/*

Women and the Pension System: the Case of Britain.

Pat Thane

Gender is an important dimension of analysis of pensions because: 1) In Britain and many other countries older women have outnumbered older men throughout the history of pensions as, on average, women have outlived men and still do.[1] 2) Women are difficult to fit into, or fare badly in, pension systems which depend on regular contributions, years of paid employment and/or levels of pay as they have been, and are, less likely than men to be employed throughout adult life and, when they are employed, tend to earn less than men. 3) Partly in consequence of these realities, older women tend to be poorer than older men. This chapter discusses the construction of the British pension system and some of its outcomes for different social groups and the different outcomes for men and women.

The making of the British pension system

The first state pensions were introduced in 1908. This followed 30 years of debate about the form pensions should take. There were strong advocates of both insurance pensions in various forms and of tax-funded non-contributory pensions. The first pension proposal to be taken seriously by the British state, in the 1870s, advocated compulsory saving into a state guaranteed pension fund by all young people between entry into paid work and marriage. Thereafter, it was recognized, saving became difficult for most working class men and impossible for most women. After official investigation, it became obvious that most young people, especially women, did not earn enough to save to fund a worthwhile pension and, in any case, many of them helped support their families with their earnings and had no surplus for saving[2]. Those who could afford to save generally already did so.[3].

A succession of government commissions investigated the issue from the 1880s.[4] The outcome, introduced in 1908, was a non-contributory, flat-rate basic pension, similar to that introduced in New Zealand in 1898, restricted to those on

1 Pat Thane, *Old Age in English History*, (Oxford, 2000), p. 479.
2 Op.Cit., pp. 196-204.
3 Op.Cit., pp. 171-193.
4 Pat Thane, 'Contributory versus non-contributory old age pensions, 1878-1908 „Pat Thane (ed.), *Origins of British Social Policy*, (London, 1978), pp. 84-106.

low incomes, who were aged 70 or over, were not currently receiving poor relief, had not been imprisoned for any criminal offence within the ten years preceding their claim and, as the Old Age Pensions Act,1908 stated, were not guilty of 'habitual failure to work according to his ability, opportunity or need, for his own maintenance or that of his legal relatives'. The latter clause proved impossible to implement and appears to have been largely ignored by administrators of pensions.

The pension was also only available to possessors of British nationality. This was a large category in 1908, since it included everyone who could prove birth within the vast British Empire, which comprised perhaps one-quarter of the world's population. However, it was very rare for very poor people from the colonies to migrate to Britain at this time. When they began to do so in substantial numbers, from the 1950s, the rules for eligibility for pensions were gradually restricted. The group most conspicuously excluded in 1908 were Jewish refugees from persecution in Eastern Europe, thousands of whom had moved to Britain since the 1880s.[5] Those who had not taken British nationality were excluded, and also the wives of non-naturalized men, even if the wives themselves were born British. This caused considerable shock to many such women, many of them widowed, when they applied for pensions and were refused and it resulted in an outcry leading to amendment of the legislation in 1911 to allow the British-born widows (only) of non-British 'aliens' to receive the pension.[6]

The main reason why British pensions were non-contributory was that the main purpose of the scheme was to relieve severe poverty among 'deserving' people in old age, i.e. those who had led respectable hard-working lives but were in poverty when too old to work for a living. The scheme did not aim to replace the incomes of workers who were better-paid during working life. It was assumed that these could provide for themselves through such voluntary mutual associations as trade unions and Friendly Societies, as most regularly employed male workers could.[7]

---

5 David Feldman, *Englishmen and Jews: Social Relations and Political Culture, 1840-1914*, (New Haven, 1994).

6 David Feldman, *Englishmen and Jews: Social Relations and Political Culture, 1840-1914*, (New Haven, 1994), p. 272. Pat Thane, 'The British Imperial State and the Construction of National Identities', B. Melman (ed.) *Borderlines. Gender and Identities in War and Peace, 1870-1930*, (London,1998), pp. 29-46.

7 Kazuko Fukasawa, *Voluntary provision for old age by trade unions in Britain before the coming of the welfare state*, (unpublished PhD thesis, University of London, 1996), E.P.Hennock, *The Origins of the Welfare State in England and Germany, 1850-1914*, (Cambridge, 2007), pp. 224-6.

Friendly Societies developed during the nineteenth century as non-profit, mutual institutions through which working people saved primarily in order to receive a weekly payment when unable to work due to sickness. Increasingly by the later nineteenth century, they also provided a small weekly payment to those unable to work due to old age, although this sum was rarely sufficient to live on. The Friendly Societies provided invaluable support for better-off working men who were, or had been, in regular employment. However, they covered no more than 6 million people at the beginning of the twentieth century[8]. According to the 1901 census, 10 million males or more were employed in manual or other low-paid occupations[9]. Also, Friendly Societies had very few female members, and male contributions generally did not cover benefits for their families. The Friendly Society experience demonstrated clearly the limitations of contributory insurance as a solution to the challenge of providing pensions for the large poor, and predominantly female, population in early twentieth century Britain. Many Trade Unions also provided sickness and, in some cases, old age benefits, but the unions which did so were also predominantly male in their membership. Neither unions nor Friendly Societies provided more than, at best, exiguous benefits for the widows of members.

Politicians recognized, and successive investigations revealed, that the core of serious poverty in old age was among women and that they were harshly treated by the only available form of support, the Poor Law. William Beveridge, who was active in British social policy-making even at the beginning of the twentieth century, opposed means-tested pensions because they were inefficient at detecting need and expensive to administer. He was initially attracted to Booth's proposals for a universal, non-contributory pension, but he recognized that this was unacceptable to the British Treasury due to the high cost and suggested – rationally, but not expecting seriously to influence the government – that the pension should be paid only to women: The principle of selection would be clear and simple and it would include all those in greatest need. After a visit to Germany, he became strongly attracted to a German style insurance pension and became strongly critical of non-contributory pensions[10].

Consequently, the first British state pensions introduced in 1908 were non-contributory because they were primarily designed to relieve poverty in old age, and the very poor, most of whom were women, could not be expected to contribute regularly to an insurance scheme. The pensions were fixed at less than the

8 Paul Johnson, *Saving and Spending. The Working-Class Economy in Britain, 1870-1939*, (Oxford, 1985), p. 57.

9 Brian. R. Mitchell & Phyllis Deane, *Abstract of British Historical Statistics*, (Cambridge, 1962), p. 60.

10 Jose Harris, *William Beveridge,* (Oxford, 1997), pp. 118-137.

estimated weekly cost of subsistence, to encourage saving and family support to supplement the pension, and were subject to stringent means and character tests, to exclude those who squandered their resources. The principles of the ancient Poor Law lived on in the new pension system. The pensions were paid from the late age of 70. It was well recognized at the time that many, probably most, older people became unfit for regular work by the time they reached their early sixties, earlier if they had worked for decades in heavy industry. The age of 70 was chosen on the insistence of the Treasury in order to cut costs: by that age many people were dead. Two-thirds of the first state pensioners were female. Throughout the history of the non-contributory pension, which lasted until 1948, remaining at a very low level of payment, three-quarters of all pensioners were female.[11]

Pensions between the wars

In 1925 the pension was supplemented by the extension of the National Health Insurance scheme (established 1911) to provide pensions between ages 65 and 70 for contributors to that scheme, who were mainly male manual workers (higher paid, white collar workers were excluded). Employed single women could contribute, but paid lower contributions and received lower benefits on the, often incorrect, assumption that they had fewer family responsibilities than most unmarried men. In reality, many single women supported siblings or older relatives. This insurance-based pension was flat-rate and fixed at the same, low, level as the non-contributory pension which continued to be paid from age 70. This expansion of the pension system was partly designed to encourage older workers to leave the labour force at a time of high unemployment. Unemployment levels were high in Britain from late 1920 until the Second World War. Such measures to reduce unemployment were encouraged by the International Labour Organization between the wars.

The Widows', Orphans' and Old Age Contributory Pensions Act, 1925, which introduced insurance pensions also acknowledged and sought to alleviate the problem of poverty due to the ending of partnerships and single motherhood. Widows were the largest group of single parents in Britain at this time and they experienced high levels of poverty. The widows' pension was paid to all widows of insured men with children under age 14 at the time of the husband's death. It was set at the same low level as the old age pension and was payable for life. Protest followed that this was unfair to women widowed at older ages who might have been out of the labour market for many years caring for husband and chil-

11 Pat Thane, *Old Age in English History*, (Oxford, 2000), pp. 194-235.

dren and would find it difficult to support themselves, especially amid the high unemployment of the 1920s. In 1929, entitlement was extended to all widows of insured men from the age of 55. This assisted a substantial group of poor older women, though still at a level too low to live on without additional resources from work, family or savings – hence the continuing need for adult children, of both sexes, to support widowed mothers.

Occupational pensions expanded in Britain between the wars, but they disproportionately benefited men. They were first introduced in the British civil service in the 1850s[12] but increasingly spread through the private sector in the inter-war years[13] Women were compelled to give up on marriage most forms of employment in which pensions were available – e.g. 'white collar' jobs in the public sector, banks etc – and were obliged to exchange their pension entitlements for lump-sum marriage gratuities. Even after marriage, most women could not rely upon lifetime support from a male breadwinner. Even the minority married to men with occupational pensions (many of which were small) could not expect to inherit that pension. Some might receive their husband's (but not the employer's) contributions, only, as a lump sum on his death. A fortunate few might receive their husband's pension for five years after his death. Women could expect to live, on average, 3–4 years longer than men and, on average, married men 4-5 years older than themselves. Hence even a relatively fortunate widow might live for several years after termination of her husband's pension.[14]

Women who did not marry did not fare better. Marriage rates at any time up to the Second World War were lower than later in the century: according to the 1931 census, in England and Wales, less than two-thirds of women aged 25-34 were married and about three-quarters of those aged 35-44.[15] Unmarried women generally had more restricted job opportunities, lower pay and lesser opportunities for saving than men, even when they had equivalent qualifications. They were less likely to be in pensionable employment. Many were carers for ageing relatives.

To highlight these problems, in 1935 the National Spinsters' Pensions Association (NPSA) was formed to demand state pensions for unmarried women at age 55. It argued that, in addition to their other disadvantages, women were often forced into involuntary retirement at earlier ages than men, for various reasons: women's poorer health; discrimination by employers against post-menopausal

12 Op. Cit., pp. 240-1.

13 Leslie Hannah, *Inventing Retirement. The development of occupational pensions in Britain.* (Cambridge, 1986), pp. 27, 95-6, 118.

14 Op. Cit.

15 Brian R. Mitchell & Phyllis Deane, *Abstract of British Historical Statistics,* (Cambridge, 1962), p. 16.

women; and the fact that many unmarried women gave up work in middle life to care for ageing parents and could not, thereafter, find employment. NPSA was founded in Bradford by Florence White, who ran a small confectionary business. Its members were mainly working or lower middle class women, including many textile workers, many of whom would have started work at ages 12 or 13. Women could exert a certain political influence at this time, after gaining the vote in 1918.[16]

A government enquiry found substance in these arguments: rates of unemployment among 'spinsters' over 45 were higher than among men of the same age, and they found it harder to regain employment; and women tended to show a marked deterioration in health from age 55, despite their longer life expectancy. The committee expressed concern about the numbers of women left in poverty after caring for elderly relatives[17]. In 1940, the state pensionable age for all women was reduced to 60. This was probably partly due to the 'spinsters'' campaign , though the official explanation was that, since wives were, on average, five years younger than their husbands, the change was designed to ensure that married couples received their pensions at similar times.

But the level of pension remained very low. Government surveys during the Second World War found appalling levels of poverty among pensioners, most of them female, even after the introduction, also in 1940, of Supplementary Assistance – a means-tested boost to the already means-tested pension. One-third of all pensioners immediately qualified for this; again, most of them female[18]. The poverty that was revealed, which horrified researchers, had often been kept private, secret even from close neighbours.

Beveridge and women's pensions

This was the situation Beveridge surveyed when he produced his influential Report in 1942. He recommended that state pensions should become universal, i.e. paid to all women at age 60, all men at age 65, and national insurance based, with contributions from employers, workers and the state. At the same time, they should remain flat-rate and minimal, 'guaranteeing just the minimum income needed for subsistence'[19] but little more. To enjoy higher incomes and 'comfort'

16 Pat Thane, 'What Difference did the Vote Make?', Amanda Vickery (ed.), *Women, Privilege and Power. British Politics, 1750 to the Present*, (Stanford, 2001), pp. 253-288.

17 *Report of the Committee on Pensions for Unmarried Women* (CMD 5991, 1939).

18 Pat Thane, *Old Age in English History*, (Oxford, 2000), p. 355.

19 *Social Insurance and Allied Services*, CMD 6404, (1942), p. 14.

in retirement, Beveridge believed that people should save, ideally through non-profit, mutual institutions such as Friendly Societies. The long legacy of the Poor Law lived on: state-assisted pensions were to remain minimal. Beveridge, it should be noted, was a Liberal, not a redistributionist socialist.

Beveridge had long been aware of the difficulties of fitting women into an insurance system and of the specific problems facing women, including the fact that not all of them experienced life-long, stable marriages. He clearly identified the main issues faced by women in seeking to provide for old age. Early in the deliberations over his report, he proposed that the needs of women should be provided for in 6 different ways:

i) Employed single women would contribute as men did for comprehensive social insurance and receive the same benefits.
ii) Married women would be entitled to a 'housewifes policy' providing lower benefits, including pensions, based on their husbands' contributions, even if the marriage ended in divorce or separation.
iii) Employed married women could choose to rely on their housewives' policy or contribute separately as employed persons, but in the latter case with lower benefits than men, on the assumption that their housing was provided by their husbands.[20]
iv) Widows would continue to draw pensions while they had dependent children, but thereafter 'every widow of working age and capacity' would be entitled to apply for a training allowance, after which she would be expected to support herself by work and to contribute to the fund.[21]
v) 'Unmarried wives', i.e. cohabitees, would be entitled to pensions on the same terms as married women.
vi) 'Domestic spinsters', as Beveridge described them, unmarried carers for elderly relatives who were not in paid work, and other categories of women, would be classed as unoccupied persons and would contribute only to receive an old age pension, i.e., they would not be eligible for sickness or unemployment benefits. The many who could not afford contributions (which would require an income of at least £75 pa) would have no recourse but means-tested public assistance. Beveridge, despite his best intentions, could not find a way to fit them into an insurance based system.[22]

---

20 The majority of employed women took the 'housewives' option i.e. paid a lower National Insurance contribution, though this lowered their pension entitlement. This opt-out was abolished with the introduction of the State Earnings-Related Pensions Scheme, SERPS) in 1978 but still affects the later life income of many women.

21 Jose Harris, *William Beveridge*, (Oxford,1997), pp. 392-3.

22 Op. Cit., p. 392-3.

Had they been implemented, these proposals would have established a framework with a greater capacity for flexible adaptation to social change later in the century, when there were higher rates of marriage break-up in Britain, from the early 1970s, than that actually established by the post-war Labour government (1945–51).

The proposals faced criticism, especially from women's organizations for not giving all women equal benefits with men. More lethally, they were opposed by the Treasury and the Economic Section of the War Cabinet on the grounds of their projected costs. Beveridge, despite his real sympathy with women's needs, had been instructed to construct a system of National Insurance and could find no way to fit into it women who did not have equivalent work histories with men. He justified his recommendations for married women on the grounds that the work of the housewife in the home was as important socially and economically as waged work and merited equal recognition in the social security system. As he put it: 'The great majority… of married women must be regarded as occupied on work which is vital though unpaid, without which their husbands could not do their paid work and without which the nation could not continue'[23]. He added, 'The position of housewives is recognized in form and in substance … by treating them not as dependants of their husbands, but as partners sharing benefit and pension when there are no earnings to share'.[24] Hence it was reasonable that the male worker's contribution should cover benefits for his partner.

Behind this approach lay not only Beveridge's concern about the relative poverty of older women, which had been clear in his writings since the beginning of the century, but also his desire to reverse the pre-war decline in the birth-rate and the consequent, projected growth in the proportion of older people in the population.[25] Beveridge believed that one important reason why housewives should be supported by the social security system was that, 'In the next thirty years housewives as mothers have vital work to do in ensuring the adequate continuance of the British race and of British ideals in the world'.[26] The Report stated:

> On marriage a woman gains a legal right to maintenance by her husband as a first line of defence against risks which fall directly on the solitary woman; she undertakes at the same time to undertake vital unpaid services and becomes exposed to new risks, including the risk that her married life may be ended prematurely by widowhood or separation … Moreover even if a married woman, while living with her husband, undertakes gainful oc-

23 *Social Insurance and Allied Services,* CMD 6404, (1942) p. 49 para 107.

24 Op. Cit., p. 52, para 117.

25 Pat Thane, 'The debate on the declining birth-rate in Britain: the 'menace' of an ageing population, 1920s-1950s', *Continuity and Change,* 5:2 (1990), pp.283-4.

26 *Social Insurance and Allied Services,* CMD 6404, (1942) p. 53 para 117.

cupation ... her earning is liable to interruption by child-birth. In the national interests it is important that the interruption by child-birth should be as complete as possible; the expectant mother should be under no economic pressure to continue at work as long as she can and to return to it as soon as she can.[27]

Beveridge's assumptions appeared to be justified by the most recent census, of 1931, which showed that that 'more than 7 out 8 of all housewives, that is to say married women of working age, made marriage their sole occupation; less than one in 8 of all housewives was also gainfully employed'.[28] Reasonably enough, he expected this situation to continue after the war.[29]

Beveridge's proposals for benefits for deserted wives and 'unmarried wives' foundered partly on moral objections from those who feared that such provision would undermine the family, partly on perceived practical problems concerning the treatment of 'guilty' wives who initiated the break-up of a marriage and, above all, on Treasury objections to the costs.[30] They were not taken up by the Labour government. Thereafter 'unmarried wives' were to treated exactly as all unmarried women, and separated and divorced women were left, as before, to try to extract support from their partners in the courts or to manage on public assistance.

Despite his reputation for having influenced the post-war welfare state in Britain and elsewhere, this was not the only one of Beveridge's proposals to be rejected by the government. He also proposed encouragement of a flexible retirement age by building in discouragement of retirement at the minimum state pension age. He suggested the incentive of higher pensions for later retirement. This was due to his concern about the declining birth-rate and consequent ageing of the population, as life expectancy also rose. To help to counter-balance the likely shrinking of the population of prime working age, Beveridge thought it essential to encourage older people to remain in the workforce.[31] The government rejected Beveridge's proposals for flexible retirement mainly because, as Britain's first-ever majority Labour government, it had long been committed to *earlier* retirement for working people. Had they adopted his proposals, the difficulties of the current Labour government in persuading voters to accept flexible retirement ages might have been avoided.

---

27 Op. Cit., p. 49 para 108.
28 Op. Cit., p. 49 para 108.
29 Op. Cit., p. 50 para 111.
30 Jose Harris, *William Beveridge*, (Oxford,1997), pp. 391-412.
31 Pat Thane, 'The debate on the declining birth-rate in Britain: the 'menace' of an ageing population, 1920s-1950s', *Continuity and Change,* 5:2 (1990).

Pensions since the Second World War

Another important proposal by Beveridge which the Labour government rejected was that the universal basic pension system should be introduced gradually, over twenty years, to enable a fund to build up which would finance a pension adequate for pensioners to live on, without requiring those without other resources to need a means-tested supplement. Beveridge was strongly opposed to means-testing and wished to protect members of the national insurance scheme from the risk of experiencing it. This did not happen. The Labour government chose to give voters an immediate rise in pensions, above the level Beveridge proposed as a starting point, but not to a level sufficient for any pensioner to survive on without a supplement from some source. They did not plan further increases. Consequently, even when the pension was first introduced in 1948, 638.000 (mainly female) pensioners had to supplement it through the new means-tested scheme of National Assistance, also introduced in 1948. Effectively, National Assistance was the successor of the Poor Law (which was formally abolished in 1948, having survived since 1601) providing means-tested relief for the destitute who had no other resource. The number of pensioners receiving National Assistance rose to almost 1 million in 1951.

Substantial numbers of pensioners (again, mostly female) have continued ever since to depend on the means-tested supplement, which has gone through a number of changes of name and detail since 1948. Still, in 2006, 1.3 million out of 1.9 million recipients of the means-tested Pension Credit (the current means-tested option, and the least punitive so far, introduced in 2003) were female.[32] Equally consistently since 1948, and a still greater cause of concern, have been the large numbers of people who have qualified for the supplement but failed to apply: still 20 % of eligible pensioners do not take up the Pension Credit, under the most humane form of administration so far devised for this supplement.

Beveridge's expectations about the post-war roles of women appeared to be borne out. Marriage rates rose and marriage became almost universal. The numbers of never-married woman fell sharply. The mean age at first marriage also fell to historically low levels, from 25,3 years for women earlier in the century (and the norm for long before), to 22,6 years in 1971[33]. This reduced the time available to most women to establish themselves in careers and accumulate pensions savings between completing education and entering marriage and childbirth, the more so because the compulsory school leaving age rose from 14 to 15

32 UK Department of Work and Pensions, *Pensions Report shows 'historical divide' faced by women*, Press Release, (3rd November, 2005).

33 Jane Lewis, *The End of Marriage*, (Cheltenham, 2001), p. 30.

in 1947 and 16 in 1972, with increasing numbers of young women staying in education past the minimum leaving age. The declining marriage age was shared by female graduates. The birth-rate also rose and births tended to be concentrated early in marriage. Social disapproval, poor availability of childcare, full employment for men and generally rising living standards ensured that in the immediate post-war years mothers of young children were rarely in the paid labour market and almost never in full-time work.

The young women who married and had their children in the nineteen fifties and sixties and did not build up pensions in their own right, and who all too often experienced divorce in the 1970s and after, are now in or approaching pension age. They account for a great deal of current poverty among older women and will do so for some time since they can expect to live into their eighties, at least.

In what is now seen as a 'golden age' of full employment between the end of the Second World War and the early 1970s, marriage also experienced an historically quite unusual golden age: life expectancy rose and the numbers of relatively young widows fell, while divorce was difficult to obtain and relatively rare by more recent standards. It was the only period in British history when the long-lasting marriage really was the norm.

However, older women, whose children had grown, were active increasingly in the workforce, indeed were encouraged out of the home and into the workplace by the post-war Labour government, which was concerned about the labour shortage. But it remained difficult, even for the best qualified women, to re-enter full-time or pensionable employment and most had discontinuous work records. Since the 1950s, increasing numbers of married women have been in paid work for increasing lengths of time, though an exceptionally high proportion of the British female workforce continues to be in part-time work which is not, or is inadequately, pensioned and is often low-paid. Women have continued to outlive men. For all of these reasons older women have still tended to be poorer than older men.

Occupational Pensions

The basic flat-rate state pension has continued at a below subsistence level to the present. Successive governments have experienced relatively little pressure to increase the pension because a high proportion of male workers rely for the bulk of their pension income on an occupational pension and have little incentive to demand higher state pensions. This key role of occupational pensions in the British system was encouraged by the Conservative governments which were in office

1951-64.[34] When Labour returned to office in 1964, it immediately increased the basic pension but could not afford to raise it to a subsistence level. It aspired to effect a long-term reconstruction of the system, to add an income related tier to the flat-rate pension, as had been Labour policy since 1957, but it was voted out of office in 1970 before this could be done. When Labour returned to power in 1974 it introduced a limited State Earnings Related Pension.[35] However, this was abolished by Margaret Thatcher's Conservative government, which was elected in 1979. British pensions have been victims of the adversarial character of the two-party, first-past-the-post, British political system.

The Conservative governments from 1979-1997 allowed the real value of the basic pension to fall still further, as they strove to cut government expenditure and as they became aware of the ageing of the population and the increased pension costs expected to result. They encouraged occupational and private pensions and reduced state regulation of both, which contributed to serious scandals of mis-selling of private pensions and to the collapse of some occupational schemes.[36]

Not until the 1980s did significant numbers of women enter employment which could potentially provide an adequate occupational pension or sufficient income to save for an adequate private pension. Yet still their chances of building a pension sufficient even for moderate comfort in old age were less than those of men, due to the persistently lower pay and promotion prospects compared with men, and discontinuous work records, of all but a minority of women.

In the immediate post-war period, some occupational pension schemes still did not admit women on the grounds that they were likely to leave their employment on marriage or on the birth of a child. Schemes which did so still often repaid the contributions as a 'dowry' on marriage. Some admitted women only at later ages than men, presumably once they were thought too old to marry. In 1965 the minimum age of admission to pension schemes varied between 21 and 40 for women, whereas for men it was normally 21.[37] In 1966, an official enquiry

---

34 Leslie Hannah, *Inventing Retirement. The development of occupational pensions in Britain* (Cambridge, 1986); Hugh Pemberton, 'Politics and Pensions in Post-War Britain', Hugh Pemberton, Pat Thane & Noel Whiteside (eds.), *Britain's Pensions Crisis. History and Policy*, (Oxford, 2006), pp. 39-63.

35 Hugh Pemberton, 'Politics and Pensions in Post-War Britain', Hugh Pemberton, Pat Thane & Noel Whiteside (eds.), *Britain's Pensions Crisis. History and Policy*, (Oxford, 2006).

36 Gordon Clark, 'The UK Occupational Pension System in Crisis', Hugh Pemberton, Pat Thane & Noel Whiteside (eds.), *Britain's Pensions Crisis. History and Policy*, (Oxford, 2006), pp. 145-168.

37 Viola Klein, *Britain's Married Women Workers*, (London, 1965), p. 126.

by industrialists and trade unionists decided that the preservation of women's occupational pensions on marriage was unnecessary.[38]

Very slowly, pension annuities for widows were introduced into occupational schemes, typically providing one-third to one-half of the husband's (often low) pension. By 1971, only one-third of private sector scheme members were eligible for this on death in service. For members who died after retirement, employers, under pressure from members, from the 1950s offered the opportunity for a male employee to take a lower pension in return for an enhanced pension for his widow: usually one-third to one-half of that paid while he was alive. Few eligible members took up this option because most initial pensions were low and the trade-off offered unfavourable.[39] Provision for widows improved due to the requirements for occupational schemes wishing to contract out of the state earnings-related scheme (SERPS), introduced in 1978, but even the best widows' pensions provided no more than half the husband 's occupational pension, which still was often low.[40]

The two pillars of state and occupational pensions did even less to provide for the growing numbers of divorced and separated women from the 1970s. Not until 2000 did women (and men where appropriate) gain the right on divorce to receive a proportion of their former spouse's pension fund and to receive benefits independently, though few such 'sharing orders' have so far been made by the courts and the advantages to women are limited.[41] Also, if the husband has a second family, it is disadvantaged by this arrangement.

Conclusion

The current problems of poverty among older women in Britain are not new. The difficulties for women of providing for their old age have been known for over a century and have never gone away, but they have been evaded by successive governments, not least because they are hard to solve without considerable public expense. But what is the alternative? Of course, women, like men, should save all that they can, but there is no evidence that large numbers of the old women at present in poverty are suffering the just reward of improvidence in early life. The

38 Leslie Hannah, *Inventing Retirement. The development of occupational pensions in Britain*, (Cambridge,1986), p. 118.
39 Op. Cit., pp. 119-20.
40 Op. Cit., p. 120-1.
41 Jay Ginn, 'Gender Inequalities: Sidelines in British Pension Policy', Hugh Pemberton, Pat Thane & Noel Whiteside (eds.), *Britain's Pensions Crisis. History and Policy*, (Oxford, 2006), pp. 91-124.

British pension system has been characterized by a state pension too low to live on and dependence on occupational and private pensions which cannot provide a comfortable old age to the low-paid and irregularly employed, most of whom are female.

Since Labour was re-elected to government in 1997, it has done little to improve the basic state pension and it has taken only mild measures to increase regulation of private and occupational pensions. It has focussed, rather, upon improving the means-tested supplement in order to help the two million or so, mainly female, pensioners left in poverty by the failings of the other two pillars. The means-tested Pension Credit, introduced in 2003, has for the first time detached means-tested supplements to pensioners from the rest of the public assistance system in an attempt to increase take-up and diminish the stigma of applying for public assistance[42]. It provides an adequate income for the poorest older people. The government has also improved other benefits for them, including providing free public transport for all over 60. But still an estimated 20% of eligible pensioners do not apply for the Pension Credit.

It is estimated that unless the pension system is substantially reformed the proportion of pensioners eligible for the means-tested credit will rise to 70% by 2050.[43] The government is currently considering a major overhaul of the pension system, following an impressively thorough official study of the issue[44], including gradually raising the state pension age to 68, increasing the basic state pension and introducing a compulsory contributory second tier.[45]

Hence, currently, of the three pillars of the British pension system, the first, the basic, flat-rate state pension is a slender, fragile pillar, not at present strong enough on its own to support any pensioner. The second, occupational and private pensions, is currently highly unstable, with schemes shifting from 'defined benefit' to less costly and less generous 'defined contribution' schemes[46] or even closing. There is widespread lack of confidence in them. The third, means-tested, pillar keeps on growing but seems unable to escape the problem of non take-up.

---

42 Rodney Lowe, *The Welfare State in Britain since 1945*, (London, 2004), pp. 409-10.

43 UK Pensions Commission, *A New Pensions Settlement for the Twenty-first Century. The Second Report of the Pensions Commission*, (London 2005), p. 142.

44 UK Pensions Commission *A New Pensions Settlement for the Twenty-first Century. The Second Report of the Pensions Commission.* (London 2005) and UK Pensions Commission, *Pensions: Challenges and Choices. The First Report of the Pensions Commission*, (London, 2004).

45 Hugh Pemberton, Pat Thane & Noel Whiteside (eds.), *Britain's Pensions Crisis. History and Policy.* 'Epilogue', (Oxford, 2006).

46 Gordon Clark, 'The UK Occupational Pension System in Crisis', Hugh Pemberton, Pat Thane & Noel Whiteside (eds.), *Britain's Pensions Crisis. History and Policy,* (Oxford, 2006).

We have yet to see whether current government proposals can provide a more secure British pensions system.

The 'Benefit Formula' in Danish Old Age Pensions

Jørn Henrik Petersen

The objective of this contribution is to analyse the development of the 'benefit formula' in Danish old age pensions. The focus is on the introduction of the People's Pension (Folkepension). It is demonstrated that the understanding of the people's pension as a basic income support programme providing flat-rate benefits to all elderly is flawed. For a discussion of the political background to the 1956 reform I refer to the contribution in this volume by Klaus Petersen and Jørn Henrik Petersen.[1]

The period of discretion

The forty years prior to the Act on relief in old age saw comprehensive debates on the conditions of the elderly. Following complex negotiations outside the parliamentary committees, the government and the moderate Liberals finally arrived at a settlement about tariffs, taxation, poor law and relief for the aged. On 9 March 1891, a bill on 'old age relief for the deserving poor outside the poor law' was introduced. The Act was adopted on 28 March, coming into force on 1 July. The content of the bill very largely depended on the political exigencies of the time.

The coverage of the Act was universal, based on citizenship rather than membership of the workforce. The same universal coverage – different from the German 1889 solution[2] reserved for the wage earners – marked the British 1908 Act.[3] In addition the Danish Act required an applicant to be a native-born subject and to have had fixed residence in the country for at least ten years. Britain – less

1 See also Jørn Henrik Petersen & Klaus Petersen, *Danish old age pensions with a focus on the Folkepension*, (forthcoming) and Jørn Henrik Petersen & Klaus Petersen, 'Folkepensionsreformen 1956', Jørn Henrik Petersen & Klaus Petersen (eds.), *13 Reformer af den danske velfærdsstat*, (Odense, 2005), pp. 97-116.

2 For a comparison of the Danish and the German Act, see Jørn Henrik Petersen, 'Altersversicherung und Altersversorgung. Ein dänischer Kommentar anläßlich des hundertjährigen jubiläums des deutschen invalitäts- und altersversicherugsgesetzes', *Deutsche Rentenversicherung*, (1989), pp. 649-63.

3 For a comparison of the Danish and British Act, see Jørn Henrik Petersen, 'The Danish 1891 Act on old age relief: A response to agrarian demand and pressure', *Journal of Social Policy*, 19 (1990), pp. 69-91.

restrictively – required applicants to have been a British subject for at least twenty years and to be a resident of the United Kingdom. The age of entitlement was 60 years in Denmark, while in Britain and Germany the age was set at 70. In Denmark the better-off were excluded by the requirement that the applicant must be without the means of providing for himself or those dependent on him for the necessaries of life – a discretionary condition – while Britain made use of a sliding scale and stipulated a fixed upper income limit.

Deservingness – serving as a substitute for contributory payments and in the Danish context termed as indirect self-help – was defined by a number of conditions.[4] Benefit levels were set according to the discretion of the local authorities, i.e. there was no explicit 'benefit formula'. Soon after the enactment, however, several local authorities, in particular the capital Copenhagen, developed a rudimentary form of 'guiding scales' by which the pension level was adjusted to the amount and kind of other income of the applicant.[5] This was a precursor of the genuine benefit formula laid down by the 1922 legislation (see below) and it was in fact, an idea imitated by Britain. In contrast, the German model, based as it was on an insurance model, made benefits dependent on previous contributions and the length of the applicant's previous working life.

The Danish debates on insurance versus tax-financed provision continued. In 1902 a commission was appointed to elaborate a proposal on 'folkeforsikring' (people's insurance). The commission had a long life partly because of its investigation relating to unemployment insurance and partly due to a high turnover in membership. The report, therefore, was published only in 1915, but the First World War had brought other and more pressing problems to the forefront. This said it is still important briefly to review the nature of the recommendations.[6]

The majority recommended that the discretionary, charity-based nature of the 1891 act be replaced by an arrangement implying that the individual had a defined legal claim under known rules. Theoretically this did not necessarily demand contributory payments, but since an unconditional right may have had demoralising effects, potentially weakening the personal sense of responsibility, the majority approved of some kind of an insurance system. Irrespective of need, the

---

4 For a specification see Jørn Henrik Petersen, 'The Danish 1891 Act on old age relief: A response to agrarian demand and pressure', *Journal of Social Policy,* 19 (1990), pp. 69-91.

5 For an in-depth analysis, see Jørn Henrik Petersen, *Den danske alderdomsforsørgelseslovgivnings udvikling I. Oprindelsen,* (Odense, 1985).

6 See Jørn Henrik Petersen & Klaus Petersen, 'Shake, Rattle and Roll! From Charity to Social Rights in the Danish Welfare State 1890-1933', Steven King & John Stewart (eds.), *Welfare Peripheries. The Development of Welfare States in Nineteenth and Twentieth Century Europe,* (Bern, 2007), pp. 149-179.

claim was a corollary to contributory payments. Nobody would be subjected to any investigation of his or her financial conditions or to any discretionary decision-making by the authorities.

The minority on the other hand strongly urged that it must be seen as a natural right of those of limited means that they would be assured of economic support in case of old age without contributory payments and without the 'humiliation' associated with collecting assistance on a discretionary basis, i.e. a demand for a genuine benefit formula with benefits financed from general taxation.

The choice was between rights ensured by contributory payments of an insurance arrangement and rights mirrored by a defined benefit scale financed by general taxation in a pay-as-you-go manner, i.e. the choice between a social insurance and a tax-transfer model.[7]

During the parliamentary session 1919/20 the Social Liberal government introduced a bill on provision in case of invalidity and another on provision in case of old age. They were both founded on non-contributory tax-financing. The spokesman of the Liberals stated that his party still sympathised with the insurance idea, but he did suggest that a compromise was possible. Referring to the issue of old age he described the solution as historically predetermined by decisions taken in 1891, and he cautiously suggested that parliament should consider the strong and profound dispute on insurance versus tax-finance as having come to an end.

In 1920 the Liberals took office and the new prime minister made it known that a bill on insurance against invalidity would be presented as soon as possible and it would be followed by a bill on provision in old age. Even so, the bill was not intended to break with the path laid out in 1891. This meant that rights in the Danish old age pension system had to be tied not to formal contracts (insurance) but to political and social 'contracts' between politicians and citizens. Nevertheless the understanding, definition and the extent of rights remained a controversial political issue in years to come.

The 'benefit formula' of the 1922 Act

Presenting the bill on old age pensions in 1922 the Liberal Minister of the Interior, Oluf Krag, said:

> It does not serve any interest to revive the debate on people's insurance versus non-contributory provision in old age. The thirty years old history in our country makes it

7 For a thorough analysis, see Jørn Henrik Petersen, *Den danske lovgivning om alderdomsforsørgelse II, 1891-1933 – fra skøn til ret,* (Odense, 2006).

natural to continue the development based on the principles originally adopted irrespective of one's opinion concerning what might have been the most desirable solution in the first place.[8]

The benefit formula proposed included not less than six scales, one to be applied in Copenhagen, two to be applied in the municipalities and three for use in the parishes. These sought to reflect living conditions in different parts of the country. Many involved in the debate voiced criticism of the number of benefit formulae. Also discussed was whether any reduction had to be proportional or progressive. The Social Democrats – being dissatisfied with the benefit level and having preferred a genuine 'people's pension' based on flat-rated benefits – endorsed the principles of the formula as such, while the Social Liberals preferred a progressive reduction ensuring advantages for smaller incomes at the cost of the higher ones. The Liberal Minister argued, parallel to the Social Democrats, that:

> The dissatisfaction voiced that persons with some income or fortune are granted a small pension is socially unacceptable. It must not be forgotten that old age pensions ought not to be a provision only for the poor. To extend benefits beyond persons in financial difficulties means that the arrangement to a greater extent assumes the character of a people's pension.[9]

He was strongly opposed by a member of his own party, who noted:

> The truth is that we are approaching a situation in which it is the duty of the public to ensure provision from the cradle to the grave.[10]

The final reading was first and foremost a debate between adherents of insurance in one form or another, and the supporters of non-contributory arrangements. The core of the argument was whether one could have a 'right' that was not paid for. In the opinion of some members the bill implied a 'right' only in a semantic sense. The Minister of the Interior, however, was unshakeable in his argument:

> The decisive [issue] is whether pension payments are to be reserved only for those who have had a genuine employment to the advantage of the collective – i.e. public servants – or whether society is not as much entitled to grant a pension free of direct charge

8 *Rigsdagstidende, 1921/22, Folketingets Forhandlinger*, col. 4126. This as well as the following quotes from the parliamentary debates have been translated into English by the author.

9 *Rigsdagstidende, 1921/22, Folketingets Forhandlinger*, col. 4759.

10 *Rigsdagstidende, 1921/22, Folketingets Forhandlinger*, col. 4771.

to those who have contributed to the development of society. It is my opinion that the latter have the same claim as have the former. This is the basic idea of the Act.[11]

The Social Liberal spokesman largely concurred. He argued:

> It does not mean anything that an individual has not paid an earmarked tax. He has paid his share by what he has contributed to society during his lifetime; not only by his work efforts but also by the general taxes he has paid to the public purse. Thus, everyone has paid his or her 'premiums' to the large cooperative society [the Danish community]. And this community repays [that debt] when the person comes of age.[12]

During the readings in parliament the number of benefit formulae was reduced to three, 'the basic amount' was reduced and the reduction was made progressive. The basic principles of the benefit formula eventually adopted are illustrated by figure 1 mirroring the calculation of the old age pension benefit in case of respectively a married couple, a single man and a single woman living in the capital of Copenhagen. Similar formulae governed the calculation of benefits in respectively the municipalities and the parishes.

Figure 1. The benefit formula of the 1922-Act for respectively a married couple, a single man and a single woman in Copenhagen.

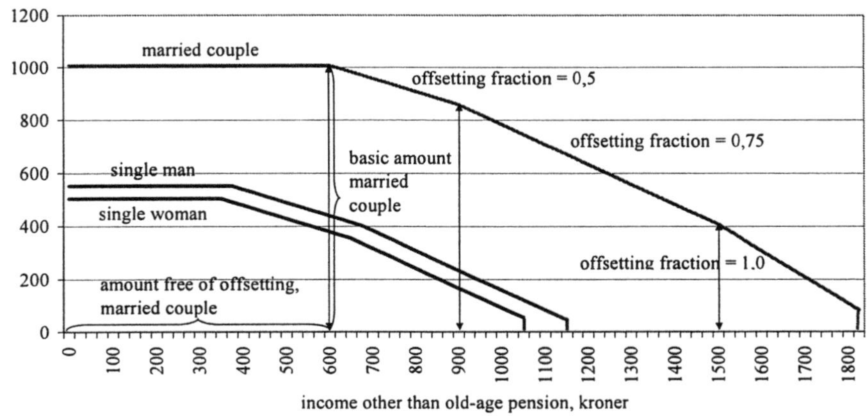

The Prime Minister, Niels Neergaard, and his Minister of the Interior, Oluf Krag, both knew that the debate on discretion versus 'rights', on insurance versus a tax-transfer procedure, had come to an end. The point of no return had been

11 *Rigsdagstidende, 1921/22, Folketingets Forhandlinger*, col. 8129.
12 *Rigsdagstidende, 1921/22, Folketingets Forhandlinger*, col. 8131-32.

passed. The opposition applauded their work as the principles were concerned, but criticised the solution with respect to the [increased] age of entitlement and the benefit levels. It was on these battlegrounds that debate over provision for the elderly was to continue in the 1920s. The 1922-reform meant that the principle of social rights was introduced in Danish social legislation.

The components of the benefit formula were a) the *basic amount* that was paid to all over and above the age of eligibility who collected incomes from other sources by an amount smaller than the *income of exemption;* b) the *income of exemption* (the amount free of offsetting) that separated those collecting the basic amount from those receiving only a reduced benefit; c) the *offsetting mechanism* the characteristics of which were defined by the use of one or more *offsetting fraction(s)* implying either a proportional or a progressive reduction; d) the *pension level at which the pension was discontinued;* e) the differentiation system regarding *sex*; f) the differentiation system concerning *marital status*; g) the differentiation with respect to *place of residence*; h) the possible *differential offsetting mechanism* as regards incomes from personal work, annuities and returns on capital.

The setting of the implied parameters, obviously, is decisive for the scheme's impact on the income distribution of the elderly. Great political attention, therefore, is attached to the benefit formula. Since the adoption of this system in 1922 Danish pension policy has been a permanent dispute on the setting of the parameters. I am not going to discuss all the parametric changes that have been implemented over the years but focus only on the basic principles of the benefit formula.

The Debate Continued

In retrospect it is obvious that the days were over for changing track in Danish pension policy. With the reform of 1922 the genuine insurance agenda was lost.

Among Conservative politicians, however, there existed an animosity towards taxation and public welfare provisions which occasionally created a breeding ground for ideas on insurance based pensions. Following the first Social Democratic government (1924-26), even the Liberal party adopted a critical attitude towards the 1922 Act, fearing that under Social Democratic rule social rights could turn into a dangerous and expensive tool.

For the session 1928-29 the Conservatives presented their own motion on 'people's insurance'.[13] The motion, marking a fundamental change of policy and

13 *Rigsdagstidende, 1928/29, tillæg A,* cols. 4173-4210.

ideology, gave rise to a lengthy debate.[14] The Liberal Minister of the Interior accepted the idea in principle, noting that

> What I am entitled to is my genuine right not only as a citizen who has accomplished my societal obligations but also in my capacity as a contributor.

Obviously, he tried to balance between on the one hand the principle of the pension as a 'right' following from the pensioners previous accomplishments (regular work) to the advantage of society and on the other hand the 'right' as the quo paid in return for the contributory quid.

The Social Democrats and Social Liberals, in accordance with past debates, supported a continuance of the principles of 1891 and 1922. Given this constellation of opposition and lukewarm support, the proposals became bogged down. A budget crisis resulted in a new election, bringing a coalition of the Social Democrats and the Social Liberals into office. K.K. Steincke was appointed as Minister of Social Affairs, thus bringing an ambitious social reformer into the limelight. For Steincke the idea of social rights was at the core of the problem.

Steincke's 'people's insurance'

Steincke, anticipating the later arguments of William Beveridge[15] and T.H. Marshall[16], urged that the 'right' to social benefits should be on a par with other rights of the citizen (civil and political), thus avoiding any demoralising feelings of humiliation and dependency.[17] He also anticipated the Beveridge approach by emphasising that a full implementation of the principle of social rights implied a social minimum to be supplemented by individual saving. To strengthen the independence and the character of the individual, he argued, one had to rely on genuine legal claims ('rights') being conditioned only by the fulfilment of a priori defined criteria.

In 1929 Steincke presented the first half of his comprehensive social reform – a bill on workers' insurance and a bill on 'people's insurance', including sickness

---

14 *Rigsdagstidende, 1928/29, Folketingets Forhandlinger*, cols. 3155-63, 4589-4637, 4781-4900.

15 *Social Insurance and Allied Services,* Command 6404, (1942).

16 Thomas Humphrey Marshall, 'Class, Citizenship and Social Development', *Essays by T.H.Marshall,* (Chicago and London, 1964), pp. 72-134.

17 Karl Kristian Steincke, *Fremtidens Forsørgelsesvæsen i Danmark,* (København, 1920), pp. 272-73.

and disablement as well as old age pensions.[18] By linking entitlement to old age pensions to membership of the sickness insurance funds Steincke had the alibi to label his proposal a 'people's insurance'. In doing so, he tried to defeat a concept traditionally used by Conservatives, i.e. an insurance-based pension system. If Steincke succeeded in adding new meaning to the concept of people's insurance the Conservative agenda would be effectively blocked and people's insurance would mean social rights. Consequently, the Conservative Party immediately countered Steincke's proposal with its own plan for a genuine old age insurance scheme. The Conservative leader John Christmas-Møller argued that

> [....] how can one understand people's insurance – well, here we have to comprehend a system by which the assistance of the old is taken care of through a form of insurance. That's the way we always have understood it.[19]

The Conservative agenda was never taken really seriously and was rejected by the other parties – including the Liberal Party – for the same reasons as in 1922.

The complicated political situation both within and outside parliament led to Steincke's reform proposals having a rocky path. On several occasions during the period 1929-1933 the proposal was discussed at length in parliament. The reform was repeatedly postponed for further investigation and negotiations. Only after the crisis settlement of January 1933[20] was the door opened. As part of the settlement, the Liberal party agreed not to block Steincke's proposal for social reform, including his proposal for an old age pension. For recipients of old age pensions the basic principles of the 1922 Act were unchanged even though some of the eligibility criteria were tightened. As mentioned above Steincke's proposal included a precondition for receiving old age pension that the individual had to have been member of a sickness insurance system. Conservative and Liberal members of parliament, therefore, could celebrate the reform as a step towards some kind of (rather clear and indirect) insurance principle. The Social Democrats and Social Liberals saw the reform as a step towards a universal tax-financed pension system and in the longer perspective this certainly became the case.

---

18 The remaining half of the reform, dealing with social assistance and unemployment insurance, was to be presented later.

19 *Rigsdagstidende, 1929/30, Folketingets Forhandlinger*, col. 4144.

20 See Jørn Henrik Petersen, *Den danske lovgivning om alderdomsforsørgelse II, 1891-1933 – fra skøn til ret,* (Odense, 2006), chapter 15.

An interlude

Despite Steincke's semantic confidence trick adherents of insurance principles persistently argued in favour of a new pension paradigm challenging the one adopted. The first years after the German occupation of Denmark 1940–45 were marked by the Social Democrats' endeavours to improve benefits – in particular for those of limited means – within the existing pension system. The Liberals and Conservatives on the other hand opted for an overhaul. In 1947, the Social Democratic government succeeded in carrying through a number of amendments, because the bourgeois parties abstained from voting. The price to be paid was the nomination of a new Commission on 'people's insurance'.[21] During the first years of the commission's work Social Democratic governments implemented a number of gradual improvements of the benefits, but – contrary to the Social Liberals – it was definitely not the objective of the party to adopt universal, flat rate benefits. The party identified 'insurance' as a system in which the 'premiums' were paid as taxation and in which the benefit of the recipients was separated from his or her previous contributions. Only when all ideas on genuine insurance-like arrangements had been given up did the party engage itself in politicising the pension system as a system. Not least the experts and civil servants serving as members of the Commission as well as external experts argued for a continuance of existing pension principles. It was eventually accepted by most parties that it was impossible to replace the existing arrangement by an insurance system. Cautiously the Social Democrats started talking about a 'general people's pension' (implying that pensions had to be paid to all citizens) and during the election campaign in 1953 the idea was politicised to such an extent that no escape was possible – the economic difficulties of the country notwithstanding. When the final report was published in 1955[22] the commission had worked for seven years without coming to an agreement. Ironically, the final report of the Commission on *People's Insurance* was entitled 'Report on *People's Pension'*. Despite concerns about the economic consequences, a motion was presented in parliament in November 1955: The Social Democrats had passed the point of no return, the Social Liberals exerted pressure and so did the organisations of the pensioners.

21 The Commission was nominated on February the 2nd 1948.

22 *Betænkning om Folkepension*, Betænkning nr. 123, (København, 1955).

Taking the first step towards a 'people's pension'. The 'minimum amount' adopted

In November 1955, two bills were introduced. The first aimed to amend the existing act on people's insurance (in Steincke's sense) primarily by increasing the basic amount and liberalising the offsetting mechanism. The second introduced a people's pension complying with a previous proposal jointly worked out by the Social Democrats and Social Liberals. With the exception of civil servants all Danes over and above the age of 67 were entitled to a people's pension. For single pensioners the pension equalled 6 per cent of the average income for breadwinners to be paid irrespective of income and fortune. The benefit was to be increased in three steps over a period of 6 years, and the Act was to be amended in the parliamentary session 1962/63. Subsequent to the first reading the bills seemed to be shipwrecked.

Figure 2. The benefit formula for a single pensioner older than 67 living in Copenhagen. The Act on people's pension 1957.

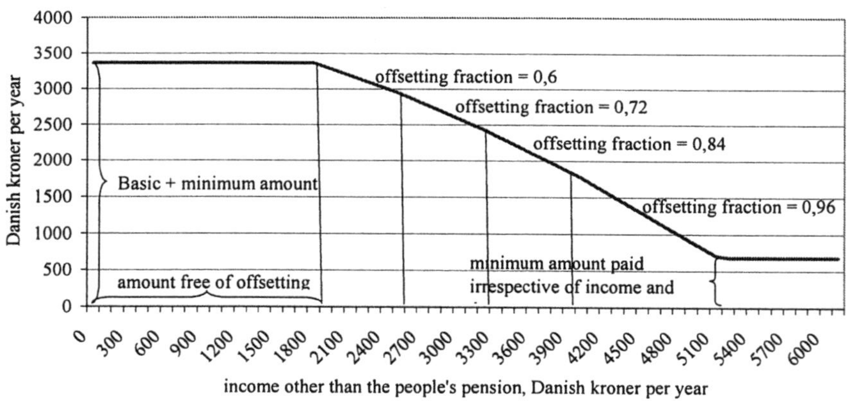

The catalyst of the political settlement was an article by a former undersecretary to the Ministry of Social Affairs.[23] His idea was simply to integrate the two bills, i.e. to let the 'people's pension' serve as a floor below which the pension could not be discontinued and letting the 'old system' overarch the 'people's pension', to entitle the system 'people's pension' and the floor 'the minimum amount'. The minimum amount, obviously, added a new parameter to the old

23 Rudolf Lassen, 'Forenklet Folkepension', *Politiken*, (November 23rd 1955); see also Rudolf Lassen, 'Noter til Folkepensionen', *Politiken*, (June 20th 1955).

benefit formula. In Lassen's view the minimum amount should gradually be increased. He saw it as the first step towards a flat rate pension.

Rudolf Lassen's idea became the core of the political settlement regarding the benefit formula.

Figure 2 shows the benefit formula for a single pensioner living in Copenhagen, but only in the case in which his or her income came from returns from capital. If it came from income from personal work and/or annuities the benefit formula made use of a so-called 'calculated income' equal to the gross income minus 1/3 of the amount free of exemption. The 'real' amount free of offsetting, therefore, was increased by 1/3, i.e. a more favourable treatment of these types of incomes compared to returns on capital. Incomes in excess of the amount free of offsetting were set off against the basic amount by a progressive scale defined over four ranges of income. Old age pensions, therefore, were still targeted towards the less well off, but all Danes with the exception of civil servants were covered and entitled to the minimum amount. The new 'minimum amount' was small, indeed, but being paid to all it served to remove the popular perception that the status of recipients of old age pension was inferior. If the pension in principle was paid to all it would not, it was argued, be seen as support for those of limited means only. Therefore, the 'take up rate' was expected to increase.

The innovations were the adoption of the *minimum amount* and the semantic change from 'old age pensions' towards 'people's pension', but the basic principles which mirrored the time-honoured paradigm remained the same. The principle of targeting the benefit to the advantage of those of limited means was maintained. The adoption of the minimum amount, however, was the first step only towards flat rate benefits paid irrespective of income and fortune.

The second step towards 'people's pension'

During the political negotiations in 1956 most spokesmen of the parties suggested to develop the idea of the 'minimum amount' so that the benefit formula was replaced by a flat rate benefit. This intent was confirmed during the parliamentary debate in November 1961 on amending the Act on invalidity- and people's pension. A commission was nominated to investigate the transition from the former pension system towards a universal, flat rated people's pension.

The commission argued[24] that the objective of encouraging saving and labour supply had gained ground to the disregard of the previous objective to target

24 *Betænkning om almindelig folkepension afgivet af folkepensionskommissionen af 1961*, Betænkning nr. 324, (København, 1963).

benefit where most needed. Four procedures for implementing a gradual transition towards 'full pensions for all', as it was termed, were presented:

- to increase the minimum amount gradually;
- to introduce flat-rate pensions for pensioners over a given age that was gradually to be lowered;
- to increase the amount free of offsetting in a number of steps;
- to reduce the offsetting fraction gradually.

Some members of the commission urged that whatever strategy was adopted the advantages were mainly benefiting people with higher incomes. They argued, therefore, in favour of measures to the advantage of the less well off partly by cash benefits and partly by benefits in kind.

In the following public debate the director of the Danish National Institute of Social Research, Henning Friis[25] saw no compelling reasons for an immediate abolishment of offsetting and expressed doubts about the postulated impact of offsetting on saving and labour supply. For Professor Jørgen Dich[26] the main reason underlying the idea was related to the interests of the better off business men in general and the farmers in particular in receiving people's pension on top of their incomes originating from sale of their enterprises. He saw the idea as complying with the post-war trend on tax- and social policies that to a growing extent mirrored an anti-equalising development.[27]

In January 1964 the government introduced a Bill implying that the basic amount as from April the 1st 1970 was to be paid to all pensioners above the age of 67 irrespective of income and fortune, so-called 'full pension to everyone'. The government followed the third strategy discussed by the commission, i.e. to increase the amount free of offsetting in five steps during the period 1965–1970 in which the minimum amount was maintained as a 'floor'. This procedure was chosen because it favoured the pensioners with the relative lowest incomes on top of the people's pension.

The transition strategy is illustrated by figure 3.

During the parliamentary readings, the Social Democratic Minister of Social Affairs saw the adoption of the 'full people's pension' paid irrespective of income and fortune as 'a historical event' and a logical move in continuation of the adoption of the minimum amount. But, he argued, there were reasons for introducing a 'pension addition' on top of the basic amount. The 'pension addition' was to some extent a concession to the internal opposition among the Social De-

25 Henning Friis, 'Den fremtidige alderspensionering', *Politiken* (June 4th 1963).

26 Jørgen Dich, 'Hvorfor skal velhavere have fuld folkepension', *Politiken* (June 29th 1963).

27 This thesis was developed in Jørgen Dich, 'Udviklingen af skatte- og tilskudspolitikken siden 1939', *Økonomi og Politik*, (1965), pp. 225-260.

mocrats arguing along distributional lines. The construction was strongly criticised by the bourgeois parties as a break with the intended principles. While the Conservatives and the Liberals had been very hesitant adherents of the idea of the people's pension in 1955/56, they had in the 1960's changed their political position so that they now strongly argued in favour of a genuine universal pension. The Minister defensively argued that over time the 'pension addition' would fade away in the wake of developing supplementary pension schemes. This argument became the fig leaf for the support of the bourgeois parties.

Figure 3. A stylized presentation of the transition towards a flat-rated basic amount 1965-1970, a single pensioner.

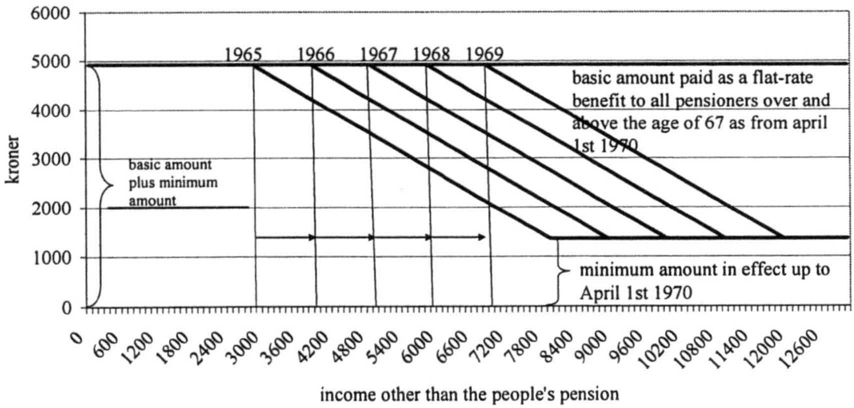

The benefit formula adopted is – for a single pensioner – illustrated by figure 4. The 'pension addition' amounted to 18.9 per cent of the maximum benefit.

The development from the 1922 pension Act over the 1956 introduction of a minimum pension towards the partly – but only partly – flat-rated nature of the 1970 system was of a great psychological and symbolic importance. By the benefit formula 'discretion' was replaced by a 'social right' to provision in old age. This was the first blow to the 'charitable' nature of the 1891 Act that in the popular understanding represented a relict from the poor law system. The second blow came with the introduction of the minimum pension implying that most Danes as from 1957 actually received people's pension. 'Universal coverage' was turned into 'universal entitlement' to the benefit – at least to the minimum amount. Even though most Social Democrats deep down in their hearts were adherents of 'targeting', and even though they were slow starters on the move that weakened

Figure4. The benefit formula for a single pensioner at April 1970.

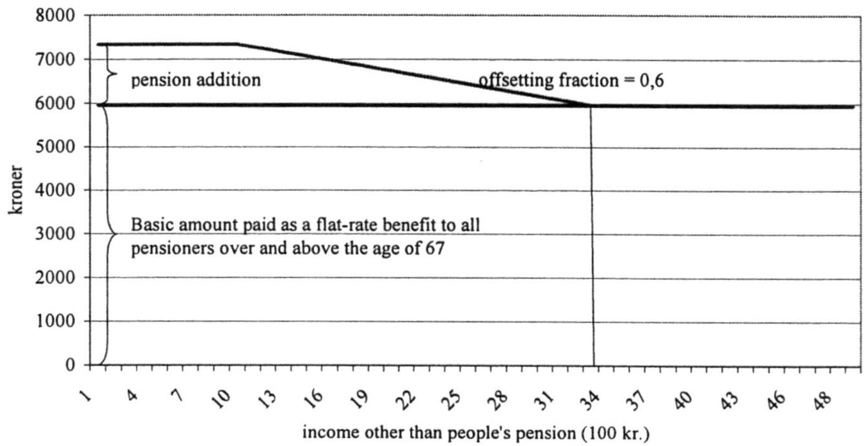

targeting, the party welcomed the minimum amount and the concept of people's pension as a political victory. To some extent this had to do with the importance attributed to the people's pension by welfare state opponents as a constitutive measure of the 'welfare state'. During the 1960s the Social Democrats came to identify themselves as the 'founding fathers' of the welfare state and the people's pension was seen as the epitome of the welfare state. The third blow, obviously, was the move towards flat-rated benefits paid irrespective of income and fortune. Had flat-rated benefits actually been adopted all Danes would have been treated equally, but for many Social Democrats that was far too generous towards the better off, so it was decided to introduce the pension addition so that equal pensions for all Danes were never adopted, but all Danes were receiving the people's pension.

Even though some Social Democrats flirted with the Swedish idea of developing 'earnings-related pensions', i.e. a pension formula in which the pension level is functionally related in one way or another to the previous income from the person's working life, the idea met with criticism from many Social Democrats.[28] It was difficult, therefore, to mobilise the party around this demand and since it was related to ideas on introducing 'economic democracy' it was also strongly op-

28 This is discussed in Klaus Petersen, 'Fordelingspolitik, samfundsøkonomi og organisationsinteresser. Den danske arbejderbevægelse og spørgsmålet om tillægspension 1963-1990', *Historisk Tidsskrift* (2002), pp. 126-169.

posed by the bourgeois parties – the corollary being that earnings related pensions were not adopted in Denmark. The pension agenda remained open.

Towards targeting within a universal frame

In 1979 the 'early voluntary retirement pay' was introduced.[29] The scheme was marketed as a 'labour market measure' to give older employees an incentive to retire at a younger age for the benefit of young workers employment options, but, obviously, it did serve as an element of the pension system. To provide further incentives to retire the benefit formula was changed as from January 1984, so that offsetting against the basic amount was re-introduced – but only in case of incomes from personal work and only for persons of age 67-69. This was a move away from the principles laid down in 1970. As from January 1st 1994 the 'income test' was extended to cover all pensioners regardless of age.

Figure 5. The benefit formula for a single pensioner 1999.

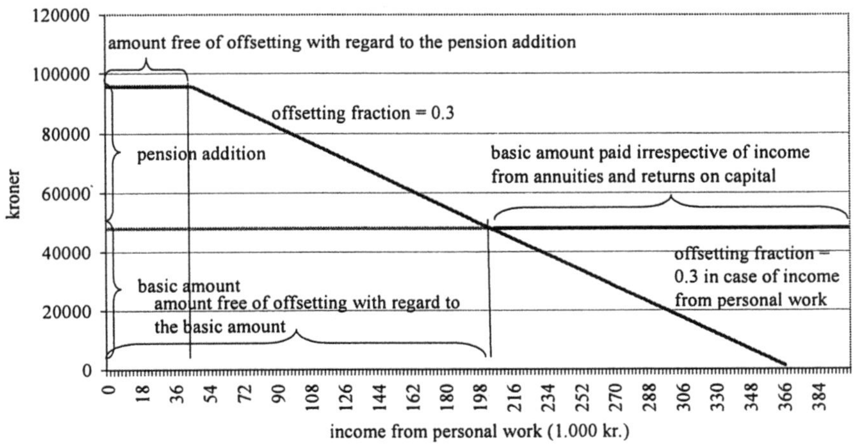

Following the 1987 and the 1993 tax reforms the benefit formula was changed in 1993. The pensioners' previous income tax exemptions were abolished and the pensions were 'grossified'. The aim was to ensure 'transparency'. It is of interest, however, that the lion's share of the increased pension was made

29 See Klaus Petersen, 'Efterløn', Jørn Henrik Petersen & Klaus Petersen (eds.), *13 reformer af den danske velfærdsstat,* (Odense, 2005), pp. 157-172.

part of the pension addition. In 1994 a so-called 'special pension addition' was introduced, but it was phased out during a five-year period in which the previous pension addition was gradually increased to amount to 49.8 per cent of the maximum benefit. As part of a political settlement on amending the 'early voluntary retirement scheme' the age of entitlement to people's pension was lowered (1999) to 65, and the offsetting fraction was reduced from 0.6 to 0.3, cf. figure 5. The endeavour to make the system transparent by making the income tax exemptions visible changed the benefit formula. It is difficult to describe the formula portrayed by figure 5 as a basic income support system providing flat rate benefits to all elderly.

Due to political pressure from 'Danish People's Party' – the supporting party of the bourgeois government that took office in 2001 – a one-off supplementary pension benefit was adopted as from 2003. The following year the one-off nature was abolished and the benefit was included in the regular benefit formula and termed 'the supplementary pension benefit'. As from 2005 the supplementary pension benefit was further increased and the offsetting mechanism was changed, so that incomes from work, annuities and returns on capital were offset against the supplementary benefit in the same (complicated) manner as were 'personal additions'.

Figure 6. The benefit formula for a single pensioner, 2006.

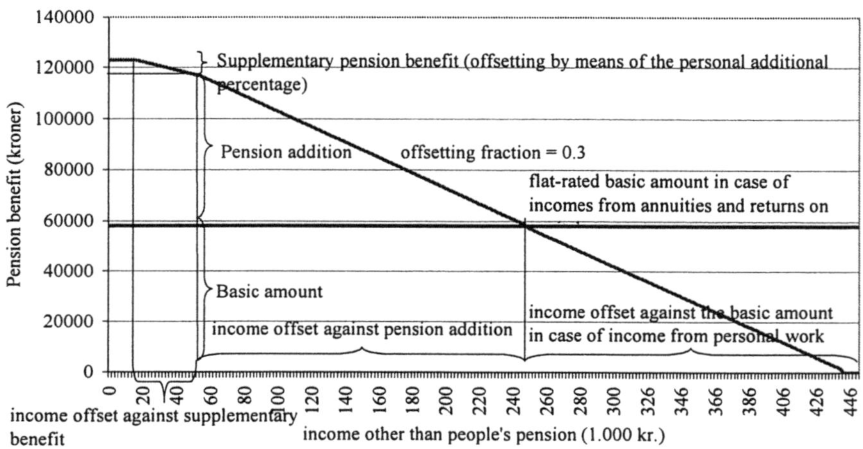

The benefit is 'income tested' for incomes below approx. DKK 247.000 and for pensioners collecting income from work the benefit is income tested for all income levels. The sum of the maximum income tested part relative to the maximum benefit is 53 per cent. The basic amount is paid as a flat-rate benefit only for pensioners who collect incomes in excess of approx. DKK 247.000 derived from annuities or returns on capital.

In 2006, 58.5 per cent of the pensioners received 'full pension addition', 29 per cent received a reduced pension addition, 7.7 per cent received the 'full basic amount', and 4.5 percent received a 'reduced basic amount only'. One may give emphasis to the fact that approx. 95 per cent received the basic amount and in consequence term the scheme a 'basic security scheme' or one may give emphasis to the fact that the scheme is 'targeted' towards approx. 60 per cent of the pensioners. However it may be, it is hardly reasonable to term the people's pension 'full pension to everyone' paid irrespective of income and fortune. It makes more sense to speak about 'targeting within a universal frame'.

Proposals for Introducing a Public 'Basic Pension' in Germany – An Issue for Two Centuries –

Winfried Schmähl

Introduction

Germany's major public pension scheme – social (or statutory) pension insurance – is a well-known example of an income-(earnings-) related pension and is designed according to the concept of insurance. Pension benefits are financed mainly by contributions that are based (mainly) on labour income (earnings). This scheme looks back on a history of more than 100 years. It was founded in 1889 and completed Chancellor Bismarck's social insurance legislation – nine months before he resigned from office in 1890. Countries with social insurance schemes similar to the German one are often labelled as countries having a 'Bismarckian' type of pension scheme. The social insurance scheme that was finally introduced at the end of the 19th century in Germany was a political compromise and differed considerably from Bismarck's original intentions for a public pension scheme: Bismarck favoured a tax-financed flat-rate pension.[1] This was, however, not the first proposal for flat-rate (basic) pensions and certainly not the last one. Although an earnings-related pension scheme was introduced – based on the concept of insurance and financed to a large extent by earnings-based contribution payments –, the alternative concept of a basic pension was discussed many times in Germany. Even in the social insurance pension scheme, a basic element was integrated from the beginning.

In this chapter, several proposals for 'basic pensions' that were made in Germany during the last two centuries will be discussed. This cannot be a comprehensive overview regarding the proposals themselves or specific elements of these proposals. It will be initially outlined that there are different meanings of a 'basic pension' in the German debate. A specific focus will be on the time after the Second World War.

1 In Bismarck's memories (Gedanken und Erinnerungen) the social pension legislation was not mentioned at all. Bismarck himself labelled the law that was finally decided as a 'geheimräthlicher Wechselbalg' – that means a child that was misshapen and foisted on him by (leading) administrators. It thus seems doubtful wether Bismarck would have been pleased that the concept of social insurance has since been linked to his name.

In 1957, in West Germany (the Federal Republic) a fundamental pension reform was decided. It was not replacing social insurance by some type of a basic pension (although such proposals were made), but was 'modernising' social insurance. The design of the German social pension insurance was changed fundamentally. Thus, the contrast to a concept of a basic pension became much more obvious. Social pension insurance became a mainly pay-as-you-go-financed scheme, aiming at income and consumption smoothing over the life cycle by intertemporal and not interpersonal income redistribution. A relatively close contribution-benefit link was realised. This was the guiding principle for reforming these public pensions in 1957.[2] It remained the guideline for several decades in West Germany as well as for transforming the pension system of the German Democratic Republic.[3]

Social pension insurance as it now exists in West and East Germany is, however, in the process of changing: Taking into consideration the political decisions in German pension policy since the year 2000, it seems to be a realistic assumption that Germany is on the way to replacing step by step income-related social insurance by some type of a '*basic* pension', *if* the already decided reform measures remain effective.

In this chapter, only some major proposals for introducing basic pensions or basic elements in the German pension formula can be mentioned, without going into details regarding the objectives, design of instruments and possible impacts.[4] Before doing this, an outline will be provided of the different concepts of a 'basic pension' relevant to the German debate.

The following characteristics of 'basic pensions' can be distinguished:

(1) A flat-rate pension, financed by
  (1a) taxes or
  (1b) (earmarked) flat-rate contributions;

---

2 Social pension insurance is by far the dominating part of public pensions (in quantitative terms) and is at present the main income source in old-age for many persons. Beside social pension insurance, there exists a separate public (tax-financed) scheme for public servants as well as a scheme for farmers that is mostly tax-financed, too.

3 This is analysed in Winfried Schmähl, 'Transformation and Integration of Public Pension Schemes – Lessons from the Process of the German Unification', *Public Finance*, 47 (1992). Supplement: Pierre Pestieau (ed.), *Public Finance in a World of Transition, Proceedings of the 47th Congress of the International Institute of Public Finance*, (St. Petersburg, 1991), pp. 34-56.

4 In the past, the author has published several articles on the topic of minimum protection in old age. Some elements of this chapter are based partially on Winfried Schmähl, 'Proposals for flat-rate public pensions in the German debate', Jos Berghman, Bea Cantillon (eds.), *The European Face of Social Security*, (Aldershot, 1993), pp. 261-280.

(2) an income-tested flat-rate pension;

(3) a means-tested public transfer payment (tax-financed) – as part of the pension scheme – to top up income to a certain level in case income (in old age or in case of disability) is defined as not being adequate.

Other dimensions of 'basic pensions' are:

(A1) A basic pension as *single* public tier (as first tier) or

(A2) *together with a second mandatory* public or private tier.

(B) A *basic element in the pension formula* of an income-(earnings-)related social insurance scheme (as an integrated part of social insurance);

(C) 'basic pension' as a politically used new expression in German for a social insurance pension without flat-rate elements that is still earnings-related, but with a *(very) low pension level.*

These elements reflect different meanings of 'basic pension' that were and are relevant in German debates.[5]

Proposals for introducing a basic pension in Germany before the end of the Second World War

In a period of fundamental reform proposals in Prussia after the Napoleonic War,[6] the German economist and statistician *Leopold Krug* (1770-1843) published in 1810 a plan to avoid poverty in old age.[7] His main idea was to introduce

5 Based on these elements, different typologies can be developed. This, however, is not intended here.

6 Labelled often as reforms by the ministers vom Stein and Hardenberg. For a summary of Prussian reforms see for instance Ilja Mieck, 'Zielsetzung und Ertrag der preußischen Reformen', Schlenker, Manfred (ed.), *Preußen – Beiträge zu einer politischen Kultur*, (Reinbek bei Hamburg, 1981), pp. 181-196.

7 Leopold Krug, *Die Armenassekuranz, das einzige Mittel zur Verbannung der Armuth aus unserer Kommune*, (Berlin, 1918). The title of his book – which I discovered some years ago – was 'The poor Man's assurance, the only means to banish poverty from our community' (own translation) and referred to the concept of insurance. Krug was influenced by physiocratic, but in particular also by classical-liberal ideas. For information on Krug and in particular his concept (also linking it to debates that took place in Germany in particular in the 1980s) see Winfried Schmähl, 'Avoiding Poverty in Old Age by an Obligatory Contribution-Financed Minimum Insurance – Leopold Krug's 'Poor Man's Insurance' of 1810 in the Light of Present Day Discussions', Jürgen Backhaus (ed.), *Essays on Social Security and Taxation*, (Marburg, 1997), pp. 16-33; a German version was published in Winfried Schmähl, 'Vermeidung von Armut im Alter durch eine obligatorische beitragsfinanzierte Mindestversicherung – Leopold Krugs Plan einer 'Armenassekuranz' von 1810', *Jahrbücher für Nationalökonomie und Statistik*, 209 (1997), pp. 323-336.

mandatory insurance with a *flat-rate contribution* to finance *flat-rate pensions* (type 1b). Two major elements were proposed:

(a) A general obligation for men and women to pay a contribution equal per head from age 20 to age 50 in order to receive a pension in principle equal per head (but increasing with age and for women only 75 % of men's pension).[8]

(b) Husbands should be obliged to finance a minimum insurance in favour of their wives in the event of widowhood and for orphans. This was seen to be a prerequisite for getting permission to marry.[9]

These obligations should avoid means-testing and benefits granted by local communities according to poor laws. This objective remained important in the German social policy debate. Krug's proposals, however, were given hardly any attention neither at that time nor later in Germany. Similar proposals were made outside Germany, for example in England.[10]

The idea behind Krug's proposals – which were remarkably well elaborated and took into consideration a lot of practical problems[11] – was individual provision for one's own old age instead of relying on public support. The concept of insurance and the link between individual contribution payment and pension benefit became a decisive element in German pension policy much later.

Before this was realised, the idea of a flat-rate pension financed by *tax revenue* (type 1a) received great attention in Germany. It was strongly supported by *Otto von Bismarck* and propagated for example by a well-known professor of public finance, *Adolph Wagner*. Bismarck's intention was to stabilise the fiscal basis of the new German Reich (which was founded in 1871). Initially, the fiscal base of the Reich was mainly depending on decisions of the different German

---

8 Among other arguments, Krug pointed out that women better can care for themselves in old age. The basic amount in the Danish pension Act of 1922 was also lower for a single woman than for a single man.

9 An intended effect was to reduce the fertility rate of people with low income and by this breaking the 'poverty circle'.

10 About 70 years later, William Blackley (1878) made proposals similar to those by Krug, but not so well elaborated and sophisticated. See William L. Blackley, 'National Insurance: A cheap, practical, and popular means of abolishing poor rates', *The Nineteenth Century*, 4 (1878). A detailed analysis is given in P. F. Aschrott, 'Das Projekt einer allgemeinen obligatorischen Alters- und Krankenversicherung in England', *Jahrbücher für Nationalökonomie und Statistik*, 15 (1887), pp. 361-385. See also Pat Thane, 'Non-Contributory versus insurance Pensions 1878-1908', Pat Thane (ed.), *The Origins of British Social Policy*, (London, 1978), comparing Blackley's proposal to other proposals in Great Britain in the late 19th century.

11 Among them was the topic how to collect flat-rate contributions and how to punish those persons that are unwilling to pay these contributions. Krug also stressed the necessity to index pensions so that their real value remains constant during old age.

states. Bismarck was therefore looking for a new revenue source – revenue from a tobacco monopoly. To make his attempt to collect additional tax revenue more attractive, he wanted to link this to a 'positive' social project, a tax-financed pension. This project was also intended to commit the workers to the new state (in times of increasing activities of the socialist movement): In analogy to the obligation of the state to pay pensions for aged civil servants and disabled soldiers, also (mainly blue-collar) workers should receive a pension.[12] This should also reduce the (local) expenditure to avoid (to some extent) poverty (although the level of flat-rate pensions was too low to avoid poverty in old age) as well as to avoid aged persons becoming dependent on the charity of relatives. The realisation of this plan, to link the introduction of a tobacco monopoly to the introduction of a public pension, failed politically in 1881. Opposition came, for example, from German states.[13]

Eight years later, the final decision on introducing a pension scheme for workers in 1889 was based on the concept of social insurance.[14] The main objectives of this reform approach remained the same as some years before in the plan to introduce a tax-financed pension, but the instruments for realising this were now different. However, in the new social insurance scheme at least one important element of the basic pension concept – although to a reduced and limited extent – was adopted, because one of the two main elements of the pension formula for calculating pensions was a *flat-rate element*, equal for every pension ('*basic amount*', 'Grundbetrag'), financed by taxes. The second element was linked to years of insurance and those earnings (up to a ceiling), upon which contribution payments (of employers as well as employees) were based ('incremental amount', 'Steigerungsbetrag').

This structure of the pension formula (type B) remained effective even after the Second World War: in West Germany until the end of 1956 and in East Germany right up until June 1990.

In the meantime, however, the concept of a flat-rate pension was still alive in the German debate on redesigning pension policy. As early as 1897, Parliament rejected a proposal to introduce a tax-financed flat-rate pension which was to be

12 Sometimes the expression 'soldier of labour' analogous to 'soldier of war' was used at that time.

13 See in particular documents published in Florian Tennstedt & Heidi Winter, 'Quellensammlung zur Geschichte der deutschen Sozialpolitik 1867 bis 1914', Karl Erich Born, Hansjoachim Henning & Florian Tennstedt (eds.), *Grundfragen staatlicher Sozialpolitik*, 1, (Stuttgart, Jena, New York, 1994).

14 Ritter gives a detailed analysis of the founding period – also in comparison to the development in England in Gerhard A. Ritter, *Sozialversicherung in Deutschland und England – Entstehung und Grundzüge im Vergleich,* (München, 1983).

supplemented by a contribution-financed pension. In the period of severe economic problems after the First World War and the hyperinflation of 1923 (which radically depreciated the real value of pensions so that means-tested social assistance mostly took over the role of financially supporting the elderly), a tax-financed pension was proposed again (but not realised).[15]

During the Nazi period, plans by the new central organisation for all employees that had replaced trade unions (*Deutsche Arbeitsfront*) were politically more important: The basis for a pension (the right to receive it) was no longer to be the contribution payment as in social insurance, but fulfilment of the duties (obligations) of a 'citizen'.[16] This basic pension for (in principle) all citizens was to replace social insurance and was to have a higher pension level than social insurance pensions. For this plan, explicit reference was made to the original ideas of Bismarck for a basic flat-rate pension.[17] These citizen's pensions were to be financed by taxes and be based on pay-as-you-go financing, while the official concept in social insurance (although by far not fully realised) was capital funding.

This 'new' approach[18] was planned to be realised after the war. The Ministry of Labour was meanwhile successful in defending the social insurance scheme and had its own plans to increase benefits, although these were only partially implemented. The ministry argued for higher benefits to realise at least a sufficient minimum protection which was still lacking. Plans to increase benefits were also stimulated by the British Beveridge Report, which was published in Great Britain in November 1942.[19] This report was carefully analysed in Germany, because social policy was an important topic in war-time propaganda. The benefit level in social insurance remained nevertheless very low up to the end of the war.[20]

---

15 See Annette Penkert, *Arbeit oder Rente?*, (Göttingen, 1998), pp. 179-191.

16 In the meaning of 'Volksgenosse', an expression opening many options to determine the characteristics of those persons that were entitled to this pension.

17 See in particular R. Crämer, 'Bismarcks Erbe in der Sozialversicherung', *Jahrbuch 1940/41 des Arbeitswissenschaftlichen Institut der Deutschen Arbeitsfront* (1941), pp. 126-148.

18 Later the plans were modified: The basic pension should be differentiated to some degree according to labour income during the last 10 years of employment, see for example Marie Luise Recker, *Nationalsozialistische Sozialpolitik im Zweiten Weltkrieg*, (München, 1985).

19 William Beveridge, *Social Insurance and Allied Services, Report by Sir William Beveridge*, (London, 1942).

20 A short overview regarding the plans during the Nazi-period is provided in Winfried Schmähl, 'Sicherung bei Alter, Invalidität und für Hinterbliebene', Bundesministerium für Arbeit und Sozialordnung und Bundesarchiv (eds.), *Geschichte der Sozialpolitik in Deutschland seit 1945-1949. Die Zeit der Besatzungszonen – Sozialpolitik zwischen Kriegsende und der Gründung zweier deutscher Staaten.* Vol. 2/1, (Baden-Baden, 2001), pp. 401-459, here pp. 411-417.

The concept of a basic pension after the Second World War: 1945–1999

The period up to the fundamental pension reform in 1957 in West Germany

After the victory of the allied troops, emergency measures to pay out pension benefits became necessary. But at the same time, reform debates were started within the different occupied zones by German experts as well as by the Allies. Although in particular the structure of the organisation of social insurance in the Russian zone was different compared to that of the three Western zones, the structure of the pension formula in principle remained as it had existed since 1889, also after the two German post-war states had been created in 1949 (the 'Federal Republic' in the Western Zones – BRD – and the 'Democratic Republic' – DDR – in the Soviet Zone). But in West Germany as well as in East Germany *minimum pension benefits* were introduced in social pension insurance into the pension formula (in addition to the already existing *basic pension amount*).[21] This increased even more the trend towards limited differences in individual pension benefits. The level of benefits in general was regarded as insufficient.

In *West Germany*, a debate about a fundamental reform of social security in general started in the beginning of the 1950s, but concentrated more and more on pension policy. The focus was on the structure and the level of benefits (and their link to earnings development), the financing (pay-as-you-go versus capital funding), the persons mandatorily included in a scheme, and on the organisation of the pension scheme.

In 1952 (one year before the second election for Federal Parliament, 'Bundestag'), the Social Democratic Party (SPD) published proposals for a comprehensive plan for social policy.[22] In this plan, a *flat-rate tax-financed pension* (type 1a) was proposed for the elderly and for permanently disabled persons.

---

21 For details of the decision process, see in particular Hans Günther Hockerts, *Sozialpolitische Entscheidungen im Nachkriegs-Deutschland – Alliierte und deutsche Sozialversicherungspolitik 1945-1957*, (Stuttgart, 1980). A description of the development in the different zones of occupied Germany is given in Winfried Schmähl, 'Sicherung bei Alter, Invalidität und für Hinterbliebene', Bundesministerium für Arbeit und Sozialordnung und Bundesarchiv (eds.), *Geschichte der Sozialpolitik in Deutschland seit 1945-1949. Die Zeit der Besatzungszonen – Sozialpolitik zwischen Kriegsende und der Gründung zweier deutscher Staaten.* Vol. 2/1, (Baden-Baden, 2001), pp. 401-459.

22 Vorstand der SPD (ed.), 'Die Grundlagen des sozialen Gesamtplanes der SPD' (published without date). (1952), Walter Auerbach, 'Modell' eines Sozialplanes – Eine Skizze', *Die Krankenversicherung*, 4 (1952) pp. 106-111, Ludwig Preller, 'Unsere Forderung auf Soziale Sicherung. Rede auf dem Parteitag der SPD in Dortmund am 26. September 1952', *SPD* (1952).

These proposals were obviously influenced by reform ideas in Sweden and Great Britain. In particular, elements of the Beveridge Report were introduced into the political discussion by the SPD-politician *Walter Auerbach* (1905-1975),[23] who during the Nazi period emigrated to London, where he encountered these ideas.[24] Also *Ludwig Preller* (1897-1974), Member of Parliament and chairman of the social policy committee of the SPD, had insight into the British situation, for example.[25] Both Auerbach and Preller argued, however, that the tax-financed flat-rate pension should be supplemented by an insurance pension financed by contribution.[26] Both types of pensions together should be sufficient to finance one's living in old age (type A2).

The published documents do not clearly show whether the flat-rate pension alone should be high enough to avoid poverty in old age (and to avoid means-tested social assistance). Both pension benefits together, however, should be higher than only a pension that can avoid poverty.[27] Thus far, the proposals of the

---

23 Then Secretary of State in the Ministry of Labour in the state of Lower Saxonia. During his exile years in London, Auerbach worked in the secretariat of the International Transport Workers' Federation and was indirectly involved in the preparation of the Beveridge Report. See Hans Günther Hockerts, 'Sicherung im Alter: Kontinuität und Wandel der gesetzlichen Rentenversicherung 1889-1979', Werner Conze & Reiner M. Lepsius (eds.), *Sozialgeschichte der Bundesrepublik*, (Stuttgart, 1982), p. 337.

24 As already mentioned, the foreign, in particular the British debates in pension policy were already carefully observed, for example, by the German Ministry of Labour in the early forties.

25 In the beginning of 1953, an Anglo-German conference on social security took place; Preller was one of the German participants exchanging ideas on the British experience and the insights for German social policy. Lünendonk (member of the Christian Democratic Party, CDU) was at that time vice president of the statutory pension insurance for blue-collar workers in Hessen and chairmain of a federal committee of the CDU for social policy. See Ludwig Preller & Heinrich Lünendonk, 'Das englische Sicherungssystem und Deutschland. Ein Briefwechsel', *Sozialer Fortschritt*, 2 (1953), pp. 102-106.

26 It is interesting to note that in the Netherlands after the Second World War the pension scheme was changed fundamentally, influenced by experiences that Dutch persons had made during their time in British exile. In particular, ideas proposed in the Beveridge Report gained influence; see Joop Roebroek & Jan H. M. Nelissen, 'Die 'heimliche Revolution'. Struktur, Entwicklung und Zukunft des holländischen Rentensystems', Michael Opielka (ed.), *Grundrente in Deutschland* (Wiesbaden, 2004), pp. 189-216.

27 The British experience was not seen as a positive example for Germany because – as Preller, for example, criticised – benefits were too low to cover a minimum subsistence level. Even if they could cover it, benefits would mostly be far below present wages. Therefore, in Germany benefits should be in a certain relation to present wages. And Lünendonk argued that after a full working life a pensioner should regularly receive a pension high enough to make social assistance unnecessary. For refe-

SPD at that time are linked to the existing *structure* of the pension formula with its basic element, but dividing the pension into two separate mandatory parts, a basic and an earnings-related one. However, the level of the (separate) basic pension (in contrast to the basic element of the existing pension formula) and the level of the two pension benefits together should be increased.

But five years later, in 1957, SPD *and* CDU[28] finally agreed on a fundamental pension reform *without* any flat-rate elements in the pension formula and without a flat-rate pension. The main reason why the SPD abandoned the idea of a flat-rate pension was that this was not popular. The same was true for an integration of different branches of social insurance within one organisation. A mostly contribution-financed 'dynamic' pension[29] linked to the development of earnings was introduced.[30] The benefit level was comprehensively increased – on average by more than 60%. The pension reform was also seen as an advantage compared to the situation in East Germany. Proposals from the insurance industry favouring a flat-rate tax-financed pension and from a working group of self-employed ('Arbeitsgemeinschaft Selbständiger Unternehmer', ASU) and even of vice-chancellor Blücher (FDP[31], later FVP[32]) were not influential in the political debate.[33] The overwhelming political majority in Parliament decided against a flat-rate pension or a flat-rate component in the pension formula.

---

rences and details see Winfried Schmähl, 'Sicherung bei Alter, Invalidität und für Hinterbliebene', Bundesministerium für Arbeit und Soziales und Bundesarchiv (eds.), *Geschichte der Sozialpolitik in Deutschland seit 1945. 1949-1957 Bundesrepublik Deutschland – Bewältigung der Kriegsfolgen, Rückkehr zur sozialpolitischen Normalität.* Vol. 3 (Baden-Baden, 2005), pp. 358-437, here pp. 383-390.

28 Christian Democratic Union (and its Bavarian Sister Party CSU).

29 Tax-financing was primarily to cover several redistributive elements in the social pension insurance.

30 Hans Günther Hockerts, 'Die Rentenversicherung 1957',Franz Ruland (ed.), *Handbuch der gesetzlichen Rentenversicherung*, (Neuwied, 1990), pp. 93-104 and Winfried Schmähl, 'Sicherung bei Alter, Invalidität und für Hinterbliebene', Bundesministerium für Arbeit und Soziales und Bundesarchiv (eds.), *Geschichte der Sozialpolitik in Deutschland seit 1945. 1949-1957 Bundesrepublik Deutschland – Bewältigung der Kriegsfolgen, Rückkehr zur sozialpolitischen Normalität*, Vol. 3 (Baden-Baden, 2005), pp. 358-437, provide many details regarding the 1957 pension reform.

31 Free Democratic Party.

32 Freie Volkspartei.

33 Winfried Schmähl, 'Sicherung bei Alter, Invalidität und für Hinterbliebene', Bundesministerium für Arbeit und Soziales und Bundesarchiv (eds.), *Geschichte der Sozialpolitik in Deutschland seit 1945. 1949-1957 Bundesrepublik Deutschland – Bewältigung der Kriegsfolgen, Rückkehr zur sozialpolitischen Normalität*, Vol. 3 (Baden-Baden, 2005), pp. 358-437, here p. 410.

There was an intensive public debate about introducing a 'dynamic' pension that was to become a *replacement* of former own earnings, and also linked to earnings development during years in retirement and financed mainly on a pay-as-you-go basis.[34] Although there was a lot of resistance against this new earnings-related concept of pension policy (even within the Federal Government[35]), a basic pension was at that time not supported by politically influential players. According to persons, who prepared the reform e.g. in the Federal Ministry of Labour at that time, foreign experience offered no guidelines for this reform concept. This new concept was formulated as a fundamental alternative to the concept of a basic pension.

After the introduction of the 'dynamic' pension in 1957

West-Germany

In the year following the fundamental pension reform that introduced a new paradigm into German pension policy, the idea of changing the system towards a tax-financed flat-rate scheme came up several times from different political quarters.

The SPD, however, did not take up its basic pension plan again, but favoured improvements within the existing system including an upgrading of low earnings (in particular those of women) for insured persons with a long earnings record (the so-called pension based on minimum income, '*Rente nach Mindesteinkommen*'). This was finally realised during the period of the first big coalition of CDU/CSU and SPD in 1972.[36]

In the sixties, the Liberal Party (FDP) proposed a tax-financed flat-rate scheme (type 1a) as the basis of a three-tier plan.[37] It must be remembered that in

34 Winfried Schmähl, 'Die Einführung der Dynamischen Rente im Jahr 1957: Gründe, Ziele und Maßnahmen – zugleich Versuch einer Bilanz nach 50 Jahren', Deutsche Rentenversicherung Bund (ed.), *Die gesetzliche Rente in Deutschland – 50 Jahre Sicherheit durch Anpassungen*, DRV-Schriften, 73. (Bad Homburg, 2007), pp. 9-28, discusses the 1957 reform in the light of experiences gained since.

35 By the Ministers of Finance and Economics.

36 See Winfried Schmähl, 'Sicherung bei Alter, Invalidität und für Hinterbliebene', Bundesministerium für Arbeit und Soziales und Bundesarchiv (eds.), *Geschichte der Sozialpolitik in Deutschland seit 1945. 1966-1974 Bundesrepublik Deutschland – Eine Zeit vielfältigen Aufbruchs*. Vol. 5, (Baden-Baden, 2006), pp. 407-481, here p. 434 f.

37 Wolfgang Mischnick, 'Gedanken zur Neugestaltung der Alterssicherung', *Betriebliche Altersversorgung*, 18, (1963), pp. 57-58. He was chairman of the FDP members

1957 the FDP rejected the pension reform in Parliament. A main argument was that private saving for old age would be negatively affected by the earnings-related social insurance scheme. The proposed flat-rate tax-financed pension (covering the subsistence level) was to be supplemented by a second mandatory contribution-financed tier (type A2). Both together should, however, only provide 'minimum protection' to stimulate additional private saving (tier three).[38]

The Central Reserve Bank (Deutsche Bundesbank) also favoured a 'basic pension'. Above this basic level, either individual voluntary saving should take place or capital funding should at least be implemented in the social insurance scheme.[39] For all these proposals no calculations were provided for the transition costs necessary when shifting from an earnings-related public scheme towards a flat-rate scheme.[40]

In the early and mid-1980s in particular, the flat-rate proposal was advanced again. This was part of a debate about the future development of pension policy in Germany, stimulated by the financing problems of the social pension insurance and particularly the ageing of the population. The issue was then presented by a prominent politician of the CDU (*Kurt Biedenkopf*) as well as by the Green Party – and again by some politicians of the FDP. They all demanded a radical change of the present public pension scheme. But differences existed between these proposals: Biedenkopf (and his main companion concerning this issue, *Meinhard*

in the Federal Parliament; more elaborated and detailedis a publication of the political foundation (Friedrich-Naumann-Stiftung) of the FDP, see Paul Ostrop, Ernst Eggers & Günter Köhler, 'Neugestaltung der Alterssicherung. Drei-Stufen-Plan zur Altersvorsorge und -versorgung', *Schriftenreihe des Instituts für politische Planung und Kybernetik (IPK)*, (Bonn undated [1969]). Some years later the plan was taken up again, but did not receive the full support of the party. Finally in 1976, the party in general decided against this concept as a guideline for pension policy, although the FDP always favoured private saving for old age.

38 A similar proposal was made in a draft version of the protestant church in 1968, but was never published, see Winfried Schmähl, 'Sicherung bei Alter, Invalidität und für Hinterbliebene', Bundesministerium für Arbeit und Soziales und Bundesarchiv (eds.), *Geschichte der Sozialpolitik in Deutschland seit 1945. 1966-1974 Bundesrepublik Deutschland – Eine Zeit vielfältigen Aufbruchs*. Vol. 5, (Baden-Baden, 2006), pp. 407-481, here p. 435.

39 Deutsche Bundesbank, 'Gesetzliche Rentenversicherung', *Monatsberichte der Deutschen Bundesbank 19*, 8 (1967), p. 33.

40 This topic was discussed in Winfried Schmähl, *Systemänderung in der Altersvorsorge – Von der einkommensabhängigen Altersrente zur Staatsbürger-Grundrente*, (Opladen, 1974) giving an estimate of transition costs, based on a simple overlapping generations model.

Miegel[41]) proposed the tax-financed pension (type 1a) as the *sole* mandatory scheme, to be supplemented by *voluntary saving* for old age (type A1). By this, more freedom of choice in spending income would be created (an argument the FDP had also used in the past).[42] It was argued that this would increase capital formation, stimulate saving and investment, and increase economic growth.

For the Green Party, the tax-financed flat-rate pension (type 1a) was mainly an element of a basic income for all and a measure to disentangle work and income.[43] The basic pension should be supplemented by a *second mandatory public* scheme (type A2). It is obvious that the specific instrument of a basic pension was proposed from different political perspectives and was linked to different objectives.

Within the CDU and the FDP (who were at that time coalition partners in government), such proposals could not command any majority. The SPD was against such a strategy, too.[44] SPD and the coalition government finally decided in 1989 on a reform 'within the system' (a few hours before the collapse of the Berlin Wall) and implemented a self-regulating mechanism in social pension insurance,[45] based on a clear definition of the benefit level that should be stabilised for the future (a defined benefit scheme).

---

41 Meinhard Miegel, *Sicherheit im Alter – Plädoyer für die Weiterentwicklung des Rentensystems*, (Stuttgart, 1981); Meinhard Miegel & Stefanie Wahl, *Gesetzliche Grundsicherung. Private Vorsorge – der Weg aus der Rentenkrise*, (Stuttgart, 1985).

42 However, transition costs are mainly neglected when underlining this possible effect.

43 See for example Michael Opielka & Georg Vobruba (eds.), *Das garantierte Grundeinkommen. Entwicklung und Perspektiven einer Forderung*, (Frankfurt/Main, 1986).

44 A detailed analysis is given in Winfried Schmähl, 'Sicherung bei Alter, Invalidität und für Hinterbliebene', Bundesministerium für Gesundheit und Soziale Sicherung und Bundesarchiv (eds.), *Geschichte der Sozialpolitik in Deutschland seit 1945. 1982-1989 Bundesrepublik Deutschland – Finanzielle Konsolidierung und institutionelle Reform.* Vol. 7, (Baden-Baden, 2005), pp. 315-388. For a comparison of the proposed concepts of Biedenkopf/Miegel and the Green Party see Winfried Schmähl, 'Übergang zu Staatsbürger-Grundrenten. Ein Beitrag zur Deregulierung der Alterssicherung?', Theo Thiemeyer (ed.), *Regulierung und Deregulierung im Bereich der Sozialpolitik, (Schriften des Vereins für Socialpolitik, Band 177),* (Berlin, 1988), pp. 83-138.

45 A detailed analysis of the reform measures as well as arguments that were relevant in opposing a shift towards a flat-rate pension are provided in Winfried Schmähl, 'Reformen der Rentenversicherung: Gründe, Strategien und Wirkungen – Das Beispiel der 'Rentenreform 1992', Bernhard Gahlen e.a. (eds.), *Theorie und Politik der Sozialversicherung*, (Tübingen, 1990), pp. 203-255. Beside economic effects of transition costs, doubts existed regarding the superiority of capital funding to pay-as-you go financing as argued by many economists. A description of the reform measures and in particular the concept of a self-regulating mechanism (decided in 1989) in English can be found in Winfried Schmähl, 'The 1992 Reform of Public Pensions in Ger-

In the 1980s another type of basic pension was presented: a flat-rate pension financed by *flat-rate contributions* (similar to Leopold Krug's proposal at the beginning of the 19th century). Here also, two different types were proposed: either as the *sole* mandatory public scheme (type 1b/A1) or *integrated* – as a floor – into the existing earnings-related social insurance scheme (type 1b/A2). The first type was recommended by some neo-liberal economists,[46] the second by some economists that were members of (or close to) the SPD.[47] This remained, however, an academic discussion. An argument against a flat-rate contribution was its highly regressive effects. Due to the high burden involved, there would be heavy pressure to earn money. Therefore, it would be difficult to work only part-time instead of full-time (as many women wished, for example). This proposal would also require additional – in particular tax-financed – measures if persons could not afford to pay the flat-rate contribution, or if they did not have the full number of contributory years to get the full (flat-rate) pension.[48] The concept of a contribution-financed flat-rate pension did not receive much attention or any political support in the German debate.

Integrating the East and West German pension schemes

In the process of German unification, two pension schemes existed, which had diverged over the years and had quite different structures. In the German Democratic Republic, the minimum elements in the pension formula of the social pension insurance had gained more and more influence and were dominating the benefit structure. They had a highly equalizing effect. To give an example: At the beginning of 1990, there was a minimum pension of 330 Mark (based on 15 working years). The possible maximum pension (for 50 working years or more) was 510 Mark. After 45 working years the minimum benefit was already 470

---

many: Main Elements and some Effects', *Journal of European Social Policy*, 3, (1993), pp. 39-51.

46 Armin Gutowski & Renate Merklein, 'Arbeit und Soziales im Rahmen einer marktwirtschaftlichen Ordnung', *Hamburger Jahrbuch für Wirtschafts- und Gesellschaftspolitik*, 30, (1985), pp. 49-67 or Wolfram Engels ea., *Reform der Alterssicherung*, (Bad Homburg, 1987).

47 Hans-Jürgen Krupp, 'Ein Vorschlag zur voll eigenständigen Sicherung der Frau', Hans-Jürgen Krupp ea. (eds.), *Alternativen der Rentenreform* ,84 (Frankfurt and New York, 1981), pp. 17-23; Gert Wagner, 'Bedarfs- oder beitragsorientierte Grundsicherung in der Rentenversicherung?', Frank Klanberg & Aloys Prinz (eds.), *Perspektiven sozialer Mindestsicherung*, (Berlin, 1988), pp. 59-94.

48 This is discussed in Winfried Schmähl, 'Beitragsfinanzierte Mindestsicherung im Alter', *Hamburger Jahrbuch für Wirtschafts- und Gesellschaftspolitik*, 35 (1990), pp. 187-205.

Mark, i.e. only 40 Mark less than the maximum benefit. The social pension insurance scheme was in fact almost flat-rate, but supplemented by several additional public pension schemes for different groups of working people.

During the negotiations between the two German governments aiming at a unification of the two state some attempts[49] were made to preserve some minimum elements of the East German pension scheme. Finally, however, the structure of the West German scheme was implemented in East Germany (with several transitional rules), increasing pension benefits remarkably for many pensioners (and introducing for the first time a dynamic pension scheme in East Germany).[50] This fundamental decision to use what was in fact the West German scheme as a blueprint for transforming the pension scheme in East Germany, was taken by CDU/CSU and SPD in West Germany together, and in principle it was supported by all players in East Germany.

The rise of a new concept of a 'basic pension' as a result of a radical paradigm shift in German pension policy: Some remarks on the future of the public pension scheme in Germany

In the years following German unification, the debate on the future of social pension insurance never stopped. At the beginning of the new century, a new coalition government (of the SPD and Green Party) finally decided on a new paradigm for pension policy: reducing the pay-as-you-go-financed social pension insurance and its benefit level and substituting for this an increase in capital-funded private pensions. For the public scheme (as well as in the area of occupational pensions) a shift from defined benefit[51] to defined contribution started. The development of the social insurance contribution rate became the decisive element. This para-

49 By players from the East as well as from the SPD in West Germany.

50 The structure of the pension scheme in the German Democratic Republic and the different steps to implement the dynamic pension scheme of the Federal Republic also in the new part of unified Germany is analysed in detail in Winfried Schmähl, 'Alterssicherung in der DDR und ihre Umgestaltung im Zuge des deutschen Einigungsprozesses – Einige verteilungspolitische Aspekte', Gerhard Kleinhenz (ed.), *Sozialpolitik im vereinten Deutschland, I, Schriften des Vereins für Socialpolitik,* 208/I (Berlin, 1991), pp. 49-95; and Winfried Schmähl, 'Transformation and Integration of Public Pension Schemes – Lessons from the Process of the German Unification', *Public Finance*, 47 (1992). The mandatory as well as supplementary voluntary public pensions were integrated in the social pension insurance.

51 This was most obvious in the objective underlying the reform measures decided in 1989, which were always to realise a constant benefit level (pensions as a certain percentage – depending on the number of pension claims – of average net earnings).

digm shift was backed by a great informal coalition of many players that, for different reasons, were interested in scaling down the public pay-as-you-go-financed pensions.[52] The interests behind this strategy as well as the instruments used for realisation will not be discussed here.[53] Instead, some consequences of this new strategy in pension policy in Germany – that will emerge gradually – will be outlined, as this sheds light on a changing concept for public pensions.

The official position is that social pension insurance will remain the most important part of Germany's pensions and that the concept of social insurance predominant during the last 50 years will not be touched. But a distinction must be made between political rhetoric and the actual results of political decisions. In the following, the focus is on the changing conceptual basis of the public pension scheme as a result of political decisions as well as of changing economic conditions. This will be illustrated by a few facts.

If the changes in the benefit level that have been politically decided during the last few years (in particular in 2001 and 2004) were already fully effective, then an 'average earner',[54] who retires at age 65,[55] would need 37 years of paying contributions to receive a pension that is just as high as the existing means-tested social assistance (assuming that the relative level of social assistance in order to avoid poverty remains as high as it is today).[56] Contributors receiving (on average during their working years) earnings below the average of all employees – and that is reality for most of female employees – would of course need a higher number of years of insurance just to get a pension as high as social assistance. For example, if the individual earnings level is about 80 % of average earnings,

52 In 2006, the coalition in government changed: a 'big' coalition of CDU/CSU and SPD came into power. The strategy in pension policy was not changed at all.

53 This is analysed in Winfried Schmähl, 'Dismantling an Earnings-Related Social Pension Scheme: Germany's New Pension Policy', *Journal of Social Policy*, 36:2 (2007), pp. 319-340. For a more detailed discussion of the first phase of the reform process – focusing also on the instruments used – see Winfried Schmähl, 'Umlagefinanzierte Rentenversicherung in Deutschland, Optionen und Konzepte sowie politische Entscheidungen als Einstieg in einen grundlegenden Transformationsprozeß', Winfried Schmähl, Volker Ulrich (eds.), *Soziale Sicherungssysteme und demographische Herausforderungen*, (Tübingen, 2001), pp. 123-204.

54 That means an insured person who received just average earnings during his/her whole earnings period. The earnings profile over the life cycle can be quite different.

55 Taking into account that the retirement age for receiving a pension without deductions will then be 67 and the deduction will remain 3.6 % per year of the (full) pension.

56 In 2001, a new branch of social assistance especially for the elderly and disabled persons was also introduced, means-tested and with the identical benefit level as before in social assistance, however with limited responsibility of children to pay back these transfers their parents received. This was mainly an attempt to give social assistance a new label.

45 years of contribution payment are needed.[57] Social assistance is a transfer payment that a person is eligible for without any saving or provision for old age.

Already at present, a great number of insured persons – including the majority of women – only have pension claims below the level that will be necessary in the future (about 2030) to receive a pension just as high as social assistance. Or, to put it the other way round: Only a relatively small part of employed persons (in particular male employees with high income) would have the chance to get a social insurance pension that is higher than the social assistance level.

In addition, it has to be taken into account that in the future, individual possibilities to accumulate pension claims will be reduced compared to pensioners that have recently retired, because many employees will have long spells of unemployment. This will lower the chance to acquire adequate pension claims. It is also important to note that even today more than 40 % of all insured persons claiming their pension have deductions from their full pension because they retire before the 'standard' retirement age (which will be gradually increased in the future from 65 to 67).[58] There is also an increase in low-paid work.

It is obvious that the legitimacy and the credibility and acceptance of such a mandatory pension scheme – where you have to pay life-long contributions but will only receive inadequate pension benefits – will be lost. Already now, faith in the public pension scheme is undermined by numerous activities of politicians, players in the financial industry, many economists and the media, all presenting a highly uniform view: the present social pension insurance is 'not sustainable' and the only way to avoid a 'pension crisis' is the shift towards private pensions, i.e. capital funding.

Taking into account the already decided measures, however, several players now declare that social pension insurance has meanwhile become sustainable (from a fiscal point of view), but social pension insurance will provide only a 'basic pension' (type C) in the future. This expression 'basic pension' refers to the benefit level of a pension scheme that is still earnings-related. It is, however, not made public for whom this will really be a basis for income in old age and

---

57 On average, 82.2 %. 40 years are needed for earnings that are on average 92.5 % of average earnings of all insured persons. At present, women mostly receive earnings below average – if the whole earnings career is taken into account. How this may change over time will not be discussed here.

58 In East Germany, about 70 % of all pensioners retiring in 2005 have pension benefits with deductions of around 12 % on average; see Martin Brussig, *Vier von zehn Zugängen in Altersrente erfolgen mit Abschlägen*, Altersübergangs-Report (2007-01).

what 'basic' means.[59] And it remains an open question who can adequately compensate the loss in public pension benefits by private capital funded pensions because, for example, in periods of unemployment there are limited financial means for private saving and also no occupational (firm-based) pension benefits can be accumulated.

The now effective political strategy in pension policy is not questioned by influential players and large sections of the population, because the effects of the new pension policy have hardly been made public in the past. Very recently, a public discussion started focussing on the danger of poverty in old-age possibly gaining importance in the future again.

What will the future of the social pension insurance scheme be in Germany if the actual political strategy remains unchanged? At present, both a mandatory public insurance scheme and a means-tested transfer scheme exist. In the insurance scheme, income testing already takes place for widow's/widower's pensions.[60] One of the possible future developments could be to merge the social pension insurance scheme in one way or the other with the already existing means-tested transfer income scheme for elderly and disabled persons in order to realise a 'basic pension' in the event of inadequate income in old age. It would be much too costly to introduce a general flat-rate pension for all the elderly.[61] But there is now a proposal – from Catholic organisations – to re-introduce a flat-rate, tax-financed element into the public pension scheme,[62] others propose (tax-financed) supplements to social insurance pensions with low pension benefits to top up and to receive benefits above the social assistance level.

Taking into account the experience and development in many countries of either flat-rate public pensions or pensions with a relatively low benefit level, capital-funded pensions (either private or firm-based) can be expected to become mandatory[63] – either by law or (quasi mandatory) by collective agreement in order to realise a higher benefit level and to avoid increasing means-tested benefits

---

59 The term 'basic pension' in Germany has become even more blurred because also a tax-privileged type of private pension (in particular attractive for self-employed persons) is called 'basic pension'.

60 Own income reduces these pensions; only the subsidised private pensions (introduced in 2001) are exempted.

61 See, for example, Hans-Jürgen Krupp & Joachim Weeber, 'Volkswirtschaftliche Aspekte eines Grundrentensystems', Michael Opielka (ed.), *Grundrente in Deutschland*, (Wiesbaden, 2004), pp. 147-165.

62 Calculations on costs are in Martin Werding, Herbert Hofmann & Hans-Joachim Reinhard, *Das Rentenmodell der katholischen Verbände*, (München, 2007).

63 Firm-based pensions are at present voluntary in Germany in the private sector.

(this would mean a shift from type C towards type A2).[64] Earnings-related pension then would mostly be from capital-funded private schemes, either an occupational (firm-based) scheme or individual private pensions. The public scheme (as the basic element of pension provision) with a low benefit level, however, will become highly redistributive – whereas many countries recently decided to realise a closer contribution-benefit link in the public pension schemes. A scheme with such a close contribution-benefit link has existed in Germany until now, but will be more and more destabilised and undermined in a process of systematic change.[65] This is a creeping process of transforming old-age security in Germany.[66]

It is not possible here to discuss the various influencing factors from the national as well as inter- and supranational level, aiming at a scaling down of public pay-as-you-go-financed pensions and substitution by capital-funded pensions. Germany has meanwhile made a political decision in the direction of this strategy. The concept of public pensions in Germany is already in a process of fundamental change, as well as the mix of public and private pensions. Linked to this is a shift in risks and responsibilities. All this will have severe consequences for income in old age, namely an increasing probability of poverty and rising income inequality in old age. Means-testing may become more important in the future.[67] This will have negative incentive effects also with regard to saving in order to fi-

---

64 Significantly increasing coverage by subsidised private pensions would burden the federal budget a lot. This would also be an argument for mandating private pensions because of the inadequate benefit level of the social pension insurance.

65 The development of private and occupational pensions is directly used (in particular by integrating specific elements into the social insurance pension formula) to scale down public pensions. For so called 'earnings conversion' – a subsidised type of employee-financed private pension organised by the firm – this is analysed in detail in Winfried Schmähl & Angelika Oelschläger, *Abgabenfreie Entgeltumwandlung in sozial- und verteilungspolitischer Perspektive*, (Berlin, 2007).

66 See Winfried Schmähl, 'Übergang zu einem Grundrentensystem: Vom radikalen Systemwechsel zur schleichenden Systemtransformation', Michael Opielka (ed.), *Grundrente in Deutschland* (Wiesbaden, 2004), pp. 119-146.

67 This is not only relevant in old age but, for example, also in the event of unemployment already now. How much social assistance will be necessary depends on total household income and not only on public pensions. The increasing female labour force participation rate will increase income of two-earners households. But unemployment will also negatively affect private saving. All these elements together – in particular changes in employment structure and earnings careers and decreasing level of public pensions – will be decisive for future development of income inequality and poverty in old age.

nance one's old age.[68] If there is no political change in pension policy, Germany is in part going back in its *public* pension scheme to its roots at the end of the 19th century. Whether such a development towards a new mix of income sources in old age will be *politically* sustainable – even if the public pensions are *fiscally* sustainable – is an open question.

Since the introduction of social insurance pensions in Germany there have been proposals for a system-shift towards flat-rate pensions from time to time. This alternative was mainly proposed in periods of (financial) problems in social insurance. But these proposals never got sufficient political support. Transition costs, although never calculated adequately, were a factor for arguing against a transition from earnings-related to flat-rate pensions. Basic pension elements, however, played a significant role within the social insurance scheme in West Germany up to 1956 and in East Germany until summer 1990. Then, a relatively close contribution-benefit link without any basic elements was introduced in social insurance. Now, a turning point in German pension policy seems to have been reached, where the idea of basic elements and basic public pensions is gaining support from politicians and other players, while ordinary people are little informed about the effects of the new pension strategy. Many politicians declare that the present social pension insurance is not sustainable, that there is 'no alternative' to redesigning social pension insurance. In the future, Public pension can only be a 'basic pension'. This new label is vague enough to be used in the political debate, and is to stimulate the population to save for their 'own' capital-funded private pensions. While the minister of labour in 2001 – at the beginning of this transformation process – declared that in the future every pensioner would be better off as a result of this new strategy, only recently some sceptical voices have been heard about the effects of the new pension strategy. In particular some fears about an increasing risk of poverty in old age have been articulated. At the beginning of 2008, a public debate started about poverty in old age in the future and in particular for future cohorts. And yet the majority of influential political

68 Experiences from the UK, for example, up to now have been totally neglected in Germany; see Jay Ginn, Uwe Fachinger & Winfried Schmähl, 'Pension reform and the socioeconomic status of older people', Gerhard Naegele, Alan Walker (eds.), *Ageing and Social Policy for Seniors in Germany and in the United Kingdom – a Comparative Overview of Policy Approaches and Research Perspectives*, (London, in print).

players, the financial and insurance industry as well as mainstream economists insist nevertheless that this strategy is 'without an alternative'.[69]

69 Finally, Germany may end up with a 'multi-pillar' concept that is close to the (original) proposals of the World Bank: A mandatory pay-as-you-go-financed basis with a low benefit level or even with more means testing, a mandatory capital-funded private pension scheme and voluntary (or subsidised) capital-funded private saving. Who wins and who loses by this shift in responsibilities, risks etc., will not be discussed here, but is a topic that has received too little attention in Germany up to now.

Pension Reforms in Europe: Convergence of Old-Age Security Systems?

Karl Hinrichs

1. Introduction

At first glance, public pension schemes seem to be easily accessible to political change, in particular, if they are predominantly financed on a pay-as-you-go (PAYG) basis as is the case in all European countries. Mediated by the state's power to tax, those schemes establish a bilateral relationship between the currently employed – liable to contributions and taxes – and the pensioners to whom the (earmarked) revenues are immediately redistributed as cash benefits. In contrast, political governance in domains of the welfare state which provide social services, such as health or child care, regularly appears to be more complicated since income and professional interests of (organised) providers play a role as well as considerations concerning the quality of services. A second glance, however, reveals that public pension schemes have usually shown strong resistance to reform and have been considered as 'a *locus classicus* for the study of 'path-dependent' change'.[1] They are the grey elephants of developed welfare states: large (in terms of social expenditure allotted to them) and hard to move in a different direction.[2]

This is so because pension schemes bridge extended time spans – from starting to earn first entitlements (most often, when entering an employment career) until the receipt of last pension before decease. At the same time, individual capabilities to adjust to institutional change decrease with proximity to retirement age and drop to zero once employment is terminated. Moreover, public schemes have created large constituencies for whom pensions are of vital significance: current pensioners are interested in ensuring their accustomed standard of living, and people of employable age want to be relieved from directly providing for their elderly parents and, ultimately, seeing their own earned entitlements materialise. Maintaining institutional trust is thus crucial. Reform attempts that aim at the scheme's *financial* sustainability also have to take into account its *social* sus-

1 John Myles & Paul Pierson, 'The Comparative Politics of Pension Reform', Paul Pierson (ed.), *The New Politics of the Welfare State*, (New York, 2001), pp. 305-333, (p. 306).

2 Karl Hinrichs, 'Elephants on the Move: Patterns of Public Pension Reform in OECD Countries', *European Review*, 8 (2000), pp. 353-378.

tainability, namely to underpin (or restore) firm expectations of secure and adequate pensions on the part of current and potential beneficiaries. Such requirements imply that pension policy actors regularly take a long-term perspective so that reforms are phased in over more than one parliamentary term and rarely touch upon 'vested rights' when retrenchments are at stake. Since attempts to impose losses are unpopular and electorally risky, political bargaining is usually characterised by the search for a broad political consensus as a major strategy of blame avoidance. Radical reforms are thus largely excluded, although a series of incremental changes may also add up to a goal shift and path departure.[3]

Undeniably, imminent population ageing was the major trigger for the pension reforms that have come about in all European countries since the 1990s and have aimed at the financial sustainability of public schemes *and* the preservation of an adequate level of income security for an increasing share of elderly people. However, the foreseeable demographic shift was not mirrored in the magnitude, direction and timing of national reform activities. Rather, these were contingent upon the discursive construction of a policy problem in view of the given architecture of public schemes and their interplay with private components, ultimately determining the level of earnings replacement after retirement. Thus, for today's reforms the origin of the schemes matters and how institutional structures of national pension systems developed over time together with a certain configuration of relevant actors involved in the politics of pension policy. These conditions influence the virulence of external and internal challenges, their perception as well as the accessible repertoire of reform levers.

In the following I will look into reform activities of a group of European countries where hitherto *earnings-related public* schemes played a predominant role in pension provision and, after showing that quite similar levers have been pulled, discuss whether some convergence can be ascertained. Subsequently, I will extend the examination to the non-public components of old-age security. Unlike – or to a much larger extent than – other arrangements of social protection (income replacement in case of unemployment or sickness, provision of health care) income security during retirement was regularly marked by a *public/private mix*, albeit to a varying degree. When comparing the development in a number of European countries it is undeniable that pension reforms have strengthened the importance of private, defined-contribution (DC) components in the retirement

3 Karl Hinrichs, 'Alterssicherungspolitik in Deutschland: Zwischen Kontinuität und Paradigmenwechsel', Jürgen Beyer & Petra Stykow (eds.), *Gesellschaft mit beschränkter Hoffnung. Reformfähigkeit und die Möglichkeit rationaler Politik*, (Wiesbaden, 2004), pp. 266-286; Karl Hinrichs & Olli Kangas, 'When Is a Change Big Enough to Be a System Shift? Small System-Shifting Changes in German and Finnish Pension Policies', *Social Policy and Administration*, 37 (2003), pp. 573-591.

income mix. Therefore, I will investigate whether this redirection of pension policy implies a break of path dependence. Finally, I will deal with the foreseeable or potential consequences of the shifted weight of public and private components in old-age security.

2. Reform Trends in Public Pension Schemes

The distinction between a *Bismarck* and a *Beveridge* approach still provides a helpful starting point to locate nations' pension systems.[4] The Bismarck approach is characterised by a public contributory social insurance scheme being the central pillar (or: tier) for providing earnings replacement in old age. In contrast, Beveridge-type systems focus on poverty alleviation through universal flat-rate pensions financed out of taxes or tax-like contributions. Status maintenance is left to the responsibility of private actors (employers and/or individuals), and those supplementary schemes are always fully funded. A large majority of countries on the European continent have belonged to the 'Bismarck camp' (almost) right from the beginning and, additionally, the USA (albeit in a 'light' version — see *Figure 1*). However, before the 1950s/1960s, benefits from established social insurance schemes were nowhere meant to be the major income resource in old age, but rather, added to earnings from continued employment, support from family members, savings etc. Only subsequently did true wage replacement materialise and 'retirement', a virtually work-free third stage of life, emerge as a universalised social institution. At some stage during their development, all Bismarck countries have introduced special (means-tested) minimum provisions for retirees.[5]

Besides the Anglo-Saxon nations (exception: USA), all Scandinavian countries started from the Beveridge approach (even before that concept was developed). Following the Swedish example, Finland and Norway (and outside Europe: Canada) topped up their people's pensions during the early 1960s with a *public earnings-related* scheme, so that they actually joined the Bismarck group. In contrast to these 'early birds', the 'latecomers', i.e. Beveridge countries which

4 Karl Hinrichs, 'Elephants on the Move: Patterns of Public Pension Reform in OECD Countries', *European Review*, 8 (2000); Giuliano Bonoli, 'The Two Worlds of Pension Reform in Western Europe', *Comparative Politics*, 35 (2003), pp. 399-416; David Natali, 'The Hybridisation of Pension Systems Within the Enlarged EU: Recent Reforms in Old and New Members', *Belgisch Tijdschrift voor Sociale Zekerheid*, 46 (2004), pp. 349-374.

5 European Commission, *Adequate and Sustainable Pensions: Synthesis Report 2006*, (Luxembourg, 2006), pp. 57-64.

Figure 1: Bismarck and Beveridge countries in pension policy

Bismarck countries
(status maintenance)

Germany
Austria
Italy
France
Belgium
(USA)

Beveridge countries
(basic security)

with (almost) universal
'topping-up'

a) *early birds* (PAYG + public)
Sweden
Finland
Norway
(Canada)

b) *latecomer* (funded + private)
Netherlands
United Kingdom
Switzerland
Denmark
(Australia)

without universal *'topping-up'*
(New Zealand)
Ireland

had confined public pensions to basic security until the early 1970s, took a different route to realising status maintenance in old age on a large scale. An earnings-related topping-up and, hence, an expansion of the system was accomplished via *occupational* pension schemes that either were mandated by law (Switzerland, Australia), or arose through collective agreements with almost universal coverage (Netherlands, Denmark). The UK pension system represents something of a (unique) 'hybrid' case.[6] Therefore, the originally large group of Beveridge

6 A national pension was introduced in 1946, and the UK had a short 'Bismarckian period', lasting from the mid-1970s until the late 1980s. During that period the *State Earnings-Related Pension Scheme* (SERPS) was legislated (1975), and the possibilities to 'contract out' were limited to employer-provided occupational pensions of the defined benefit (DB) type. In 1988, SERPS was substantially cut back and contracting-out extended to further alternatives (DC type occupational pensions and personal pension schemes). Meanwhile about three in four employees have turned away from SERPS (in 2002 renamed into *State Second Pension – S2P*) so that the public scheme clearly plays a minor and decreasing role in providing earnings replacement for British pensioners; see David Blake, 'Contracting Out of the State Pension System: The

countries, where provision for supplementary retirement income beyond public minimum pensions is left to the responsibility of private actors, has shrunk to two countries, namely Ireland and New Zealand. In both countries occupational or personal pension schemes have not (yet) been mandated.

In the *latecomer* countries, the second pillar is private, fully funded and extensively regulated in order to protect employees' claims and, most often, it enjoys certain tax privileges (fiscal welfare). These countries adopted a *multipillar approach*, i.e. a diversification of the structure, funding and administration of benefits, well before it was forcefully propagated by the World Bank, because 'third pillar' pensions resulting from voluntary individual provision regularly also play a substantial role in the retirement income mix. The *latecomer* or multipillar countries are firmly located in this camp, and no changes in the basic structure of their pension systems have taken place or are imminent. The pressure on their public schemes due to population ageing is less pronounced, as they are regularly on a smaller scale than in Bismarck countries. Therefore, it is more interesting to focus on reforms which occurred in traditional and second-generation (*early birds*) Bismarck countries over the last two decades and which aim at stabilising the contribution rates or, at least, containing their future increase. From a comparative perspective, five trends are clearly discernible.[7]

First, the *contribution/benefit link* has been tightened. Benefit formulae were changed in such a way that earnings liable to contributions (or the contributions themselves) over the entire employment career are taken into account where previously a certain number of years in covered employment sufficed to attain a 'full' pension and the benefit level was determined by earnings achieved during a number of 'best years' or 'last years' prior to retirement.[8] Calculating pensions

---

British Experience of Carrots and Sticks', Martin Rein & Winfried Schmähl (eds.), *Rethinking the Welfare State: The Political Economy of Pension Reform*, (Cheltenham, 2004), pp. 19-55. Because the latest pension reform will further enhance private provision through 'personal accounts', the UK clearly belongs to the group of multipillar countries; see Department for Work and Pensions, *Personal Accounts: A New Way to Save*, (Norwich, 2006).

7 Karl Hinrichs, 'Elephants on the Move: Patterns of Public Pension Reform in OECD Countries', *European Review*, 8 (2000); OECD, *Reforms for an Ageing Society*, (Paris, 2000); OECD, *Pensions at a Glance: Public Policies Across OECD Countries. 2007 Edition*, (Paris, 2007), pp. 55-62; European Commission, *Adequate and Sustainable Pensions: Synthesis Report 2006*, (Luxembourg, 2006), pp. 112-21; Mika Vidlund, Old-Age Pension Reforms in the EU-15 Countries at a Time of Retrenchment. Finnish Centre for Pensions, *Working Paper 2006:1* (Helsinki, 2006).

8 The strictest (and most transparent) link between lifetime contributions and benefits occurs in so called 'notional defined contribution' (NDC) schemes, which mimic a fully funded plan (with growth of covered wages defining the 'interest rate') but actually operate on a PAYG basis. Among others, Italy, Sweden and Poland have shifted

this way neutralizes the effect of different career earnings profiles. Thus, the trend toward the lifetime average principle diminishes internal redistribution and implies lower public pensions, especially for workers who cannot produce a complete full-time career. Such re-commodification provides an incentive to work longer (if possible) in order to attain a pension level that approximates to one's needs.

Second, other reform elements explicitly aim at *raising retirement age*, either by gradually increasing the standard retirement age (mostly for women when it was lower than for men and for employees in the public sector if a lower eligibility age existed before) or by closing pathways to early retirement, including a more restricted access to disability pensions. Beside applying more uniform rules valid for the entire workforce and raising the earliest eligibility age, a further lever to increase the exit age was the introduction or extension of flexibility for long-term insured to retire within a defined 'age window': individual decisions to claim a public pension before reaching standard retirement age imply permanent (and more or less actuarial) deductions, while prolonging working life beyond that age is rewarded with corresponding bonuses.[9]

Third, in all countries applied *indexing formulae* have been modified. Lower initial pensions come about by changed methods of valorisation: past earnings that enter the benefit formula and determine pension entitlements when claimed for the first time are no longer revalued in line with average earnings growth, but according to the inflation rate (e.g. France) or a combined index (e.g. Finland). Additionally or alternatively, demographic parameters – further life expectancy at retirement age (e.g. in all Nordic countries and Austria) – became incorporated in the formula by which the benefit level is determined at the time of retirement. Thus, rising longevity will not lead to an implicit expansion of the system due to prolonged benefit receipt, but rather, result in lower pensions for subsequent cohorts of retirees. Finally, changed indexing formulae of current pensions may imply quite substantial long-term savings of pension expenditures due to the 'basis effect'. A (partial) exclusion of retirees from improved standards of living of the working-age population is attained when pensions are adjusted according to the consumer price index instead of wage growth, the portion of inflation in a mixed

---

their public employment-related schemes to this almost actuarial method of benefit calculation.

9 Karl Hinrichs & Paula Aleksandrowicz, 'Reforming European Pension Systems for Active Ageing', *International Social Science Journal*, 190 (2008), pp. 585-599; European Commission (Social Protection Committee), *Promoting Longer Working Lives Through Pension Reforms. First Part: Flexibility in Retirement Age Provision*, (Brussels, 2007).

indexing formula is increased, or the (declining) contributor/pensioner ratio is taken into account (as in Germany).[10]

Fourth, the only expansionary trend of reforms in Bismarck countries was to incorporate *unpaid family work* into the benefit calculation, so that raising children and/or taking care of frail relatives now result in (higher) pension entitlements.[11] The applied procedures and the produced benefit increases vary widely. These 'family credits' partly compensate for other benefit cuts (as a result of changed benefit formulae particularly affecting women or setbacks of survivors' pensions), but improve women's pension level relative to men because of their – on average – shorter employment record and thus reduce horizontal disadvantages. The costs of these improvements are mostly covered by tax revenues. This is also true for further benefit components (if retained at all) that have not been earned through contributions out of own earnings and which are meant to ensure socially adequate pensions. Myles and Pierson call such relief of the insured collectivity through subsidies out of general tax revenues as 'rationalising redistribution'.[12]

Fifth, there is a discernible trend to give *pre-funding of pensions* greater weight in public schemes which, in principle, operate on a PAYG basis. For the sake of containing the future rise of contribution rates, in some countries the public schemes are or will be temporarily furnished with higher capital reserves by different means – either a higher rate is charged than currently necessary (Canada and Finland), revenues from privatising public enterprises or state budget surpluses are set aside in earmarked funds and will be infused later (Belgium and France), or other publicly owned funds (in Norway, assets accumulated in the *Petroleum Fund*) are used for this purpose.

All changes that appear in the five trends[13] may be categorised as 'parametric reforms'[14] or, as Peter Hall calls them, first and second order changes whereby

---

10 According to Börsch-Supan and Wilke, the inclusion of this so called 'sustainability factor' in the benefit (adjustment) formula makes the German public pension scheme an NDC system 'look-alike' whereas it was a defined-benefit system before; see Axel Börsch-Supan & Christina Wilke, 'The German Public Pension System: How It Will Become an NDC System Look-Alike', Robert Holzmann & Edward Palmer (eds.), *Pension Reform: Issues and Prospects for Non-Financial Defined Contribution (NDC) Schemes*, (Washington, DC, 2005), pp. 573-610.

11 Matthias Meißner, 'Familienarbeit in der Alterssicherung in Europa', *Deutsche Rentenversicherung*, 61 (2006), pp. 507-525.

12 John Myles & Paul Pierson, 'The Comparative Politics of Pension Reform', Paul Pierson (ed.), *The New Politics of the Welfare State*, (New York, 2001), p. 324.

13 Several of these reform trends also extend to the *latecomer* countries. In order to keep in check future spending increases of their basic pension schemes, they have taken action with regard to raising the retirement age (e.g. Denmark, the UK, Australia, in

either *levels* are adjusted (e.g. the standard retirement age) or an *instrument* shift takes place (e.g. the method of indexing benefits).[15] Will those reform trends imply that some convergence of public pension schemes within the group of Bismarck countries has happened or will come about after they have taken full effect? The bulk of comparative welfare state research during the last decades was about advancing convergence (or persistent divergence) and the relationship of structure and agency as explanatory variables. The question of growing similarity of policies over time depends on the criteria defined for convergence and whether one is able to identify one or several common forces that cause such a process.[16] If one focuses on instruments and their setting it is obvious that public pension schemes have become more similar because comparable changes of instruments have taken place and their concrete setting has been narrowed. In a few cases, one has clearly borrowed from the 'tool box' of neighbour countries (e.g. Finland, Norway and also Poland, which have adapted elements from the innovative pension reform in Sweden).[17] In general, however, the adoption of similar reform elements was less the result of deliberate emulation of other countries' reform efforts, but rather the result of an internally *finite menu* of institutional adjustment options that could be applied in contributory, earnings-related PAYG schemes. Such a limited menu of reform options thus favoured *parallel developments* when predominantly cost-containing changes were at stake.[18]

Switzerland only for women) or modified indexing procedures (Netherlands). Furthermore, Ireland, the Netherlands and New Zealand also build up reserve funds to partly cover future outlays of their basic pension schemes. In Denmark and, to some extent, also in Australia, basic pensions are now (more strictly) tested against rising retirement income from maturing second and third pillar plans. Further countries with a Bismarckian pension system (like Portugal, Slovenia and Spain) which are not looked at in detail here have carried out reforms that conform to the aforementioned trends and also encourage supplementary private provision for old age (see below).

14 Sheetal K. Chand & Albert Jaeger, 'Reform Options for Pay-as-you-go Public Pension Systems. World Bank, *Social Protection, Discussion Paper no. 9927* (Washington DC, 1999).

15 Peter A. Hall, 'Policy Paradigms, Social Learning, and the State: The Case of Economic Policymaking in Britain', *Comparative Politics*, 25 (1993), pp. 275-296.

16 See Bent Greve, 'Indications of Social Policy Convergence in Europe', *Social Policy and Administration*, 30 (1996), pp. 348-367; Christoph Knill, 'Introduction: Cross-National Policy Convergence: Concepts, Approaches and Explanatory Factors', *Journal of European Public Policy*, 12 (2005), pp. 764-774 (pp. 768-9).

17 Karl Hinrichs, 'Enlarging Freedom of Choice: Pension Reforms in the Nordic Countries and Germany', Björn Hvinden & Håkon Johansson (eds.), *Citizenship in Nordic Welfare States: Dynamics of Choice, Duties and Participation in a Changing Europe*, (London/New York, 2007), pp. 200-215.

18 See Colin J. Bennett, 'Review Article: What Is Policy Convergence and What Causes It?', *British Journal of Political Science*, 21 (1991), pp. 215-233 (pp. 220-1, 231);

The *Open Method of Coordination* (OMC) explicitly started as convergence policy, meant to enhance 'transnational learning' and the transfer of 'best practice' among EU countries. However, by this process hardly any potential reform lever or innovation in the pension area will be detected that national policy experts are not aware of already and that they have not checked for political and practical feasibility to address similar challenges within the given institutional setting of their own country.[19] Nor is there any 'best practice' of how to attain a consensual pension reform or to overcome political veto points. For these reasons, the practical impact of disseminating information through the OMC process on national policy formation is expected to be low.[20] Rather, one may expect that similar pressures (e.g. demographic change or globalisation) pose distinctive policy problems which, when dealt with in different pre-existing institutional contexts implying correspondingly different courses of issue processing and dissimilar actor constellations, translate into policy changes that will primarily *revise initial diversity* instead of *reducing* it. To that extent, domestic politics determined which concrete pension reform element was actually accessible at all and how it was implemented (timing, magnitude, affected groups).

When considering the five reform trends as 'parametric' changes, does this mean that the impact of particularly the first three trends on present and future pensioners' retirement income will be limited? Indeed, most single reform elements seem to be small, and the effects are hardly visible at first because they phase in gradually. However, it is the cumulative impact that will result in sometimes considerably *lower* and more *unequally* distributed public benefits.[21]

Katharina Holzinger & Christoph Knill, 'Causes and Conditions of Cross-National Policy Convergence', *Journal of European Public Policy*, 12 (2005), pp. 775-796 (pp. 786, 791-2).

19 One has to bear in mind that exemplary reforms like in Sweden (1994/1998), Italy (1995) and Germany (1989 and 2001) were legislated *before* the OMC process started.

20 See e.g. Schludi, Martin, 'Chances and Limitations of 'Benchmarking' in the Reform of Welfare State Structures – the Case of Pension Policy', Paper presented at the Amsterdam Instituut voor Arbeidsstudies, (Amsterdam, 8 May 2003); Martina Eckardt, 'The Open Method of Coordination on Pensions: An Economic Analysis of Its Effects on Pension Reforms', *Journal of European Social Policy*, 15 (2005), pp. 247-267.

21 Karl Hinrichs & Olli Kangas, 'When Is a Change Big Enough to Be a System Shift? Small System-Shifting Changes in German and Finnish Pension Policies', *Social Policy and Administration*, 37 (2003). For example, the combined impact of employment career changes and pension reforms in *West* Germany shows up as a decrease of the *average* pension awarded to *newly retired men* as a percentage of the 'standard pension' (assumed: 45 years of insurance, always earning an average wage). Between 1990 and 2006, it dropped from 94.5 to 74.1 per cent while the standard replacement ratio remained about the same (figures calculated from database of the public pension

Therefore, the combination of first and second order changes may in fact express that, at least in some Bismarck countries, a *paradigm shift* (or third order change) has taken place and materialised as a path departure. In fact, there is a *sixth trend*, namely, to expand private components in order to compensate for lower wage replacement induced by the first three reform trends mentioned above. In the next section I will therefore look into this development and evaluate whether it actually amounted to a break with an established path.

3. Entering a New Path: Social Insurance plus Obligatory/Subsidised Supplementary Provision

Figure 2 is a modified version of the first one that includes recent institutional developments, namely, the shift towards a greater weight of private components within the retirement income mix. On the right-hand side there is hardly any change. Ireland is moving closer to the group of *latecomers* as occupational pension coverage is on the rise – although at present only just exceeding 50 per cent of all employees.[22] As mentioned before, the *latecomers* have shown less reform activities – at least, no substantial changes in the overall structure of their pension systems have taken place. The UK, however, is an exception as pension policy remains a permanent construction site but still fails to provide a decent standard of living for former low-wage earners and a considerable part of elderly women. Based on the report of the Pensions Commission, further reconstruction is underway, aiming at improved income protection for pensioners within a multipillar system.[23]

---

administration – *DRV*). It means that, even in *nominal* terms, the *average* monthly amount has been declining since the year 2000 (€ 883; 2006: € 790). This example supports the argument that the true impact of reforms cannot be adequately read from a comparison of *standard replacement rates* over time or between countries (see OECD, *Pensions at a Glance: Public Policies Across OECD Countries. 2007 Edition* (Paris, 2007), for a calculation of those rates for different earnings levels).

22 Department of Social and Family Affairs, *Green Paper on Pensions*, (Dublin, 2007), pp. 51-2. In view of work-based pension plans having decreased to a participation rate of less than 15 per cent, the New Zealand government launched a voluntary savings plan (*KiwiSaver*) in 2007 that is tax subsidised and automatically enrols all new employees (as long as they do not refuse).

23 Pensions Commission, *Implementing an Integrated Package of Pension Reforms: The Final Report of the Pensions Commission*, (Norwich, 2006); Department for Work and Pensions, *Security in Retirement: Towards a New Pensions System*, Cm 6841, (Norwich, 2006); Department for Work and Pensions, *Personal Accounts: A New Way to Save*, (Norwich, 2006).

Figure 2: Shifts between different arrangements of pension systems

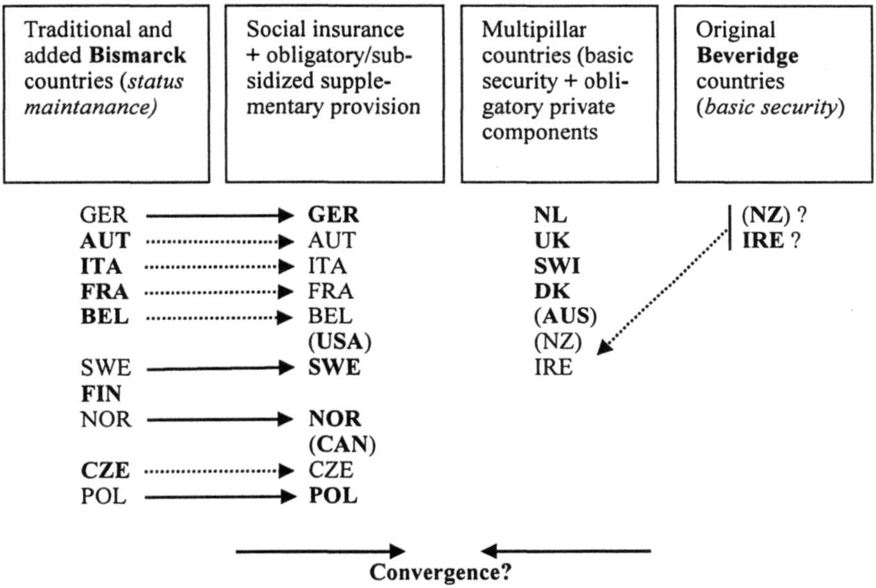

Until recently, the multipillar concept had not gained much ground in old and new Bismarck countries. Despite much rhetoric about the 'three-pillar model' in Germany, quite generous benefits from the public pension scheme secured true earnings replacement in old age (after a complete employment career) for the majority of workers and had largely crowded out other sources. Occupational pension plans covered only a minority of employees and were on the decline for several decades. Only for former high-wage earners did occupational pensions and income from individual provision make a significant contribution to total retirement income. A similar, but cross-nationally varying predominance of public pensions was also true for Austria, Belgium, Finland, Italy, France (with quasi-public occupational pensions on top of the general scheme) and – with some reservations – for Sweden, where collectively agreed occupational pensions supplemented the combined (and relatively generous) benefits from the basic (flat-rate) and earnings-related (*ATP*) schemes.

An increasing number of countries within this category show a clear tendency in old-age security policy to more or less explicitly abandoning the objective of status maintenance via public pensions alone, i.e. from the nation-specific target level at which it had been realised so far.[24] The public component, designed as a social insurance scheme, will remain dominant for a long time. However, it will provide benefits at a lower level than before and, moreover, require a prolonged working life (see section 2). If one looks at individual countries within the Bismarck group, it is almost certain that, after a series of reforms, only the semi-public Finnish pension scheme (all relevant details are legally fixed but the implementation left to private carriers) will stick to the principle of status maintenance.[25] While pension policy in France is only reluctantly facilitating voluntary private pension plans[26], Sweden, Poland and Germany have carried out a paradigm shift – or such change is possibly imminent (e.g. the Czech Republic).[27] However, when aiming at financial sustainability of their public schemes through various retrenchments, national governments have not fully withdrawn from the goal of preserving an adequate level of income security in old age. They pursue it by *other means* – mandating or encouraging supplementary *private provision* – but will not necessarily attain the *same results* as before, namely, firmly foreseeable pensions and limited inequality in old age (see next section). The objective of this overall trend, however, is that retirement income from private, fully funded components is designated to compensate for lowered pensions from social insurance schemes which are moving towards basic security.[28] Therefore, the

24 Traditionally, the retirement income mix in the USA and Canada has been somewhat different, because the respective earnings-related public scheme offers a lower replacement rate. Already for workers earning an average wage, additional private provision (via the employer or individually) is required for not risking an excessive decline of the accustomed standard of living. In both countries, private provision is not mandatory but tax-favoured, and private pension coverage is quite high, particularly in Canada (OECD, *Pensions at a Glance: Public Policies Across OECD Countries. 2007 Edition*, (Paris, 2007), pp. 76-80). Thus, these two non-European countries are grouped in the second column of *Figure 2*.

25 Karl Hinrichs & Olli Kangas, 'When Is a Change Big Enough to Be a System Shift? Small System-Shifting Changes in German and Finnish Pension Policies', *Social Policy and Administration*, 37 (2003).

26 Christelle Mandin & Bruno Palier, 'The Politics of Pension Reform in France: The End of Exceptionalism?' Giuliano Bonoli & Toshimitsu Shinkawa (eds.), *Ageing and Pension Reform Around the World*, (Cheltenham, 2005), pp. 74-93 (pp. 87-9).

27 Poland and the Czech Republic are included here because they had a long social insurance tradition, and Bismarckian traits survived during the communist era. Both countries maintained a purely public DB pension scheme after the transition in 1990. In 1999, Poland turned to a multipillar system.

28 In a comment on the findings of the first edition of *Pensions at a Glance*, the OECD admitted that there is a 'lower limit of politically acceptable replacement rates through mandatory systems' and the present levels do 'not appear to leave a huge degree of scope for further cuts in pension entitlements beyond the reforms that are already in

question arises whether these countries entering the multipillar track are coming closer to the *latecomer* countries as far as the structure of their pension systems is concerned.

Sweden was the first country that, based on a broad inter-party compromise, not only reformed both components of its public pension scheme[29] but also added a further component. The so called *premiepension* is part of the public pension system, however, during the accumulation period (i.e. before annuitisation) it is carried through by privately managed pension funds. 2.5 of a total contribution rate of 18.5 per cent are mandatorily diverted to build up financial assets in individual investment accounts. Contributors are given extended options to freely choose up to five from nearly 800 registered pension funds (and to switch between them). The level of the accruing *premiepension* is dependent on contributions and the actual performance of the pension funds chosen. The reformed Polish pension system has clearly borrowed features from the new Swedish system: the PAYG social insurance scheme applies the NDC principle, and the contribution share devoted to the fully funded mandatory but privately managed pillar is even higher (7.3 of total rate of 19.52 per cent). Norway has also followed the Swedish example. In 2006, a compulsory supplement to public pensions (*Folketrygden*) was introduced. However, unlike the Swedish *premiepension* it comes as an employer mandate to offer occupational pensions based on a minimum contribution rate of two per cent (which may be matched by the employee) so that about 70 per cent of private sector workers became covered for the first time. This stipulation precedes the passing of the 'big' pension reform during the current parliamentary term. It will include all elements mentioned in section 2 but, most likely, benefit levels are going to decline less than in most other countries.

In Germany, the 'fixed contribution principle' was adopted in 2001, when it was stipulated that the contribution rate to the public scheme must not exceed 20 per cent until 2020 and 22 per cent until 2030. This means an explicit surrender of status maintenance as a key goal. Voluntary savings of up to four per cent of gross salary for a so called *Riester-Rente* are rewarded with state subsidies or tax breaks and destined to *compensate* for a gradually declining public pension level. At the same time, legislative changes concerning occupational pensions intend to increase coverage, first of all, by encouraging (tax-favoured) earnings conversion based on collective agreements. Similar legislation went into effect in Belgium in

---

place in the 'average' OECD country' (OECD, *Solving the Pensions Puzzle*, OECD Policy Brief, (Paris, March 2005), p. 4).

29 The universal flat-rate scheme was transformed into a 'guarantee pension' that is tested against the public *inkomst* and *premie pension*. The earnings-related tier (*ATP*) was changed to the NDC principle (see above, *n. 8*).

2003 in order to spread occupational pension coverage via agreements between the social partners. Meanwhile, they extend to almost half of the workforce.[30] The voluntary approach to private supplementary pensions topping up declining public benefits is pursued in other Bismarck countries: in Austria and Italy benefits from already existing end-of-service allowance schemes (*Abfertigung* and *Trattamento di Fine Rapporto*) enjoy tax advantages if transferred to pension funds whereby in Italy workers are automatically enrolled unless they formally refuse. Additionally, Austria is subsidising private pension savings similar to the *Riester-Rente* since 2003 (and attained a surprisingly high take-up rate of about 30 per cent), as does the Czech Republic, where currently 37 per cent of the working-age population make payments into designated pension funds (sometimes with an employer match).[31] The voluntary approach, however, is bound to fail if people abstain from participation and ultimately have to rely on public pensions alone. This is less likely to happen when complementary pension provision implies no additional burden for employees, as in Austria and Italy, where the function of already established severance pay schemes has been changed.

All in all, we can observe an extension of the retirement income *system* in a number of (old and new) Bismarck countries via the addition of new, fully funded components while, at the same time, there is a relative decline of PAYG financed public pensions. It means differential growth of the incipiently small private schemes and the established public scheme. Therefore, this mode of institutional change is called 'layering'.[32] Beside assigning new functions to the different components of the pension system, this path-altering dynamics affects the politics of pension policy, since new actors who had occupied a more or less marginal position so far have now gained a real stake in this policy domain, such as the financial service industry, public authorities regulating an emerging welfare market and its products, organisations protecting pension savers' interests, or Ministries of Finance when it comes to tax-favoured pension savings. They have to deal with new themes and conflicts (concerning regulation and supervision of private pensions, the amount of tax expenditure, etc.) in new arenas or, old ac-

30 Jozef Pacolet & Veronique Coudron, 'De staat van den verzorgingsstaat in Belgie omstreeks 2005', *Belgisch Tijdschrift voor Sociale Zekerheid*, 48 (2006) pp. 589-621.

31 The Czech Republic will probably implement a major pension reform in 2009. The report of a reform commission that included representatives from all five political parties in parliament revealed quite opposed positions. In spring 2008 the details of the deliberated policy changes are not yet recognisable.

32 Wolfgang Streeck & Kathleen Thelen, 'Introduction: Institutional Change in Advanced Political Economies', Wolfang Streeck & Kathleen Thelen (eds.), *Beyond Continuity*, (Oxford, 2005), pp. 1-39 (pp. 22-4).

tors, such as the social partners in Germany and Belgium, acquire new roles when negotiating collective agreements on occupational pensions.

Moreover, the principles that determine retirement income are changing, which will produce grave consequences. In Bismarck countries, so far, the length of covered employment and the earnings level have been taken into account when calculating public pensions. The applied 'defined benefit principle' (DB) made the level of security largely foreseeable for future retirees. Due to the first and third reform trends mentioned in section 2 this will less be the case – in particular where there was an approximation or complete switch to the NDC principle, as in Sweden or Italy. As regards the growing importance of supplementary components, uncertainty about the level of monthly pension payments is even larger because they are dependent on the accumulated assets to be converted into an annuity at the time of retirement. The amount of contributions is decisive, as are individual decisions about the portfolio and the state of financial markets at the end of a person's working life. People who voluntarily or compulsorily provide for old age through private pensions are thus exposed to considerable investment and financial market risks, and rising longevity may imply a (much) lower annuity than expected when assets are eventually converted.

This is so because, in addition, occupational pension plans are rapidly converted to DC plans, whereas traditionally the benefit level was calculated according to the length of service and the final wage (or average salary while working for the plan sponsor). In those DB plans, the employers have to bear investment and longevity risks. Increasingly, they are avoiding these risks by paying a certain, mostly lower percentage of the wage into pension funds and not taking responsibility for the level of accruing pensions. In the UK, this process has progressed very far, as it also has in the USA, where '401(k) plans' (named after a corresponding section in the income tax code) are becoming increasingly prevalent.[33] Participants in '401(k) plans' convert parts of their earnings into pension savings (to which employers may – and often do – add further contributions) and, to a varying degree, they have a say in how accumulating funds are to be invested. The difference between occupational and personal pensions is thus blurred, as is also the case with those earnings conversion plans in Germany that represent an alternative to the *Riester-Rente*. In Sweden, the traditional arrangement of occupational pensions as DB schemes was no longer compatible with the

33 Paul Bridgen & Traute Meyer, 'When Do Benevolent Capitalists Change Their Mind? Explaining the Retrenchment of Defined-Benefit Pensions in Britain', *Social Policy and Administration*, 39 (2005), pp. 764-785; Alicia H. Munnell, 'Employer-Sponsored Plans: The Shift from Defined Benefit to Defined Contribution', Gordon L. Clarke, Alicia H. Munnell & J. Michael Orszag, (eds.), *Oxford Handbook of Pensions and Retirement Income*, (Oxford, 2006), pp. 359-380.

DC principle that applies for both components of the mandatory system. The social partners have renegotiated the contractual schemes and, except for benefit elements favouring high-wage workers, adopted the DC principle as well. Consequently, employees have been given choice as to the investment decisions.[34]

From a comparative point of view, there is thus a definite trend to shift the weight of pension components designed to ensure status maintenance in the direction of the defined contribution principle and pre-funding. Thereby, the *costs* and the *risks* for participants in the reformed pension system increase. The *costs* of a partially privatised system are higher, because fees charged by private fund managers considerably exceed the administrative costs of comprehensive public schemes. The *risks* to attain an aspired level of old-age security are transferred to the future retirees. In view of the development of financial markets after the year 2000, those risks are unquestionably real ones. For example, the sudden increase in the employment rate of people aged 60 and older after the millennium in the USA indicates that a large number of them postponed retirement because they were hit by a declining value of their assets invested in '401(k) plans' or individual retirement accounts.[35] In the Netherlands, due to the turbulence on financial markets, the predominant DB type occupational pension schemes became seriously imbalanced. The pension funds corrected this by suspending indexing of current pensions and raising the contribution rates for employers and employees[36] and, subsequently, by moving away from full-fledged DB plans and changes of indexing methods.[37] Similarly, second-pillar pension funds in Switzerland experienced considerable shortfalls in terms of future obligations after the year 2000, so that the guaranteed interest rate on contributions had to be decreased several times.[38] Given these incalculable risks, it is all too understandable that employers try to get rid of them and, hence, private households are increasingly

34 Karl Hinrichs, 'Enlarging Freedom of Choice: Pension Reforms in the Nordic Countries and Germany', Björn Hvinden & Håkon Johansson (eds.), *Citizenship in Nordic Welfare States: Dynamics of Choice, Duties and Participation in a Changing Europe* (London/New York, 2007).

35 Andrew D. Eschtruth & Jonathan Gemus, 'Are Older Workers Responding to the Bear Market?', Center for Retirement Researche at Boston College, *Just the Facts on Retirement Issues*, no. 5 (Chestnut Hill, MA, September, 2002).

36 De Nederlandsche Bank, 'Dutch Pension Sector: Sustainability Under Pressure', *Quarterly Bulletin* (December 2004), pp. 65-74.

37 Eduard H.M. Ponds & Bart van Riel, 'Sharing Risk: The Netherlands' New Approach to Pensions', Center for Retirement Researche at Boston College, *Issues in Brief*, no 5 (Chestnut Hill, MA, 2007).

38 Joseph Steiger & Hans Nussbaum, 'Pensionskassen in Unterdeckung – die wichtigsten Ergebnisse der Erhebung BSV 2005', *Soziale Sicherheit (CHSS)*, (2006, no. 1), pp. 31-34.

turned into 'shock absorbers of the last resort', as was remarked by the International Monetary Fund.[39]

As regards the third pillar of old-age security, private households always had to bear the immediate consequences of their investment decisions. However, individual provision is gaining increasing weight in the retirement income mix of almost all European countries, not least because employees anticipate lower levels of public benefits and many react accordingly (if their current disposable income leaves sufficient latitude for additional savings). This is also the case in Germany, where about 11.5 million employees have taken up a contract for the *Riester-Rente* (summer 2008). Increasingly, savings are being invested in private pension products which, unlike low-interest savings accounts, contain more risks.[40] In international comparison, the third pillar of old-age security is of different significance in the retirement income mix. In Anglo-Saxon countries and also in Scandinavia, tax-favoured acquisition of owner-occupied housing is part of the welfare state edifice and, accordingly, plays in important role in the retirement income mix.[41] However, private households investing in owner-occupied housing as one component of future old-age security are also exposed to considerable market risks, such as fluctuations in housing prices or mortgage rates.

Shifting the retirement income mix towards contribution-defined components and, concomitantly, the transfer of various risks to private households entail consequences that are not only relevant for the question of convergence, but also the question of whether this development actually means a path departure in pension policy, at least in some European countries. According to Peter Hall, a radical policy change is the outflow of a preceding paradigm shift. Such a policy paradigm combines goals and techniques within an intellectual framework (ideas and standards) for interpreting the rationales for a policy and defining its problems.[42]

---

39 International Monetary Fund, *Global Financial Stability Report: Market Developments and Issues. April 2005*, (Washington DC, 2005), p. 89.

40 Remsperger, Hermann & Stöß, Elmar, 'Spar- und Anlageverhalten in Deutschland: Trends und Perspektiven', *Deutsche Bundesbank. Auszüge aus Presseartikeln*, 44 (19th October, 2005), pp. 4-8.

41 Home-ownership represents a consumable asset (due to an 'imputed rent' that is not actually paid). If home-ownership among elderly households is fairly widespread (as in Norway, for example) it facilitates fixing a lower standard pension level and supporting the minority of (elderly) tenants by targeted housing allowances. For this reason, a simple comparison of replacement rates for workers after an assumed 'standard' career (see OECD, *Pensions at a Glance: Public Policies Across OECD Countries. 2007 Edition*, (Paris, 2007)) is somewhat misleading when evaluating the financial situation of elderly households.

42 Peter A. Hall, 'Policy Paradigms, Social Learning, and the State: The Case of Economic Policymaking in Britain', *Comparative Politics*, 25 (1993), p. 279.

Until recently, in Bismarck countries, the prevailing pension policy paradigm rested on cognitive and normative beliefs about the superiority of the social insurance approach, widely shared among political and social actors. Frank Bönker lists a number of non-exclusive conditions favourable for the competing multipillar approach to gain ground.[43] Probably most important have been (1) an apparent exhaustion of the (single-pillar) social insurance approach that is running out of options to effectively/credibly address the long-term financial problems, and (2) the fit of the competing paradigm with ideological traditions (e.g. the empirically incorrect three-pillar concept in Germany that nevertheless had always been present in the public discourse). Further factors supporting an *ideational change* were (3) a rearrangement of established policy communities (sometimes caused by a change in government or the replacement of policy experts and administrators after long tenure), certain interest groups becoming powerful enough to modify interpretative frames, or (individual) policy entrepreneurs successfully contributing to the destruction of the once coherent policy paradigm. In some cases, (4) positively perceived arrangements/reforms in peer countries have helped to spread the new paradigm via transnational communication and learning.[44] In that regard, critics of the *OMC* process exactly fear its normative repercussions since the main impetus for a coordination of national pension strategies came from actors (the Economic Policy Committee and the ECOFIN council) committed to containment of public expenditure, strengthened work incentives, a larger role of privately managed funded schemes etc.[45] The socially oriented actors whose prime concern is to maintain adequate pensions worry about a potential loss of established national values and priorities if a strict orientation towards financial sustainability is prevailing and finds expression in corresponding benchmarks and indicators.[46] It is unclear to what extent the power struggle at the EU level on

43 Frank Bönker, 'Changing Ideas on Pensions: Accounting for Differences in the Spread of the Multipillar Paradigm in Five EU Social Insurance Countries', Peter Taylor-Gooby (ed.), *Ideas and Welfare State Reform in Western Europe*, (Houndmills, Basigstoke, 2005), pp. 81-99.

44 See also Katharina Holzinger & Christoph Knill, 'Causes and Conditions of Cross-National Policy Convergence', *Journal of European Public Policy*, 12 (2005), pp. 790-1.

45 Martin Schludi, 'Chances and Limitations of 'Benchmarking' in the Reform of Welfare State Structures – the Case of Pension Policy', Paper presented at the Amsterdam Instituut voor Arbeidsstudies, (Amsterdam, 8 May 2003) pp. 23-4.

46 This is more likely to happen since, after EU enlargement in 2004, the number of member countries having implemented a multipillar system has increased. They will definitely prefer indicators to be established that their pension arrangement can comply with best. See Martin Schludi, 'Chances and Limitations of 'Benchmarking' in the

ideas of a sustainable and modernised pension system has actually trickled down, but it may have confirmed some national policymakers in their determination to take the multipillar approach as a point of reference and to speak up for it at home with stronger backing.[47]

However, the respective national policy discourse and pension politics in Bismarck countries determined whether the multipillar paradigm was adopted in a largely uncontroversial fashion, as in Sweden, Germany and, to some extent, also in Italy and Norway. In others, it was much more contested (France and Austria, where cuts in public pensions were at stake), or the social insurance paradigm did not crumble away at all (Finland).[48] Although it is not easy to define what constitutes a path departure, one may reasonably argue that it happened in countries where the old paradigm was replaced and, consequently, pension reforms went beyond 'normal policymaking'[49] and implied a discontinuity in policy. Such a third order change materialised where the objectives assigned to the respective pillars were modified (here: status maintenance no longer the prime goal of the public pillar) and private households are now expected to take on more self-responsibility and risks (here: a greater weight of fully funded DC components and less emphasis on distributive criteria when benefits are calculated). This was clearly the case in Sweden and Poland, where the structural change came about as a 'big bang', and in Germany. There, the system shift was the result of a series of incremental reforms. In other Bismarck countries (e.g. Italy, to some extent, also Austria and the Czech Republic), first and second order changes concerning the public pillar have substantially eroded its generosity but,

---

Reform of Welfare State Structures – the Case of Pension Policy', Paper presented at the Amsterdam Instituut voor Arbeidsstudies, (Amsterdam, 8 May 2003) pp. 30-1.

47 See also Karen M. Anderson, 'The Europeanization of Pension Arrangements: Convergence or Divergence?' Caroline de la Porte & Philippe Pochet (eds.), *Building Social Europe through the Open Method of Co-ordination*, (Brussels, 2002), pp. 251-283; Martina Eckardt, 'The Open Method of Coordination on Pensions: An Economic Analysis of Its Effects on Pension Reforms', *Journal of European Social Policy*, 15 (2005).

48 Frank Bönker, 'Changing Ideas on Pensions: Accounting for Differences in the Spread of the Multipillar Paradigm in Five EU Social Insurance Countries', Peter Taylor-Gooby (ed.), *Ideas and Welfare State Reform in Western Europe*, (Houndmills, Basigstoke, 2005); Karl Hinrichs, 'Alterssicherungspolitik in Deutschland: Zwischen Kontinuität und Paradigmenwechsel', Jürgen Beyer & Petra Stykow (eds.), *Gesellschaft mit beschränkter Hoffnung. Reformfähigkeit und die Möglichkeit rationaler Politik*, (Wiesbaden, 2004); Karl Hinrichs, 'New Century – New Paradigm: Pension Reforms in Germany' Giuliano Bonoli & Toshimitsu Shinkawa (eds.), *Ageing and Pension Reform Around the World*, (Cheltenham, 2005), pp. 47-73.

49 Peter A. Hall, 'Policy Paradigms, Social Learning, and the State: The Case of Economic Policymaking in Britain', *Comparative Politics*, 25 (1993), p. 279.

so far, the emphasis put on partial privatisation (expanding occupational and personal pensions) has been much weaker. The present development, however, also points to 'hybridisation'[50], namely a move towards the structure of pensions systems realised in latecomer countries (see *Figure 2*).

4. The Turn towards a Multipillar Approach: Some Consequences

In view of the trend towards the multipillar approach described in the previous section, four consequences – related to very different aspects – deserve to be highlighted.

(1) When comparing *expenditures on old-age security*, those of the different public schemes are usually taken into account (sometimes weighted with the share of the population aged 60 or 65 and older). To get a rough impression of the welfare *state's* involvement in this area of social protection, this might be sufficient.[51] However, when it comes to financial sustainability, it becomes increasingly meaningful to include the 'tax expenditure' (foregone taxes) that is linked to mandatory and voluntary contributions to privately-managed pension plans. In a number of countries examined in this chapter, these tax allowances or direct subsidies imply a very significant financial burden for state budgets.[52] What is more, because low-income employees participate less often and/or contribute lower amounts, those tax advantages generally produce regressive distributive effects. However, current mandated and voluntary *private* social spending as measured by Adema and Ladaique[53] – of which pensions are the largest component –

50 David Natali, 'The Hybridisation of Pension System Within the Enlarged EU: Recent Reforms in Old and New Members', *Belgisch Tijdschrift voor Social Zekerheid*, 46 (2004). See also Giuliano Bonoli, 'The Two Worlds of Pension Reform in Western Europe', *Comparative Politics*, 35 (2003).

51 A decreasing variance of European countries' public pension spending would hardly be a sufficient indicator for convergence. If there have been changes in expenditure (as a percentage of GDP), they reflect the balance of political decisions on program expansions and restrictions reached (very) long ago; furthermore, recent reforms will only produce their full effect with an extended time-lag. Likewise, the income situation of today's retirees is the result of institutional arrangements and individual behaviour oriented to those rules, incentives, or obligations when they were of working age.

52 See Kwang-Yeol Yoo & Alain de Serres, 'Tax Treatment of Private Pension Savings in OECD Countries', *OECD Economic Studies*, 39 (2004), pp. 73-110. One has to bear in mind that, at the same time, a sizable income tax claim on future pension payments is built up if pensions are taxed upon receipt, albeit normally at a lower rate.

53 Willem Adema & Maxime Ladaique, 'Net Social Expenditure, 2005 Edition', *OECD Social, Employment and Migration Working Papers*, no. 29 (Paris, 2005).

does not fully reflect the ongoing shift to private pensions. Those figures refer to *benefits* paid from private pension plans, but as long as they are immature, current *contributions* incurred by employers or private households far exceed the magnitude of current benefits in all Bismarck countries that have only recently turned to the multipillar model with an increasing weight of pre-funded components.

(2) Due to the enduring trend to shift the retirement income mix to fully funded, contribution-defined components, the actual level of old-age security becomes an issue that is no longer decided within *national boundaries* alone. Established nation-specific notions about an adequate level of basic security or wage replacement are becoming less relevant, while the country's position in international competition is gaining in importance. Therefore, public pension reforms attempt to restrain the growth of non-wage labour costs even if that implies lower levels of income security in old age. Again, the EU comes in as further factor, since first-pillar schemes are part of national public budgets. In the event of an emerging deficit, via the Growth and Stability Pact, new pressure may be put on public pension schemes. For example, in Italy the aspired access to the European Monetary Union substantially influenced the pension reform of 1995 and eased its legislation.[54] Inasmuch as occupational and private pension provision expands and is also designated to explicitly (or, at least, implicitly) perform social policy functions, regulatory interventions to protect future pension savers (from providers' mismanagement, excessive administrative fees etc. or from the temptation to prematurely consume their accumulated assets) are becoming ever more necessary. Recently, attempts have been made in a number of countries to regulate the growing welfare markets for partly novel pension products through a large array of legislation or decrees from supervisory authorities, and the more the EU member states *themselves* shift the weight of their pension systems towards funded elements of the second and third pillar, Community law increasingly defines the regulatory frame.[55]

A second and equally important aspect relates to the still growing volume of pension assets that is not only invested in the respective home market but, after financial markets have been liberalised, pension funds spread financial holdings

54 Maurizio Ferrera & Elisabetta Gualmini, 'Reforms Guided by Consensus: The Welfare State in the Italian Transition', *West European Politics*, 23 (2000), pp. 187-208.

55 Martina Eckardt, 'The Open Method of Coordination on Pensions: An Economic Analysis of Its Effects on Pension Reforms', *Journal of European Social Policy*, 15 (2005); European Commission, *Adequate and Sustainable Pensions: Synthesis Report 2006*, (Luxembourg, 2006), pp. 130-2; Markus Haverland, 'When the Welfare State Meets the Regulatory State: EU Occupational Pension Policy', *Journal of European Public Policy* 14 (2007), pp. 886-904.

worldwide. For example, in France the PAYG principle was utterly uncontested. Impressed by the transnationalisation of pension funds' activities, President Chirac demanded the development of fully funded plans in France so that in future French employees will not have to work for the pensions of elderly Americans because U.S. pension funds had bought shares in French firms on a large scale.[56] Nevertheless, worldwide investment of pension savings is viewed as advantageous because of risk diversification. The International Monetary Fund[57] and others, however, assume there are considerable risks involved in such a 'global asset allocation process' that may affect the income of retirees in numerous countries at the same time. In particular, there is much concern (but inconsistent theoretical and empirical evidence) about potentially declining market prices of financial investments when in all Western countries large birth cohorts will start to retire around the year 2020 and to consume their pension savings and an 'asset meltdown' may occur.[58]

(3) Regularly, benefits from earnings-related public pension schemes are not strictly based on the individual equity principle (although more than in the past — see section 2), but also contain some redistribution for the sake of social equality. If the share of public components in the retirement income mix declines and, related to it, the redistributive effects in favour of persons with otherwise low pensions decrease as well, then the *individual capability* to additionally provide for old age increasingly determines the actual income situation during retirement. On the one hand, the ultimate wage replacement rate is contingent on the ability to continuously pay mandatory or voluntary contributions into private pension plans for a maximum period of time – it is i.a. important to stay on in employment until age 65 or even beyond. Longer spells of unemployment, poor health, or impaired job opportunities for older workers may in a socially selective manner foil such individual compensation strategies. On the other hand, the capability to make provisions for old age varies by income level. Therefore, the degree of earnings disparity is of crucial importance, and if it is rising (as is the case in most Western countries), income inequality during employable age will trans-

---

56 Bruno Palier, 'Tracking the Evolution of a Single Instrument Can Reveal Profound Changes: The Case of Funded Pensions in France', *Governance*, 20 (2007), pp. 85-107 (p. 98).

57 IMF, *Global Financial Stability Report: Market Developments and Issues. April 2005*, (Washington DC, 2005), p. 5.

58 Sylvester J. Schieber & John B. Shoven, 'The Consequences of Population Aging for Private Pension Fund Saving and Asset Markets', Michael D. Hurd & Naohiro Yashiro (eds.), *The Economic Effects of Aging in the United States and Japan*, (Chicago/London, 1997), pp. 111-130; Hans Fehr & Sabine Jokisch, 'Demographischer Wandel und internationale Finanzmärkte', *Perspektiven der Wirtschaftspolitik*. 7 (2006), pp. 501-517.

late into an even larger inequality in old age. This assertion may imply that pension reforms have less led to a similarity of the institutional *structures* of pension systems (or will do so in future) than to a convergence of reform *outcomes* when income inequality among retirees in (almost) all European countries will further increase.[59]

(4) Mandatory membership in public pension schemes and/or in DB occupational pension plans has largely relieved employees from retirement planning and the need to assess the risks of welfare markets. The changing configuration of pension systems goes along with a higher degree of self-responsibility, and the enlarged role of DC-type components increases the demand for *individual risk management* or 'do-it-yourself social policy'.[60] At the same time, the transfer of market risks is associated with more freedom of choice to decide about provision for old age according to one's preferences and degree of risk aversion. To behave as active consumers making informed choices presupposes knowledge about different pension products and their respective risks as well as a long planning horizon, since decisions (not) made are becoming of individual significance only years or decades from now. However, private pensions are complex products and most people are not well prepared to make such rational choices. In fact, studies in behavioural economics have provided ample empirical evidence that one has to reckon with persisting financial illiteracy, inertia to take action at all (or too late)[61], or people making bad choices that are costly to revise. Even in the UK and the USA where, for a long time, the majority of employees have had to make far-reaching decisions about their future retirement income situation, in general, financial literacy is not very developed, has hardly improved over time and is still positively correlated to income and education level.[62]

---

59 This expectation of growing inequality is not limited to pensioners belonging to the same birth cohort, but rather, extends to older and younger cohorts among the retirees as private pensions are regularly not indexed to inflation (or average wage growth). An inflation rate of merely two per cent p.a. reduces the purchasing power of a pension by about one quarter after 15 years in retirement.

60 Rudolf Klein & Jane Millar, 'Do-It-Yourself Social Policy', *Social Policy and Administration*, 29 (1995), pp. 303-316.

61 Where private pension coverage is not mandatory, in order to overcome myopia and procrastination, 'automatic enrolment', i.e. participation in a pension plan unless the worker explicitly contradicts, has become a widespread instrument, e.g. in Italy, New Zealand, USA, and (soon) the UK.

62 IMF, *Global Financial Stability Report: Market Developments and Issues. April 2005*, (Washington DC, 2005), pp. 74-87; for further references see Karl Hinrichs, 'Active Citizens and Retirement Planning: Enlarging Freedom of Choice in the Course of Pension Reforms in Nordic Countries and Germany', Universität Bremen, Zentrum für Sozialpolitik, *ZeS-Arbeitspapier*, Nr. 112004 (Bremen, 2004).

As a largely unforeseen consequence of implemented reforms, additional *paedagogical interventions* nevertheless become necessary to improve the competencies of individual actors who (have to) enter this welfare market. Thus, the development towards multipillar pension systems goes along with an *extension of the modes of welfare state intervention*.[63] Among the European countries, the debate on how to impart financial literacy to future retirees has probably been most intense in the UK[64], but in other countries having entered the 'multipillar track' financial education has become a matter of growing concern as well, since governments have learned that simply sending out information (e.g. statements about future entitlements) is not sufficient to assist people making informed choices.[65] Apparently, there exists a negative relationship between the degree of regulation and the necessity to impart 'financial literacy': if regulatory efforts in fact produce more transparency and limit freedom of choice on an easily comprehensible scale, the need to develop the relevant competencies is reduced. At least in Germany and Sweden, the perception has grown that broadly developing financial literacy is facing high hurdles, and this has led governments to search for less complex settings of individual decision-making through re-regulation of privately managed pension schemes. In view of the initially low take-up rate, the German pension reform of 2004 contained a simplification of rules related to the *Riester-Rente*. In Sweden, a committee that evaluated the *premiepension* system came forward with a number of proposals that, among other things, focused on a reduction of the bewildering range of almost 800 pension fund alternatives and on im-

---

63 Here I am referring to Kaufmann's distinction of four modes of welfare state intervention; see Franz-Xaver Kaufmann, *Sozialpolitik und Sozialstaat. Soziologische Analysen*, (Opladen, 2002), pp. 69-127. Public pension policy is, first of all and still, an *economic intervention*: money is redistributed in order to improve the income situation of individuals who are not able anymore or no longer expected to earn a living through employment. As well, *regulatory interventions* in order to improve the legal status of future retirees are not new. For example, they have defined and secured the claims of employees to occupational pensions (e.g. vesting and portability rules) or settled the rights and obligations of parties to a life insurance contract. The fourth mode, which Kaufmann calls *ecological intervention,* is largely irrelevant here. It aims at ameliorating opportunities for individuals and households and relates to facilities providing social services within reach of potential clients.

64 E.g. Department for Work and Pensions, *Simplicity, Security and Choice: Informed Choices for Working and Saving*, Cm 6111, (London, 2004).

65 See also OECD, *Improving Financial Literacy: Analysis of Issues and Policies*, (Paris, 2005). Germany is one of a few countries whose National Strategy Report 2005 produced for the 2005 *OMC* process contains a section on measures to improve financial education, see Bundesregierung, *Nationaler Strategiebericht Alterssicherung 2005*, Deutscher Bundestag, Drucksache 15/5571, (Berlin, 2005).

proving guidance for largely ignorant participants to encourage active and better choice.[66]

5. Conclusion

During the last ten years, the dynamics of pension reforms in Europe has obviously increased. In a number of countries, public pension schemes that had been geared towards status maintenance arrived at 'critical junctures' where they became less resistant to profound changes, and in quite a few countries a clear path departure has occurred. While all Bismarck countries have pulled quite similar reform levers, it is questionable whether there was an unequivocal convergence in the institutional structure of *public* schemes. Some countries, most clearly Sweden, Germany and Poland, embraced a multipillar approach as a point of reference and moved closer to a group of countries that have arranged their pensions system as a combination of basic security via public pensions and privately managed (employer-related and individual) plans on top, providing wage replacement in old age. Such an institutional extension (or: 'layering') has changed the politics of pension policy and also extended its scope, since regulatory interventions have been intensified and the issue of financial education is entering the political agenda. The ascertained dynamics of pension reforms largely contradicts notions of welfare state resilience and especially of old-age security as the most immovable object.[67] Those notions of resilience have been obtained from looking back to social policy developments during the 1980s and early 1990s. If one takes into account the more recent institutional changes, it becomes obvious that in some Bismarck countries 'old politics' actors' (notably trade unions and Social Democratic parties) *ability* to defend the status quo has largely collapsed, or their *willingness* to do so has faded.[68] In contrast, the rise of a new paradigm of old-age security policy has prepared the ground for path-breaking changes initially producing small outcome shifts that, however, will intensify over time.

---

66 See Statens offentliga utredningar, *Svårnavigerat? Premiepensionssparande på rätt kurs*, SOU, 87 (Stockholm, 2005).

67 Paul Pierson, 'The New Politics of the Welfare State', *World Politics* 48 (1996), pp. 143-179.

68 Karl Hinrichs, 'Alterssicherungspolitik in Deutschland: Zwischen Kontinuität und Paradigmenwechsel', Jürgen Beyer & Petra Stykow (eds.), *Gesellschaft mit beschränkter Hoffnung. Reformfähigkeit und die Möglichkeit rationaler Politik*, (Wiesbaden, 2004).

Pensions Can be Cut

Einar Overbye

Pensions can be cut

Public old-age pensions provide security against the risks accruing from longevity, i.e. the risk of living so long that private resources dry up. Most voters are inclined to regard themselves as high risks in this regard. At the same time, the old are the core group of what used to be called the 'worthy poor'. For these and related reasons, an influential hypothesis in the welfare literature has been that pensions, once introduced, can never be significantly reduced. The perceived vote loss will prevent democratically elected politicians from attempting cutbacks, and if they none the less should try, they will commit political suicide. This is a theoretically well-founded hypothesis. It is also able to meet the Popperian criteria for a scientific hypothesis: It can be falsified. If one or several countries successfully cut public pensions, the hypothesis is wrong.

During the 1990s, that was precisely what happened. Originating in Latin America, large-scale pension reform, including changes to less expensive systems, spread to Central and East European countries. Thus the hypothesis is wrong: pensions can be cut.

The pension reforms of the 1990s and 2000s have also weakened another influential hypothesis: that pension reform is 'path-dependent'. Path-dependence connotes that the structure of previous institutional arrangements impact on how reformers perceive political alternatives, that they structure the field of vested interests reformers find themselves in, and more generally that they limit the scope for future political reforms. With particular regard to pay-as-you-go based pensions, the fact that one generation will have to pay twice (once to finance the pension claims of older generations and once to fund their own pensions) was assumed to create a lock-in effect that prevented a shift toward funded public pension systems. However, when Sweden changed the public pension system in the late 1990s, Sweden moved from a pay-as-you-go defined benefit system to a notational and partially funded defined contribution system. This change must not *necessarily* be regarded as a break with the past, since Sweden still maintains earnings-related public pensions (although significantly reduced, and of a very different design). But then again, if this design shift is not sufficiently dramatic to be recorded as mainly on the not-path-dependent side, what is? If everything is path-dependent no matter what happens, the path-dependency hypothesis turns into a tautology[1].

The not-path-dependent nature of pension reforms in Latin America and Central/Eastern Europe is even more obvious. Path-breaking reforms originated in Chile in 1981. The design change involved a shift from pay-as-you-go defined-benefit to less generous funded defined-contribution pension schemes. In defined-contribution schemes, contributions are typically defined as a percentage of earnings, and benefit levels depend on the number of contributions, plus accrued interests. Chile was a dictatorship at the time the change was made, but democratically elected governments in Argentina (1994) Bolivia (1997) Colombia (1994) El Salvador (1998) Mexico (1997) Peru (1993) and Uruguay (1996) have changed their mandatory pension systems along Chilean lines. So have Bulgaria (2002), Croatia (2002), Estonia (2002), Hungary (1998), Kazakhstan (1998), Latvia (2001), Lithuania (2004), Poland (1999) and Slovakia (2005).[2] The massive shift away from pay-as-you-go defined benefit schemes to (sometimes fully funded) defined-contribution schemes can be labelled many things, but hardly path-dependent, unless the hypothesis is watered down to something that is trivial and non-falsifiable.

Structure and agency in the struggle for pension reforms

A revised theory of pension reform must solve two puzzles. First, how to explain why cuts in public pensions have indeed been possible, despite the widespread opinion (in the political science community) that a perceived loss of voters would

1 I am concerned here with path dependence interpreted as a specific *hypothesis:* that the design of a public pension system will never be radically altered once it has become well-established, and that all later changes will be incremental. This interpretation is in line with the intuitive definition of the concept. It is rather different, however, from Paul Pierson's terminology in his influential 2000 article in *American Political Science Review*. Pierson treats path dependence as a general *approach* to the study of political change. Pierson puts forward several interesting theoretical assumptions, but there is a long way from the theoretical assumptions underlying an 'approach' to testable implications. For the purpose of this article, path dependence is defined as a *specific hypothesis* about political change, not as a *general approach* in the study of political change.

2 Colin Gillion ea., *Social security pensions. Development and reform*, (Geneva, 2000). Einar Overbye, 'The redistributional impact of a World Bank 'pension regime', Jochen Clasen (ed), *What future for social security?*, (Hague, 2001), pp. 179-95; Carmelo Mesa-Lago & Katharina Müller, 'The politics of pension reform in Latin America'. *Journal of Latin American Studies*, 34 (2002), pp. 687-715.

prevent this from happening. Second, how to explain why not only pension cuts, but path-breaking design changes as well, have not been blocked by voters and/or entrenched interest groups. The purpose of this article is to suggest a solution to these puzzles.

Pension cuts and path-breaking reforms do not make themselves. They are advocated and fought through the political decision-making system by change agents (political entrepreneurs) acting in a very competitive environment. Struggles over pension reform takes place in settings that make it more-or-less easy for advocates of reform to gain acceptance for their view. Important structural factors include the design of the previous pension system, the overall economic situation, demographic trends, and the history of financial markets. Such factors do not determine the outcome of the struggle over reform, but they make it more or less easy for change agents to argue their case, and similarly make the case for status quo more or less difficult to defend.

The design of the existing pension system

If large groups are outside the public pension scheme to begin with, they have no interest in defending the old scheme. Due to large informal sectors, many Latin American workers were not covered by public retirement schemes in the first place.[3] In Bolivia (where only 12 percent of workers were covered by the old scheme), the new defined contribution schemes extended coverage to larger groups of workers, although contribution evasion is widespread.[4] To the extent that new defined-contribution schemes are strictly contribution-based (no tripartite financing), no tax money is siphoned away from taxpayers (outsiders without pension coverage) to 'insider' groups. In these circumstances, advocates of change can argue that a defined-contribution system creates a more equitable system.

A related factor why radical reform and a shift to defined-contribution schemes have been particularly widespread in Latin America concerns the administrative efficiency of the old schemes. In Argentina, El Salvador, Mexico and Uruguay, the pension systems were de facto bankrupt or close to bankruptcy before the reform.[5] In some cases, administrative costs were suspiciously high.[6] Fraud and mismanagement is in principle easier to deal with in defined-contribution than in

3 Colin Gillion ea., *Social security pensions. Development and reform*, (Geneva, 2000), pp. 533.

4 Carmelo Mesa-Lago & Katharina Müller, 'The politics of pension reform in Latin America', *Journal of Latin American Studie*, 34 (2002), p. 702.

5 Op. Cit., pp. 694, 696, 697, 699.

6 World Bank, *Averting the old age crisis*, (Oxford,1994).

defined-benefit schemes, since a defined-contribution scheme provides a clearer link between money in and money out. If incoming money should be lost along the way, individuals can take legal action against the administrators. This is more difficult in pay-as-you-go based defined-benefit schemes, where there is no formal link between contributions and benefits – no name tag that follows the money as it moves through the administrative apparatus. The new schemes do not necessarily perform better – that is an empirical question[7]. But limited coverage and inefficient administration can easily make defenders of the status quo look like spokespersons of privileged groups and/or inefficient managers. While making it possible for advocates of change to present themselves as those who speak for underprivileged outsiders, rather than to be perceived as selfish politicians bent on depriving worthy pensioners of their bread and salt.

The economic situation

A sudden economic crisis prior to, or during, a reform process, limits resistance to change among political elites. Crises-conscious voters often support politicians who demonstrate initiative and ability to act, also reducing the risk of vote loss by embracing reform. Economic crises helped facilitate the path-breaking pension reforms in Central and Eastern Europe, following the regime shifts and the economic recessions that ensued. In many Central and East European polities, runaway inflation combined with inadequate indexing (due to tight government budgets) eroded confidence in old-style public pension provision. Mistrust in the state fuelled support for private or quasi-private alternatives. Pride in 'our established way of doing things' was also weak, since the fall of communism ushered in new political elites with no prestige invested in defending previous pension arrangements.

Demographic trends

Most Western countries (and many Eastern countries) will experience rapid population ageing over the next 30 years. Population ageing implies that pension costs will grow automatically unless pension generosity per claimant is cut back.

7 A factor working in the other direction is the high administrative costs to run funded defined contribution schemes. However, if several administrators have to compete with each other for the right to administer the funds, competitive pressure should at least in theory weed out the most fraudulent and/or incompetent of them.

Most pension cuts that have been implemented will not lead to *reduced* pension spending, only to a *slowdown in the growth* of pension spending. Population ageing makes it possible for advocates of change to argue that pension spending threatens to crowd out other types of public spending. If voters accept this way of framing the issue, cuts are made more acceptable among voters.

Financial markets

Pension reforms demand a long time horizon. The time from first contributions are paid till the last benefits are awarded may span 60 years. The 20th century experienced two world wars, punctuated by a general depression and followed by a long period with administered low interest rates in many countries. To provide even a simple annuity through funded systems in those circumstances was difficult. Hence proponents of funded defined-contribution pension schemes were hard put arguing the advantages of funded schemes during most of the 20th century. Pay-as-you-go defined benefit schemes appeared safer, since it is the power to tax which ultimately underwrites the pension promise. This began to change in the 1980s, when most OECD countries abandoned administrative controls on credit markets (if they had such controls in the first place). This ushered in an era of larger international capital flows and higher real interest rates.[8] Pay-as-you-go defined-benefit schemes secure against the risk of future low interest rates, but these schemes also lack an upside: if interest rates stay higher than expected, this does not lead to higher pensions. If voters believe that real interest rates will stay high in the future, they may prefer funded defined-contribution rather than pay-as-you-go defined-benefit pension schemes. Again, the point is not whether this sanguine view bears out: the point is whether it is shared by a sufficiently large group of politicians, opinion leaders and (ultimately) voters, at the time the reform proposal is going through the politicised stage of the decision-making process. If optimism is sufficiently widespread, agents of change may frame a shift from defined-benefit to defined-contribution as a something-for-nothing opportunity: lower contribution rates today plus higher benefits tomorrow. As the Thomas-theorem states: If people believe that a situation is real (here: that interest rates will stay high), then it is real, in its consequences (here: a shift from defined benefit to defined contribution pension schemes gains political support).

8 Svein E. Gjedrem, 'Økonomiske perspektiver', *Foredrag på Norges Banks representantskapsmøte 17 febuary 2005*, (Oslo, 2005).

Swedish path-breaking reforms: A closer look

Pension reforms have been less path-breaking in West European countries than in Latin American and Central/East European countries. Most West European countries still maintain pay-as-you-go based pension schemes where 'contributions' are de facto earmarked taxes. In these defined benefit schemes the pension level is calculated as a percentage of final or average earnings (or average earnings during last 5 years); usually between 60 and 70 percent of the earnings base. In such schemes, the link between formal contributions and benefits is looser than in defined contribution schemes. West European countries have initiated cutbacks, but usually in an incremental (path-dependent) fashion. Typical reforms include less generous indexing rules, extended contribution periods, increased formal pension ages and limited access to early retirement schemes.[9] Even the few European countries without mandatory earnings-related pensions have implemented incremental cutbacks and design changes: Denmark now moderately means-tests the previously flat-rate people's pension, and the extensive layer of Danish occupational pensions increasingly consists of defined contribution rather than defined benefit schemes[10].

---

9 For example, Spain has extended the number of contribution years from 20 to 25, and the reference period for benefit calculations from 8 to 15 years. Extensions of contribution years and/or reference periods have also taken place in Austria, Finland, France, Greece and the UK: Colin Gillion ea., *Social security pensions. Development and reform*, (Geneva, 2000), pp. 585-6; Vic P. Stathopoulos George & Jorge Garces, 'Squaring the welfare circle and government ideology: Greece and Spain in the 1990s', *International Social Security Review*, 52:4 (1999), pp. 47 ff. By extending the number of contribution years and using career average rather than final salary as the reference period, defined benefit schemes become more similar to defined contribution schemes as far as the relationship between life-cycle earnings and future pension benefits is concerned.

10 Overbye assumes that once a country has introduced mandatory superannuation benefits, or an extensive network of occupational superannuation, a flat-rate basic pension (if this existed in the first place) will gradually be subjected to increased means-testing. The underlying argument is that once widespread superannuation is in place, the majority do not have to rely on a high, flat-rate basic pension to satisfy their demand for income-maintenance in later years. Hence political entrepreneurs bent on means-testing the minimum benefit are likely to face gradually less resistance to such proposals as the superannuation systems mature. See Einar Overbye, 'Mainstream pattern, deviant cases: The New Zealand and Danish pension systems in an international context.' *Journal of European Social Policy,* 7:2, (1997). It must be acknowledged, however, that means-testing in the Danish basic pension system is still very limited, and so far only concerns the pension supplement: Erik Mortensen, *Social leksikon 2003-2004*, (København, 2003), pp. 110-11.

The less path-breaking nature of West European pension reforms stems from structural conditions that make it more difficult for agents of change to frame a radical break with the past as desirable. West European countries have generally maintained broad-based, fairly effectively run public pension schemes, and they have been spared sudden economic crises and dramatic regime shifts. However, one West European country – Sweden – has implemented a pension reform that represents a dramatic break with the past design. Sweden scrapped the defined benefit-principle and introduced public pensions that, at least nominally, are tied to the number of contributions an individual makes during his/her entire working career. The Swedish system also includes a genuinely funded component invested in financial markets. The path-breaking Swedish reform is effective in creating future cost-control, since the shift to a defined-contribution scheme freezes the amount spent on pension (the contribution rate) as a percentage of wage costs. Since the population is steadily ageing, pushing up pension costs, this freeze on contributions will probably lead to reductions in annuity payments per pensioner in the future.

How was Sweden able to move outside the path? Some of the facilitating factors mentioned above were also present in the Swedish case. Sweden experienced a sudden and intense recession in 1991-92, creating a 'something must be done' atmosphere among the political elites. The Swedish pension reform was agreed on 'in principle' in 1994, and was introduced by Parliament in 1999. The period 1994-1999 coincides with high interest rates, plus a stock market boom. In a situation with high interest rates and booming stock markets, funded defined contribution schemes promise to give everybody higher future pensions, at lower contribution rates. However, other structural factors facilitating path-breaking reform elsewhere were missing in Sweden. Most importantly, the previous Swedish pension system was well-run and encompassed a solid majority of the population. Besides, far from copying a (perceived) successful design from another country, Sweden was the innovator of the notational defined-contribution approach. Being the first to tread a new path is a particularly challenging task for any change agent. How was the reform proposal none the less carried through the democratic decision-making system? The Swedish case highlights some particularly difficult-to-copy aspects of facilitating factors: cultural context, personal chemistry and political skill.

Wilensky[11] draws a distinction between consensus democracies (democratic corporatism countries) and majoritarian democracies (fragmented/decentralised democracies). Consensus democracies usually employ election systems based on proportional representation, and the political culture is characterised by compromise and give-and-take. Majoritarian democracies usually employ winner-takes-all election systems, and a more confrontational political style. It is easier to get consensus on certain frames if politicians, trade unions and media are used to co-operation, and trust each other not to break informal deals, even if there should be short-term (vote) gains from defecting. The small Scandinavian democracies are famous for their social-corporatist arrangements, which a less enthused observer than Wilensky once labelled someone-have-talked-together democracies[12]. This tradition of talking together at the top represents a cultural factor which may explain why Sweden introduced a more radically path-breaking pension reform than other West European countries.

In his masterly analysis of the 1959 Swedish pension reform, Molin[13] distinguishes between a not-politicised and a politicised stage in a political decision-making process. In the non-politicised stage, political initiatives move around between actors and agencies in the form of sketches, drafts, research and committee reports. A political initiative usually enters the politicised stage when it is put on track to become a decision in Parliament. Not all political initiatives become politicised, however: the odds that the proposal becomes politicised increases if clear alternatives are formulated and communicated to the public, and the parties position themselves differently – which was very much the case in the 1959 reform. An advisory referendum, dissolution of Parliament and new elections were part of the process that led the Social Democrats to victory against vehement opposition from the non-Socialist parties[14]. The 1999 Swedish pension reform, by

11 Harold Wilensky, *Rich democracies*, (Berkeley, 2002), pp. 85ff.

12 Personal conversation with unknown scholar from a majoritarian (English-speaking) country, at some conference during the 1990s.

13 Björn Molin, *Tjänstepensionsfrågan. En studie i svensk partipolitik*, (Göteborg, 1965).

14 The defeat divided and discouraged the non-Socialist parties for at least a decade, while 'the 1959 pension victory' gained almost mythical status in the Social Democratic collective memory. None the less, despite the tremendous political prestige the Social Democrats had invested in the 1959 reform, they were willing to reach for a broad consensus when – in 1992 – structural factors (such as the 1991/92 Swedish economic crisis) had convinced the party leadership that a major overhaul was desirable. Incidentally, the 1959 path-breaking reform (introducing public superannuation in Sweden) displays yet another difficult-to-copy factor that can influence the out-

contrast, is a textbook example of how competing politicians – through informal agreements – can *prevent* a political initiative from reaching a politicised stage in the decision-making process, precisely by abstaining from formulating and communicating clear alternatives to voters, and by abstaining from positioning themselves differently with regard to the main reform proposal. The Swedish pension reform was prepared by a high-level, inter-party working group which met between 1992 and 1994. Lundberg describes the meetings as follows:

'The will to compromise was apparent in the way the pension committee worked, which in my interviews was described as very close and trusting ('fortroendefull'). The idea was first to agree in the committee. Then the agreement had to be anchored in the respective party leaderships. Only after that were mass media and the general public to be informed. [The shared opinion was that] No one would win on a new-principled fight over pensions. Thus the wish was to keep the discussions of the working group away from the public at any price. Even the internal discussions in the parties were held under strict control. ... Officially, the committee did not work to create a new system but to 'reform' 'improve' and 'modernise' the old. The Social Democrats made this an absolute condition for even considering participating in the committee. It was strictly ruled out even for the Conservatives to say something different.'[15]

Personal chemistry

It further turned out that the committee members representing the two most antagonistic parties, the Social Democrats (Anna Hedborg) and the Conservatives (Margit Genser), liked each other. Quote Hedborg:

'I think it played a role that Margit Genser represented the Conservatives. She is a very independent and systematic person. She loves logic. If you challenge her with a very logical line of reasoning she cannot resist it – and I am a little like that, too. Könberg [representing the Liberal party] is also a bit like that. We are all very issue-oriented, somewhat engineering types ... Somehow I think it was a

---

come: pure luck. After the election, the Social Democrats were one vote short of pushing their proposal through Parliament. However, a renegade MP from the Liberal party announced he would vote with the Social Democrats. The new system was carried through Parliament with a one-vote majority.

15 Urban Lundberg, 'Socialdemokratin och 1990-talets pensionsreform', Joakim Palme (ed.), *Hur blev den stora kompromissen möjlig?*, (Stockholm, 2001), pp. 30-31 [own translation].

very lucky mix of persons. Both that we were the persons we were and that there were not more of us.'[16]

This favourable personal chemistry created a 'we' identity among the committee members. Bonding between high-level committee members, making them present a united front vis a vis outsiders, is rare even in Scandinavian politics. It helped bring about the path-breaking outcome. It is a factor difficult to reproduce in other settings, illustrating the element of *unpredictability* that cultural-psychological factors induce into a policy making process.

The important theoretical point is that elite-elite interaction during a reform phase involves a complex social process. Actors must find out if they can trust opponents to stick to informal deals. The core structure resembles an assurance game. Each elite must decide if it can trust other elites to cooperate, or if it should deflect and reap the benefits of attracting disaffected voters. Reputations for being cooperative or uncooperative (which depend on political culture and traditions) act as signals in this game. Elites can also use strategies such as self-binding (publicly announcing their intentions), or bonding (engaging in joint committees) to signal their intentions to other players. Deceptions can be part of this game, but the community of elite politicians is somewhat similar to a village community, in the sense that most elite politicians also meet and interact the day after the reform has been voted on in parliament. As in a village community, social controls (backed by the risk of social ostracism) discourage blatantly disloyal behaviour, and help make informal agreements stick.

The Swedish reform encountered no voter revolt. This illustrates Zaller's point that if most parties and media agree how to frame an issue, media effects on political opinions are much stronger than in situations without party or media consensus on how to frame an issue.[17] If all elites and opinion leaders can be taken on board, not only have disaffected voters nowhere else to go – they are also less likely to perceive themselves as dissatisfied in the first place.

Political skill

It is not absolutely certain that benefits will be lower in defined-contribution schemes than in defined-benefit schemes, even if contribution rates are lower. Since the whole point of defined-contribution schemes is that benefits are not de-

16 Op. Cit., p. 32.

17 John Zaller, 'The myth of massive media impact revived: new support for a discredited idea', Diana C. Mutz, Paul M. Sniderman & Richard A. Brody (eds.), *Political persuasion and attitude change*, (Ann Arbor, 1996), pp. 52ff.

termined in advance, no one in Sweden – at the time the new scheme was introduced – could say for certain that the new pension design was a less generous design. If interest rate projections are sufficiently optimistic (and in the 1990s many were very optimistic), future benefit levels can in fact increase. By introducing a brand new scheme, Swedish political elites probably dampened protests more effectively than if they had incrementally changed benefit formulas in the old scheme. Thus path-breaking design change is not necessarily the design change that encounters most resistance. By switching to a defined contribution scheme it became more difficult, also for experts, to say who would end up as winners or losers. If no one is sure if they win or lose, resistance to change is minimised. In the Latin American context, Mesa-Lago and Müller similarly argue that 'strategic bundling' of reform packages increases complexity and lowers visibility, making it more difficult for interest groups or voters to determine if they are going to win or lose.[18]

Summing up: Why do voters accept path-breaking, pension-cutting reforms?

The no-cutbacks-are-possible hypothesis, as well as the all-changes-are-path-dependent hypothesis, is based on an underlying premise that voters' preferences are derived from their narrow pension-political interests. The fact that cuts as well as path-breaking reforms have been implemented shows that this underlying premise is too simple. A competing theory assumes that most voters are 'rationally uninformed' on political issues.[19]. This theory builds on the insight that the impact of any one vote is zero, unless the election should otherwise result in a tie. Since this possibility is so miniscule that it will be disregarded by rational actors, voters have limited incentive to gather information about reform proposals (including pension reform proposals). From a cost-benefit perspective, the act of voting in an election is a low cost/low benefit act. Since the incentive for inde-

---

18 Carmelo Mesa-Lago & Katharina Müller, 'The politics of pension reform in Latin America', *Journal of Latin American Studies*, 34 (2002), p. 712. See also Paul Pierson, *Dismantling the welfare state? Reagan, Thatcher and the Politics of Retrenchment*, (Cambridge, 1994), p. 21.

19 Joseph A. Schumpeter, *Capitalism, socialism and democracy*, (New York, 1996 [1942]), pp. 261-2; Anthony. Downs, *An economic theory of democracy*, (New York, 1957), pp. 244-7; Philip E. Converse, 'Public opinion and voting behavior', Fred I. Greenstein & Nelson W. Polsby (eds.), *Handbook of Political Science: Nongovernemental politics*, (Reading-Massachusetts, 1975), pp. 93-4; Geoffrey Brennan & James M. Buchanan, *The power to tax*, (Cambridge, 1980), pp. 22-23, 28ff.

pendent information-gathering is limited, it is easier to influence low cost/low benefit acts than to influence acts where individual costs and benefits are high (as when buying a car or a house: the costs involved when performing such acts are high, and so are the individual consequences of making a wrong decision).

To elaborate the premise of rationally uninformed voters, the act of voting in an election has more in common with a speech act (expressing a political opinion) than with costly decision acts (such as buying a new car or a house). To cast a vote and to express a political opinion are both virtually cost-free and of little consequence. The similarities between voting and expressing political opinions may imply that political preferences are influenced by what people perceive as the *socially desirable* position to adopt. A main rationale for expressing political opinions is to signal to one's peer group(s) opinions and views regarded by others as acceptable, thus enhancing one's reputation as a person others can trust.[20] Empirical studies of political opinions have indeed found a strong social desirability bias in the opinions people express.[21] The emerging study of political persuasion and attitude change show several examples indicating that people attach importance to be seen as holding socially desirable views.[22] Voting might similarly be motivated by voters' reputational interest to be perceived as well-meaning citizens, rather than by their economic self-interest in a narrow sense[23]. If so, public opinion about pension reforms (and subsequent voting) is likely to be influenced by whether reforms are perceived as socially desirable.

---

20 Einar Overbye, 'Making a Case for the Rational, Self-Regarding, 'Ethical' Voter ... and solving the Paradox of Not Voting in the process', *European Journal of Political Research*, (1995).

21 T. deMayo, 'Social desirability and survey measurement. A review, *Surveying subjective phenomena*, (New York, 1984)

22 Howard Schuman & Stanley Presser, 'Public opinion and public ignorance: The fine line between attitudes and nonattitudes', *American Journal of Sociology* ,85:5 (1980); Tom W. Smith, 'Nonattitudes: A review and evaluation', *Surveying subjective phenomena*, (New York, 1984); Shanto Iyengar, 'Framing responsibility for political issues: The case of poverty,', *Political Behaviour*, 22:1 (1990); James H. Kuklinski & Norman L. Hurley, 'It's all a matter of interpretation', *Political persuasion and attitude change*, (Michigan, 1996); Dennis Chong, 'Creating common frames of reference on political issues'; Diana C. Muntz ea. (eds.), *Political persuasion and attitude change*, (Michigan,1996).

23 As an added subtlety, notice that in situations where perceived narrow self-interest and perceived common interest should collide there is little risk involved in voting according to the perceived common interest, since the impact of one vote on the election result is negligible anyhow Einar Overbye, 'Making a Case for the Rational, Self-Regarding, 'Ethical' Voter ... and solving the Paradox of Not Voting in the process', *European Journal of Political Research*, (1995).

The above does not imply that old-fashioned self-interest plays no role in forming voters' opinions on pension reform. Most voters live in social environments consisting of people similar to themselves (most pensioners mostly know pensioners, for example). Hence their reputational interest in coming across as committed to the common cause of their social environment often coincides with their own economic interests[24]. Besides, most people have an uncanny ability to convince themselves that what they perceive as their own interest happens to be in the common interest. None the less rational ignorance, as well as reputational concerns, makes voter preferences more fluid and malleable than the straightforward self-interest hypothesis suggests.

In conclusion, the majority view on pension reform is likely to depend on who gets the upper hand in the defining-the-situation game. Is the situation defined in such a way that a responsible and caring person should be expected to support the reform, in order to make room for even worthier social programmes, plus secure the long-run stability of the economy? If this emerges as the dominant definition of the situation, resistance to the reform will be limited to a minority. Or is the defining the situation-game won by political entrepreneurs who portray supporters of reform as selfish taxpayers who do not want to grant the worthiest of the worthy poor (the old) a decent living standard? If so, the reform will meet widespread opposition.

Concluding comment

The successful implementation of pension reforms during the 1990s and 2000s shows that the scope for elected politicians to change policies is quite large. Limited initial knowledge means that many voters do not have 'internal preferences' on many policy issues, and can be persuaded depending on how new information is presented (framed). The impact of framing on public opinion is particularly large if political elites agree to present reforms in the same way.

Success is likely to go to political entrepreneurs that can get their policy proposals to appear socially desirable. This is so partly because voters have limited incentive to pay the information costs to know their narrow economic interests, but also because voters have a reputational interest to be perceived by others as concerned with the common interest rather than their narrow economic interest.

Is wide scope for reform good or bad news for democracy? This is also an issue that can be framed in different ways. If democracy is perceived as a system

24 Explaining the correlations between social characteristics (gender, class, ethnicity, region, religious outlook etc. etc.) and voting behaviour.

where internal individual preferences are somehow aggregated into collective outcomes, some pension reform processes may appear democratically questionable, including the very tightly controlled Swedish reform process. However, this perception of democracy overestimates the initial clarity of individual preferences, and underestimates the influence of opinion leaders, politicians and other definers of the situation on the preference-formation process itself. If one instead adopts a Schumpeterian view of democracy, where voters at more-or-less regular intervals get to decide which among competing elites that are allowed to rule until the next election, tightly controlled reform processes are perhaps less problematic. One may even argue that successful pension reforms indicate that ruling politicians are able to stand up to vested interest groups as well as to assumed 'selfish' older voters – contrary to predictions made within the democratic overload-tradition.[25] Real-life democracy may not correspond to its ideal type, but at least successful reforms show that democracy is not a frail political system that works only on sunny days. And they definitely show that Schumpeterian political entrepreneurship is alive and well in the modern welfare state, implying that new path-breaking reforms are bound to happen also in the future.

25 Samuel Brittan, 'The economic contradictions of democracy', *British Journal of Political Science*, 5:2, (1975); Edgar K. Browning, 'Why the social insurance budget is too large in a democracy', *Economic Inquiry*, XIII (1975).

Increasing Longevity and the Welfare State

Torben M. Andersen

Introduction

A core element in the welfare state is the entitlements offered to elderly citizens to old age care and pensions. This was one of the first elements in the development of what today is understood by a welfare state, and political debates often focus on the conditions offered by society to the elderly as an indication of the extent to which the welfare state is fulfilling its main goals. Over the years, the entitlements of the elderly have gradually been extended. This applies both to pensions (see below) and to the level and extent of health and old age care. Thus, today, an average Dane at the age of 65 can expect to enjoy a retirement period which is 7 years longer than a person at the age of 65 could expect in 1960. This proves that old age care and pensions have shifted from being a question of provisions for the economically and physically weak (lack of work capability) and old citizens to a question of welfare for the broad population in a third life phase post-labour market participation. Thus, to the majority of the population, retirement is a voluntary decision in the sense that it is not induced by an inability to work.

This development can easily be explained by the improvements in living conditions and, not least, material well-being. This has created room for a choice between further material improvements and non-material activities which, in broad terms, are usually termed leisure. The increase in the demand for leisure is driven by the fact that growth in income improves the opportunity set, and it shows up in terms of shorter working hours, longer vacations, and earlier retirement. The tendency towards a longer retirement period is therefore a common phenomenon across all western countries. In addition, the improvements in material well-being as well as advances within life sciences have expanded the opportunity set for treatments and increased demand. Since the need for health care is strongly age-dependent, it follows that this aspect is particularly visible for the elderly part of the population.

A challenge faced by all Western countries[1] is the increase in longevity. While longevity has been on a trend increase for the past centuries, the driving

1 Longevity is on the rise globally except in Africa and Russia, where it is decreasing. A primary reason for this is HIV/AIDS.

force has shifted from being a decline in child mortality to being a shift in mortality rates for elderly people, cf. figures 1a. and 1b.

Figure 1a. Survival rates, Denmark 1981/82, 2004/05 – males

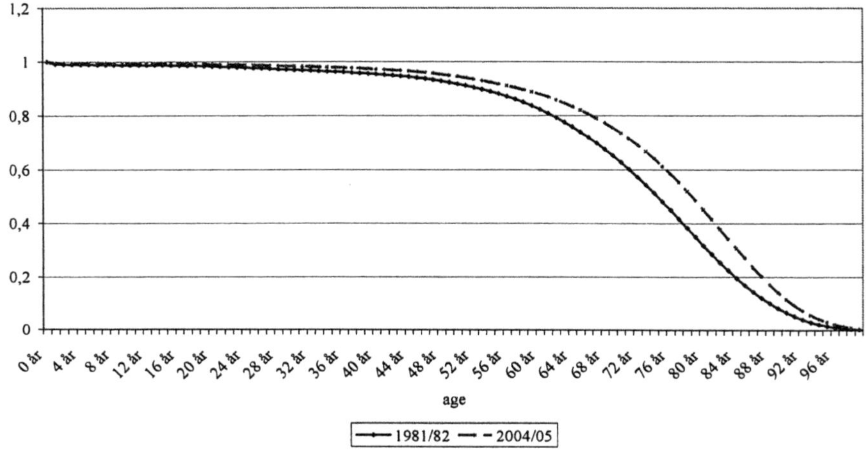

Figure 1b. Survival rates, Denmark 1981/82, 2004/05 – females

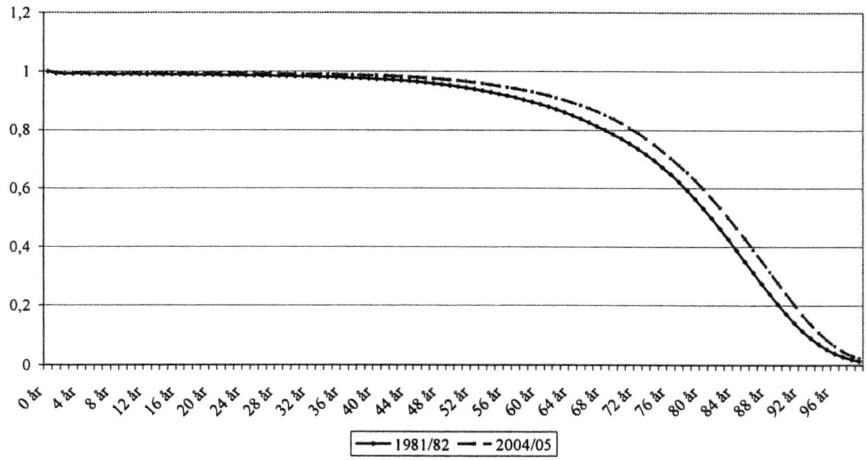

Note: Survival rates as depending on age as averages for 1981-1982 and 2004-2005.
Source: Danmarks Statistik, Statistikbanken

The increase in longevity is rather substantial. At the beginning of the 20th century, an average Dane had a 50% chance of becoming 65 years old, and at the beginning of the 21st century, the probability had increased to 80%.[2] The remaining expected lifetime for a person at the age of 65 was, at the start of the 20th century, 12 years, at the start of the 21st century, it is 17 years; and according to the most recent projection, it will be more than 20 years in 40-50 years time.[3]

The increase in longevity is in itself a significant welfare improvement and an indication of the options provided by increases in material well-being and advances in medicine. As an illustration, life expectancy is weighted by 1/3 in the human development index constructed by UNDP, and increasing longevity is an important factor for the trend increase in the index. However, the increase also raises important policy issues, especially in a welfare state with a strong commitment as regards conditions offered to elderly citizens.

Extended welfare arrangements of a universal nature cause a strong life-cycle dependency in the average person's position as either a net-contributor to or a net-beneficiary from welfare arrangements. This is a straightforward implication of the 'cradle-to-grave' character of the welfare model. The average person will be a net-beneficiary as young and old, and a net-contributor during his/her working ages. A particularly challenging issue is increasing longevity. Since the public pension system in Denmark provides given benefits from statutory pension ages (and early retirement ages) and for the remaining lifetime (effectively a life annuity), it follows that increasing longevity, other things being equal, increases the 'benefit period' relative to the 'contribution period'. It is a straightforward implication that increasing longevity brings the financial viability of the financial contract at stake if retirement ages remain unchanged. Hence, there is a policy choice to be made on how to adjust to the options created by improving longevity.

From a policy perspective, it is a particularly problematic aspect that there is no immediate mechanism precluding a postponement of the adjustment to the projected increase in longevity. This is so since the change comes gradually, and therefore expenditures will outpace revenues only slowly but persistently. Since there is no strict pay-as-you-go condition, this will, in the first place, cause an upward trend in public debt levels. In short, the costs of adjustment will be pushed into the future. This raises important intergenerational distribution issues, since it implies that future generations will have to contribute to the financing of the consequences caused by current generations obtaining a longer longevity. This is due to the fact that it is impossible to reverse the retirement decision, and

---

2 Velfærdskommissionen, *Fremtidens velfærd kommer ikke af sig selv, Analyserapport*, (Copenhagen, 2004).

3 DREAM, *Befolkningsprognose*, (Copenhagen, 2006).

because the longer period spent as a beneficiary of the social contract does not show up until late in life, since the increase in longevity is driven by a rightward shift in mortality rates, cf. figures 1a. and 1b.

Postponement of adjustments is not only a financial issue but may also have political implications for the social contract. A key explanation of the support for the social contract[4] is that it rests on a combination of i) trust across generations, in the sense that current generations in the working age group accept to be net-contributors in the expectation that future work age groups will be willing to support them when they become older – the intergenerational social contract, and ii) intergenerational altruism, implying that any generation cares about the well-being of both preceding and future generations. The viability of the system is thus critically dependent on continuous support in terms of maintaining trust and altruism. In other words, the social contract involves a chain letter element across generations. With a growing population this scheme works smoothly, since the number of young tax payers will always grow by more than the number of the old (for given retirement/pension ages). Hence, for a given tax rate levied on income, it follows that pension (or other expenses on the old) can grow by the sum of population growth and productivity increases (dynamically efficient economy). On top of this, there is an insurance element in the sense that all the old are covered irrespective of their labour market history.

However, if population growth slows down due to lower fertility, or the group of retirees increases due to increasing longevity, it follows that a system of given contribution rates, benefit levels and retirement ages is not financially viable. If taxes are to remain unchanged, pensions will have to decline relative to wages, or alternatively, if pensions must remain unchanged relative to wage income, tax rates will have to increase. In short, the social contract across generations needs to be adjusted

This paper discusses the challenges faced by public pension systems in the broad sense of age-dependent benefits (pensions and early retirement) and service provisions (health care, old age care etc.) when longevity increases, and some possibilities for adjusting the social contract to deal with these problems. The paper is organised as follows: Section 2 briefly outlines the demographic changes, while Section 3 considers the intergenerational social contract embedded in the welfare state. Section 4 discusses pros and cons of various ways of adapting the social contract to increasing longevity, including pre-funding and

4 For a survey of the literature on the political economy of social security, see e.g. Vincenzo Galasso & Paola Profeta, 'The political economy of social security: a survey', *European Journal of Political Economy*, 18, (2002); Casey B. Mulligan & Xavier Sala-i-Martin, 'Political and Economic Forces Sustaining Social Security', *Advances in Economic Analysis & Policy*, 4:1, Article 5, (2004).

making parameters of the system contingent on longevity. Section 5 ends by discussing some political economy aspects of reforms of the social contract.

2. Demographics

Most countries face an upward trend in the dependency ratio (the ratio of young below age 15 and old above 64, relative to the work age population).[5] Figure 2 shows the projected paths for the old age dependency ratio for Denmark from a recent projection.[6] The demographic old age dependency ratio increases from

Figure 2. Old age dependency ratio – Denmark 1981-2100.

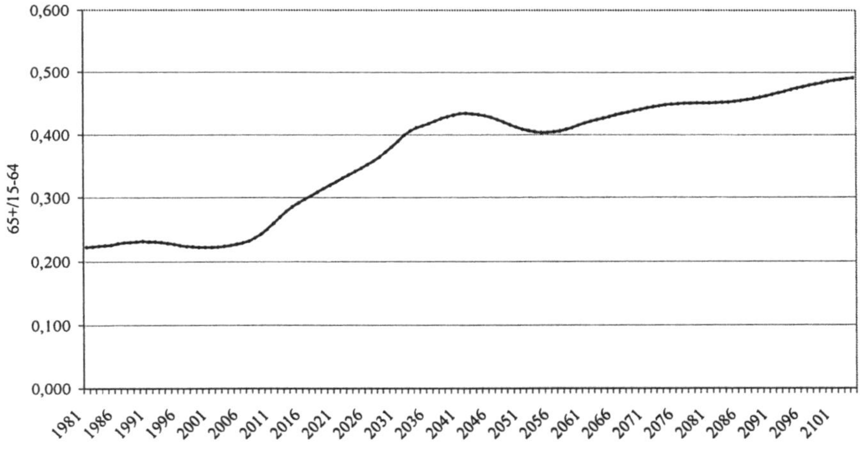

Note: Old age dependency ratio defined as the age group 65 and more relative to the age group 15 to 64.
Source: DREAM, Befolkningsprognose (2006).

about 0.25 to 0.4 within the next 3-4 decades, followed by a slight fall, and subsequently it raises somewhat. It is a key property that the increase is permanent, and the long-run perspective is thus almost a doubling of the old age dependency

5 IMF, *World Economic Outlook – The Global Demographic Transition*, (Washington, 2004).

6 DREAM, *Befolkningsprognose*, (Copenhagen, 2006).

ratio. The projection here is very similar to recent projections for Sweden and Norway.[7]

Much debate on the ageing problem has focussed on the effects of the baby-boom generation approaching retirement. This is a phenomenon generated by swings in fertility (high in the decades after WWII and low since the 1970s) that induces a subsequent increase in the dependency ratio. In debating the consequences of increasing dependency ratios, it is important to distinguish between the effects of the changes in fertility and the upward trend in longevity. In a demographic sense, the former is a transitory phenomenon, since the dependency ratio will (for given pension ages and longevity) be constant for a given fertility level. Hence, a period with a high fertility level (the 1940s and 1950s) and the implied baby-boom effect will, with a delay of 5 to 6 decades, show up as an echo effect in the dependency ratio. If the fertility rate remains fairly stable at the new level, the dependency ratio will stabilise at a lower level after 8-9 decades. However, this is not the case with the changes induced by increasing longevity (under the assumption that future spikes in mortality due to epidemics and the like are ruled out). The projected increases in longevity are permanent (see figures 3a. and 3b.), and therefore the implied increase in the dependency ratio is permanent (for given age criteria).

Figure 3a. Life expectancy at birth past and projected, Denmark 1901-2100.

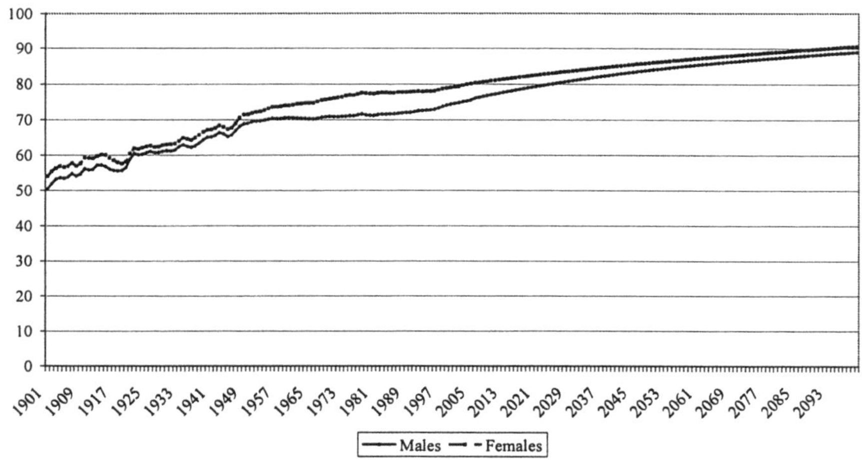

7 T. M. Andersen, 'Ageing and globalisation in the Scandinavian welfare model', *Ageing Horizons*, 4, (6th November, 2006).

Figure 3b. Remaining life expectancy at the age of 60 past and projected, Denmark 1901-2100.

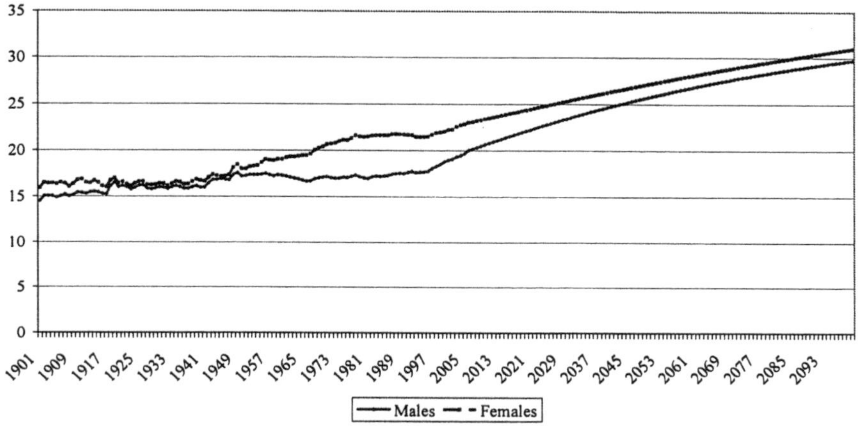

Source: DREAM, Befolkningsprognose (2006).

3. The Social Contract

The social contract refers to two key facts concerning the welfare state. The first is that entitlements are individual, and since the main provisions include child care, education, health care and pensions, it follows that there is a strong age dependency in the use of welfare state provisions. Secondly, welfare activities are mainly financed in a Pay-As-You-Go (PAYG) manner; that is, current tax revenue should cover current expenditures. The main source of tax revenue is (direct and indirect) taxation of labour income, and it therefore follows that the larger share of tax revenue is generated by the population in working ages active in the labour market. Hence, there is also a strong age dependency in contributions made by the average person to the financing of the welfare state. Combining these two facts, it follows that the average person is mainly benefiting from welfare arrangements as young and old, and mainly contributing to their financing in their working ages. In Figure 4, the age dependent net contributions to public finances are shown for Denmark.

Figure 4. The social contract. Age dependent net contributions to the public sector.

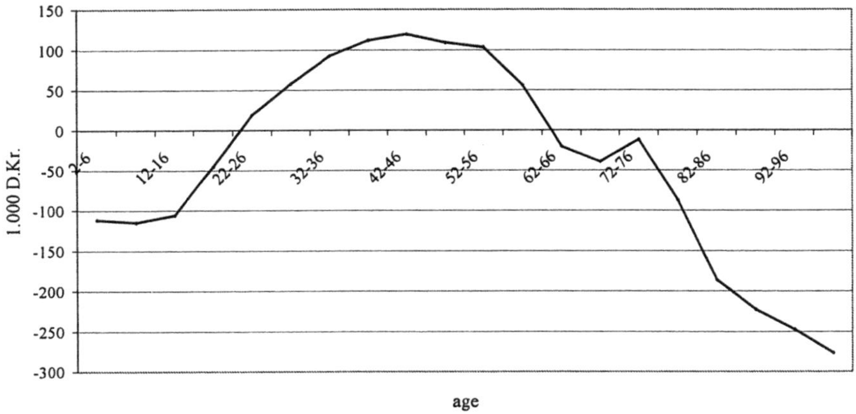

Source: Velfærdskommissionen (2004).

The inverted U-form of the age-dependent net contributions captures the social contract in a lucid way. The particular form is not specific to countries with an extended welfare state, but the amplitude of the figure is. In Figure 5 below, the changes in the social contract are displayed for Sweden for selected periods from the 1930s and to the present system. The figure shows several interesting points. First, alongside the expansion of the welfare state, the amplitude of the inverted U-figure has increased, i.e. larger net benefits are received as young and old, and larger tax payments are made in the working years. Second, the extension of the welfare state has in particular implied that the net-benefits to elderly citizens have been extended. Finally, it is seen that policy changes in Sweden in the 1990s have somewhat muted the amplitudes of the figure, in particular for elderly people.

Combining the demographic shifts in Figure 2 with the properties of the social contract captured in Figure 4 immediately reveals that a financial problem will arise. Current welfare arrangements are not financially sustainable in the wake of the increase in the dependency ratio. The order of magnitude of the financial problems is substantial, and deteriorating public finances will lead to systematic deficits.

Figure 5. The development in the social contract in the Swedish Welfare State, 1930-2014.

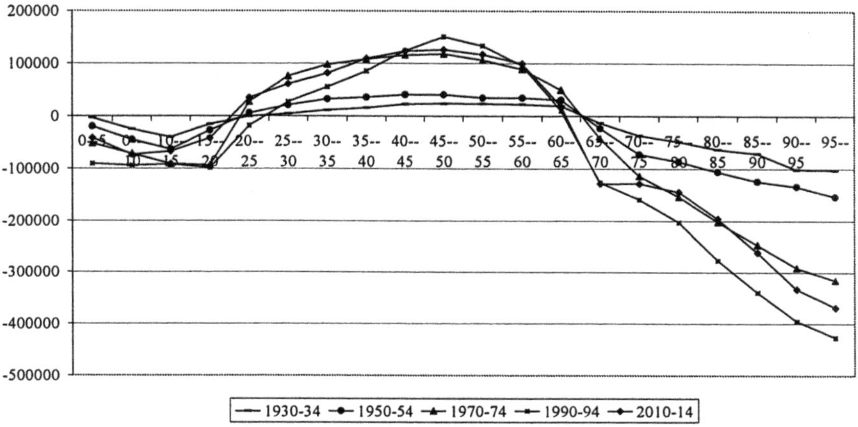

Note: Calculated as averages over 5-year intervals, i.e. 5-10 is the age groups above 5 years and below 10 years. For comparison, the numbers are in 2006 prices and corrected for GDP growth.
Source: Pettersson, T., Pettersson T., och Westerberg A., Generationsanalyser – omfördelning mellan generationer i en växande välfärdsstat. Expertgruppen för Studier i Samhällsekonomi (ESS), 6, (Stockholm 2006).

In a recent assessment for Denmark[8], Velfærdskommissionen finds that the problem amounts to a deterioration of public finances (primary balance) of about 4 percentage points of GDP between now and 2040[9]. For Norway, the demographic consequences for public finances are among the most dramatic for OECD countries. According to estimates, the deterioration in public finances in 2040 is above 6 percentage points of GDP.[10] The sustainable use of petroleum wealth

8 Velfærdskommissionen, *Fremtidens velfærd kommer ikke af sig selv, Analyserapport*, (Copenhagen, 2004); Velfærdskommissionen, *Fremtidens velfærd – vores valg, analyserapport*, (Copenhagen, 2006).

9 A more recent evaluation shows that the sustainable problems are worse mainly due to an updated projection of the increases in longevity. However, the recent welfare reform increasing the retirement age implies that the permanent budget improvement in percentage points of GDP is reduced from 4.0% to 2.2%. See DREAM, *Langsigtet økonomisk fremskrivning 2006 – med vurdering af velfærdsreform*, (Copenhagen, 2006).

10 Pensjonskommissjonen, *Moderniseret Folketrygd – Bærekraftig Pensjon for Fremtida*, NOU (Norges Offentlige Udredninger), 1, (Oslo, 2004); Dennis Frederiksen ea.,

can finance about ¼ of the expenditure rise due to ageing. For Sweden, estimates by the OECD show that the increasing dependency ratio will continuously deteriorate public finances, and the deteriorations of the budget balance between now and 2050 amount to 4½ percentage points of GDP.[11]

4. Reform avenues

The upward trend in the dependency ratio to a permanently higher level and the implied financial problems make it necessary to discuss possible policy reforms. Postponement of adjustment would create risk at the level of citizens concerning the future welfare arrangements they can expect as well as a shift of some burden of adjustment to future generations. In the following, several avenues for reforms are discussed. First, a so-called pre-funding strategy aiming at consolidating public finances in advance of the increase in the dependency ratio is considered. Next, various ways of introducing automatic adjustment mechanisms into the social contract to make it less vulnerable to changes in longevity are considered.

4.1. Prefunding

Since the demographic shifts are evolving gradually and leading to a permanently higher level for the dependency ratio, it may seem obvious in due time to ensure a sufficient consolidation of public finances to prepare for the increase in the dependency ratio. This may be termed a pre-funding strategy since the aim is to consolidate public finances in advance of the increase in the old-age dependency ratio. The pre-funding strategy can be found in various forms, of which the 'pragmatic' and the 'once-and-for-all' versions are the two most frequently discussed.

The pragmatic version has its starting point in the fact that the public sector is currently running surpluses (as is the case in e.g. Denmark and Sweden). Given the projected increase in the dependency ratio and the implied financial problems, it makes intuitive sense to lower debt to create more leeway to handle the demographic changes. This can also be phrased in the way that if current surpluses are used to either expand expenditures or lower taxes, it will inevitably be a policy change which soon will have to be redressed when the demographic

---

Makroøkonomiske virkninger av pensjonsreformer – Beregninger baseret på forslag fra Pensjonskommisjonen, Working Papers, Statistics Norway, (Oslo, 2005).

11 OECD, *Economic Surveys – Sweden*, (Paris, 2005).

changes become more substantial. Hence, to avoid variation in welfare arrangements and tax systems over time, it is recommendable to pursue a pragmatic pre-funding strategy, using current favourable public finances to reduce public debt levels. This is in fact what has been implied by the so-called 2010-plan[12] in Denmark, aiming at a halving of public debt (as a fraction of GDP) from 2001 to 2010. In Sweden, a pre-funding strategy is implied by the requirement in the 'finanspolitiske ramverk' of running a budget surplus of at least 2% of GDP over the business cycle.

The more restrictive or ambitious version of the pre-funding strategy asks at what level public balances would have to be to ensure that in the long run (i.e. in present value terms) there is equivalence between revenues and expenditures. This strategy is therefore of a once-and-for-all nature in the sense that it makes one permanent adjustment to ensure fiscal sustainability. This requires permanent budget improvements which for Denmark have to be close to 4% of GDP, and for Sweden 2% of GDP. Such a strategy has several consequences. It implies a once-and-for-all change in parameters of the social contract to ensure long-run financial viability. It is a consequence of the upward trend in the dependency ratio that this strategy, for a considerable number of years, will imply a substantial consolidation of public finances, and therefore eventually accumulation of a rather high net wealth. This wealth is needed to finance future expenditure increases due to the permanently higher dependency ratio.

To assess this pre-funding strategy, it is important to distinguish between increases in the dependency ratio caused by changes in fertility and changes in longevity.

Changes in fertility are bygones in a demographic sense. The drop in fertility and the implied baby-boom effect cannot be undone. This leaves a fiscal problem in the sense that there is a change in the dependency ratio to take care of. There is a case for some consolidation or pre-funding in relation to this, since the burden would otherwise shift to future generations. Consolidation prior to retirement for these generations effectively implies that these cohorts come to contribute to the financing of the financial consequences of this shift (i.e. indirect savings via public sector consolidation), whereas in the absence of consolidation, the burden would rest on future tax payers. Whether this is a fair distribution depends on

12 When the plan was formulated, the demographic changes were mainly attributed to the baby-boom effect, and therefore it was considered to have a large temporary component. The pre-funding strategy at that time was thus foreseen to deal with a large part of the demographic challenge. Later, it has been recognized that the demographic change is permanent, and therefore pre-funding is only an element in 'preparing for the demographic changes'.

both who should take responsibility for the drop in fertility, and how the consequences of fertility changes should be distributed across generations.

For the case where households are infinitely lived (via an operative bequest mechanism) longevity is thus not an issue, and Floden shows that changes in the dependency ratio should mainly be addressed by a consolidation of public finances, that is, a pre-funding.[13] In this case, all generations come to contribute equally to the financing needed to ensure fiscal sustainability. This result is driven by a consumption smoothing or sharing argument, i.e. the burden is distributed (almost) equally across generations.[14]

Increasing longevity raises different issues, since future generations are expected to enjoy the pleasures of increased longevity, i.e. this has a forward-looking aspect. Current generations would thus, under a consolidation strategy, contribute to the financing of future generations with longer longevity. It is not clear that this is fair. In Velfærdskommissionen, it is shown that a pre-funding strategy would imply that generations with (relatively) low longevity would come to contribute considerably to the financing of expenses caused by later generations having longer longevity.[15] Under the reasonable assumption that longer longevity is assessed positively, this intergenerational distribution profile is not justified.

4.2. Demographic contingencies

The adjustment of the social contract to changes in longevity involves fundamental issues of intergenerational distribution as already brought forward in the discussion of the pre-funding strategy. Clearly, there is no definite solution to this distributional issue. In a recent report from the UK Pensions Commission, a rather explicit stand is taken on the issue of longevity, retirement and intergenerational distribution:

---

13 Martin Flodén, 'Public saving and policy coordination in aging economies', *Scandinavian Journal of Economics*, 105, (2003).

14 Norway is an example of a country where a substantial pre-funding is taking place based on oil and gas revenue. The situation is thus different to the extent that the pre-funding is based on "extra income", and moreover, time-consistency problems have been attempted solved by the establishment of the oil fund (accumulation takes place outside public records in the traditional sense) and the rule (handlingsreglen) for the use of the money. For Norway, this has worked reasonably well so far, although there has been some deviation from the rule.

15 See Velfærdskommissionen, *Fremtidens velfærd kommer ikke af sig selv, Analyserapport*, (Copenhagen, 2004); Velfærdskommissionen, *Fremtidens velfærd – vores valg, analyserapport*, (Copenhagen, 2006).

Over the long-run fairness between generations suggests that average pension ages should tend to rise proportionately in line with life expectancy, with each generation facing the same proportion of life contributing to and receiving state pensions.[16]

To get a handle on the intergenerational distribution issues raised by the trend increases in longevity, it is useful to consider the stylised situation of the choice made by a social planner solution in the case where all generations are weighted equally, i.e. the social planner has neutral generational preferences (the welfare of all generations are assigned equal weight). In this case, it can be shown[17] that the social optimum implies that

* all generations enjoy the same consumption possibilities
* all generations spend the same share of life as active in the labour market (retirement age is proportional to longevity).

The first part shows that there is considerable inter-generational redistribution to ensure that all have the same consumption possibilities, but the second part shows that generations are going to contribute to the social contract relative to their longevity (as suggested by the quote from the UK Pensions Commission given above). In particular, the latter part suggests a gradual change in pension/retirement ages alongside increases in longevity, ensuring that future generations with longer longevity contribute to the financing hereof by retiring at a later age (but still having the same proportion of lifetime in and outside the labour market).

It may seem intuitive that if the financial problems are created by increases in longevity, then these problems can be neutralised if pension and retirement ages are explicitly linked (index) to longevity. This is, however, not quite so simple, and indexing retirement/pension ages one-to-one to longevity does not automatically ensure fiscal sustainability of the social contract. To see this consider a pension scheme for which the old receive a transfer equal to

$$b(T-R)$$

where b is the benefit, T longevity and R the retirement age (= length of working life). If the annual labour market income is y it follows that total consumption possibilities (disregarding discounting) is

$$Ry+b(T-R)$$

16 UK Pensions Commission, *A New Pension Settlement for the Twenty-First Century*, (London, 2005), p. 4.

17 See Torben M. Andersen, *Social security and longevity,* Working Paper, (Aarhus, 2006).

or in per period terms

$$(R/T)y+b(1-R/T)$$

If consumption possibilities per period should be unchanged and the retirement age proportional to longevity T, i.e.

$R/T = r = \text{constant}$

it follows that the transfer is given as

$$Tb(1-r)$$

and therefore proportional to longevity T, i.e. generations with longer longevity need some transfer if the period by period consumption possibilities and the relative retirement age should both be independent of longevity. Or to put it differently, for all generations to have the same consumption possibilities and relative retirement age, it is necessary to have transfers from generations with low longevity to generations with longer longevity.

Using the insights from above in the empirically relevant case where longevity is on an upward trend, it follows that there is need for some pre-funding. That is, current generations will have to contribute to future generations with longer longevity. This is so since, although they gain from the increase in longevity, it also follows that their consumption possibilities (in flow terms) will be lower, and this gives a rationale for some redistribution towards generations with relatively lower consumption. This is therefore exactly the opposite of what is implied by postponing adjustment, since that would leave future generations with a larger debt level, and thus imply that the intergenerational distribution profile is tilted in the opposite direction of what is implied by the optimal policy. This is one way of showing the consequences of delays in reforms. The extent of pre-funding driven by these inter-generational distribution issues may, however, be modest. In Andersen[18], the needed pre-funding is considered for a case where there is a trend increase in longevity of 0.2% per year for the next 50 years/generations[19] in a stylised overlapping generation model. It is found that the required pre-funding creates a wealth level of approximately 10% of GDP after 50 years (primary budget surpluses in initial years below 0.5% of GDP assum-

18 Torben M. Andersen, *Social security and longevity,* Working Paper, (Aarhus, 2006).

19 Roughly the order of magnitude implied by UN forecasts. See United Nations, *World Population in 2300*, (New York, 2004).

ing initial debt to be zero). The reason why the level of pre-funding is relatively modest is that the optimal policy implies that the effective retirement age is proportional to longevity, and in this way, generations with longer longevity come to contribute significantly to the financing of the consumption demands this creates. Hence, the numbers shown here suggest that ensuring that retirement moves proportionally to longevity will deal with the large share of the financial problems arising from increasing longevity.

This raises the important question of how to ensure that actual retirement ages follow longevity. It is here interesting to compare recent reforms in Denmark and Sweden addressing demographic pressures, since they both include mechanisms to address this problem, but different approached have been adopted.

4.3 Indexing pension and retirement ages to longevity

The Danish pension system is for pillar I a defined benefit (DB) scheme stipulating given benefits[20] from a statutory pension age and for the remaining lifetime. The pension age is currently 65 (recently reduced from 67). In addition, there is a voluntary and contribution based (though heavily tax subsidised) early retirement scheme (efterløn) accessible between the age of 60 to 65.

In a recent reform (2006), it has been decided to i) make discrete increases in the entitlement age for early retirement from 60 to 62 in steps of 6 months over the years 2019-2022, and similarly to increase the pension age from 65 to 67 in steps of 6 months in the period 2023-27, ii) index these statutory ages to the life expectancy of persons aged 60 from 2025. The objective for the indexation is to maintain an expected pension period of 19½ years across generations with different longevity.

The latter aspect is particularly interesting since it introduces an explicit index clause related to longevity into the social contract. This is an additive indexing formula in the sense that the expected retirement period is kept constant in terms of expected duration (R=T–a), i.e. increases in longevity are spent in the labour market, and we have that the relative retirement age is

$$R/T=1-a/T$$

That is, the relative retirement age is increasing with longevity, and therefore the transfer is decreasing with longevity.

20 The pension has three layers: a base pension, and two supplements for which there is means testing. Benefits are indexed to wages according to 'satsreguleringsloven'.

4.4 Making benefits contingent on longevity

After the major reform in the 1990s, the Swedish system is a so-called notional-defined contribution scheme.[21] This scheme is a PAYG scheme in which actual benefits are individualised based on contributions. Individual contributions are thus credited to and accumulated on individual accounts, but they are notional in the sense that the account determines the share of benefits implied by the PAYG scheme. Actual benefits therefore depend on the notional pension wealth, the rate of return of the PAYG scheme, and life expectancy at retirement. The latter is important since it implies that benefits are annualised based on the retirement age and expected longevity.

The notional-defined contribution scheme thus implies that benefits are adjusted to actual developments in both employment and longevity.[22] For the present discussion, this has two important implications. First, there is a direct link between benefits and longevity, and agents deciding to have an invariant retirement age despite increasing longevity will not be able to claim (in present value terms) a larger benefit as opposed to a defined benefit scheme with a stipulated (and constant) retirement age. Secondly, if aggregate employment falls, e.g. because many decide to retire early, benefits will also be lowered. In this sense, the notional-defined contribution scheme has two important sources of adjustment mechanisms.

From an individual perspective, the Swedish system is also an additive adjustment scheme in the sense that the benefit flow is unchanged if the retirement period is invariant (assuming a constant interest rate).

4.5 Adjusting statutory pension ages or benefits to longevity?

A comparison of the Swedish and Danish systems hinges critically on the importance of a statutory retirement age, which, in turn, poses the question why a social security scheme should include a statutory pension/retirement age. There are several arguments in favour of a statutory retirement age. One is that agents tend to be myopic and therefore underestimate the need for savings and the consequences of retiring early. This is in particular due to the fact that in a welfare

21 See Axel Börsch-Supan, 'From traditional DB to notional DC systems: The Pension Reform Process in Sweden, Italy and Germany', *Journal of the European Economic Association*, 2-3, (2005); Edward Palmer, 'The Swedish Pension reform Model: Framework and Issues', Working paper, *Social Insurance*, 1, (2000).

22 Germany has introduced a sustainability factor, implying that benefits are dependent on the dependency ratio.

state, there is a 'bail-out' problem, since agents without savings always will be entitled to some minimum living standard. A particular issue may be the extent to which agents tend to underestimate longevity, especially in a period with a trend increase. In such a period, individual savings and retirement plans may imply too little savings and too early retirement. The statutory pension age can to some extent overcome this and be a signal of the appropriate retirement age.

A further aspect is that the individual retirement age is affected by the tax distortion, while the statutory retirement age is not. The tax distortion implies that the private incentive to retirement is stronger than it is to society. Hence, there seems to be an argument for having a statutory retirement age. However, this argument may be too simple since this does not preclude retirement before the statutory retirement age based on private savings. Against this, it may be argued that it is not relevant/possible for groups with low savings. Moreover, the statutory age may serve as a signal/norm as is indicated by the evidence that few retire before the statutory retirement age. However, this may change due to the build-up of substantial pension savings.

The retirement/pension decision is affected by a tax distortion (composite tax rate made up of direct taxation and eventual loss of benefits and means testing). This distortion is clearly less in a system where benefits are contribution-based and adjusted to the expected retirement period. In this sense, the Swedish system leaves better incentives for later retirement than the Danish. In both systems, there is, however, still a tax distortion or tax externality, implying that if a generation decides to retire later, it will create room for either lower taxes or higher benefits, and vice versa.

The actuarial scheme as adopted in Sweden makes it an individual choice to adjust the retirement age to (expected) longevity, but there is a clear signal via the fact that benefits are adjusted to expected longevity. The problem of myopia etc. mentioned above may still apply here. In addition, there is a question of how low a benefit level that can be offered to retirees. In a welfare state, there is a clear minimum level, and this may be reached if agents do not adjust the actual retirement age (say due to strong norms) to the actual path for longevity[23]. This may create a future tension in the system if large groups of pensioners are considered to have too low benefit levels, irrespective of whether it is caused by an underestimation of longevity or that they did not take proper account of the projected increase in longevity. To put it differently, the actuarial system may need a

23 The effect is striking. Postponing retirement from the age of 61 to 65 would imply a benefit level which is about 30% higher, cf. Edwars Palmer, 'The Swedish Pension reform Model: Framework and Issues', Working paper, *Social Insurance*, 1, (2000).

lowest possible retirement age to make it viable. In Sweden, the minimum age at which there is a pension entitlement is 61, and it is not linked to longevity.

An important question is whether the actual retirement age will follow the statutory pension and early retirement ages. There are two reasons to question this. First, a large group of future pensioners would have a substantial additional pension income from mandatory labour market pensions as well as individualised savings. Hence, an income effect in the retirement decision may cause more to want earlier retirement. Second, there may be a preference shift where an increasing number of people want to enjoy more leisure activities in their 'third phase of life'. In short, an increase in statutory pension ages may not automatically lead to a corresponding increase in actual retirement ages.

The preceding discussion has implicitly relied on the assumption that retirement is a voluntary decision in the sense that the individual makes a choice between later retirement, and thus increased lifetime income, or increased leisure. For a significant group, retirement takes place before normal retirement due to loss of work ability due to physical or psychological problems. In Denmark, a fraction of the age group of 60 has retired on disability pension, and before the age of 65 (the statutory pension age), more than 60% of a cohort has retired from the labour market. The social contract implies that if the welfare state should be able to provide for groups losing work ability or retiring earlier, it follows that adjustments would have to be made in the form of higher taxes or later retirement for the more able. Assuming that work ability is decreasing with age, it follows that the retirement/pension age of other groups would have to increase by more than the increase in longevity. Only in the unlikely case where work ability depends on remaining lifetime would the system be neutral to such changes. Otherwise, the retirement age would have to increase by more than longevity.

For both the Danish and the Swedish scheme, it is important to note that they only deal with one side of the financial problems arising from ageing, namely, pensions. Equally important are expenditures on health and old age care which are strongly age-dependent. Hence, a financial problem is bound to arise unless longer longevity to an extreme degree is driven by more 'healthy' years, implying that age dependent health care activities for the larger part of the elderly are postponed to a later age. In addition, it could be mentioned that new and improved treatments as well as a strong income effect on the demand for health related activities are likely to be strong upward driving forces for health expenditures.

4.6 Pre-funding or gradual adjustment?

There is a strong case to be made for the introduction of automatic adjustment mechanisms to deal with changes in longevity. This includes concerns for intergenerational distribution, but also the pragmatic fact that this makes policies less dependent on projections of future paths for longevity. However, as noted above, many countries are in an initial situation with high debt levels and with room for consolidation of public finances, and this gives an argument for some pre-funding in terms of reductions of public debt levels before the demographic shifts get significant effect.

There is, however, also an issue of credibility in relation to the choice of policy strategy. This applies to both strategies. The adjustment mechanism relies on future changes, but will they be enacted? In the Danish case – with future, rather large, discrete changes in retirement and pension ages – there is clearly a political risk that these may be overturned if there e.g. is a severe downturn in the years preceding the large upward steps in the early retirement/pension ages. The pre-funding strategy has the advantage of being based on current actions which can be observed. However, it also has a time-consistency problem[24]. Is it likely that policy makers can maintain such a pre-funding strategy, implying systematic budget surpluses and possible building-up of public net-wealth (or very low debt levels), and at the same time keep a very strict policy allowing no improvements (better services or lower taxes)? While this may not be that problematic at initial high debt levels, problems may arise when debt levels become smaller (in international and historical comparison) and especially if public wealth is being accumulated.

5. Concluding remarks

Models on political economy teach us that intergenerational social contracts are supported by the trust the contributing agents have in being able to benefit from a similar scheme when they get old as well as intergenerational altruism. Accordingly, it is important to guard these elements, and the key to this is to undertake reforms in due time which are transparent and considered fair. If not, uncertainty will arise and depreciate trust in the system, and intergenerational imbalances

24 The US experience in recent years can also be taken to show that initial favourable public finances contributing to coping with fiscal sustainability problems were not time-consistent.

may develop which diminish the support for the social contract embedded in the welfare state.

Yet, there is often substantial opposition to reforms, and proposals are often categorised as retrenchments of welfare arrangements. The success by which the latter argument has been marketed in the debate is interesting when the fact is that the whole issue is arising because opportunities improve in the sense that agents can expect a significantly longer longevity. The discussion of the need for reforms is not a question of shifts in political preferences, but rather changes caused by changed fundamentals, namely the gains from increasing longevity.

What are the major obstacles to reforms? In some cases, poor information and confused debates have caused misperceptions about the issues at stake. More importantly is probably the intergenerational distribution issue which is quite simple, namely that postponement of reforms will shift burdens to future generations. Hence, present generations will gain and future generations will lose if reforms are postponed, and therefore the political system may be inclined to delay reforms. However, this argument is most relevant for the pre-funding strategy because the adjustment mechanism will tie the adjustment to the generations that will actually gain from increased longevity. Hence, such reforms do not carry any immediate costs, and may therefore be easier to implement. This may explain why such reform elements have already been implemented in Sweden and Denmark.

The Democratic Deficit of Pension Reform: The Case of Sweden

Urban Lundberg

Pension reforms raise both technical and political questions. The former concern how to design a pension system that offers older people decent living conditions without burdening the economy, the latter why reforms deemed essential from an economic viewpoint fail to materialise for political reasons. In recent years, these issues have generated a considerable body of literature. The Post War pension systems in the industrialised world, according to an almost unanimous research community, must now adapt to new circumstances and conditions. If this is to happen, however, recalcitrant interests must be overcome and crucial decisions be taken.

The Swedish pension reform of the 1990s has acquired a highly exclusive status in the literature. The reason for this is that it appears to solve both the technical and the political problems. It is viewed both as an innovative solution to the ageing society dilemma and as a triumph for the Swedish political system. At a dramatic stage in the country's economic development, Swedish politicians managed to rise above narrow party interests.

An aspect of the Swedish reform that has received less attention, however, both in pension research and in the general discourse, is the democratic context in which the technical solutions are drawn up and the political decisions taken. This is the theme of the present chapter. How are interventions in the national pension scheme deemed essential by the experts but opposed by the electorate to be justified? A critical observer might suggest that pension research in recent years has suffered from a 'Machiavellian' bias. The focus has been on policymakers and experts and their attempts both to establish economic stability and to keep down costs in the social sector without the loss of governmental power. Questions concerning the workings of democracy and its status as a source of public legitimacy are seldom discussed. Democracy in the general sense of the word becomes something to be overcome or manipulated rather than something to be protected and deepened for its own sake.

The democratic problem may be associated with two powerful and interrelated trends in the modern world. Firstly, economic and cultural globalisation, which means there is greater dependence on decisions reached in other parts of the world, and secondly, the ageing populations of industrialised countries, which according to the experts means that those of us living today will make increasingly heavy demands on the resources of future generations.[1] The growing share of older people in the population is viewed as the main challenge to welfare and democracy, and it is this trend that forms the basis of the present chapter. Particular attention is focused on the decision-making process that led to the Swedish pension reform of the 1990s. This is discussed in terms of the Swedish political system in general and of the Social Democratic Party's special role in Swedish political culture in particular.

Veto points and the constitutional order

In the beginning of the new century, the experts are predicting a previously never experienced ageing of the population in industrialised developed countries. Specifically, this means that the relative burden of older people on welfare systems will increase, while the younger will have to assume greater responsibility both for their own social welfare and for that of previous generations.[2] A further problem is that there are no historical parallels that enable us to assess how this development might affect economic and social structures in society. The process of decreasing mortality rates followed by decreasing fertility rates and longer life expectancy is a unique phenomenon in world history. But it is already clear that the pressure on the welfare systems to redistribute between young and old will increase dramatically in the future. If our welfare is to survive, it is claimed, we will need to engage in a process of continuous change and adapt public institutions both to constantly shifting age structures and to constantly shifting social and economic conditions.[3]

---

1 In Anglo-Saxon literature this dilemma is labelled 'squaring the welfare circle', see Guiliano Bonoli, Vic George & Peter Taylor-Gooby, *European Welfare State Futures. Towards a Theory of Retrenchment,* (Cambridge, 2000).

2 Elmar Rieger & Stephan Liebfried, *Limits to Globalization,* (Cambridge, 2003); Paul Pierson, 'Coping with Permanent Austerity. Welfare Restructuring in Affluent Democracies', Paul Pierson (ed.), *The New Politics of the Welfare State*, (New York, 2001); Duane Swank, *Global Capital, Political Institutions and Policy Change in Developed Welfare States,* (Cambridge, 2002). For Swedish figures, see Långtidsutredningen, *Alternativ finansiering av offentliga tjänster*, Apendix 7, (2003).

3 See Thomas Lindh, 'Offentlig sektor och åldersfördelningen', Bo Malmberg & Lena Sommestad (eds.), *Befolkning och välfärd. Perspektiv på framtidens välfärdspolitik,* (Stockholm, 2002); Långtidsutredningen, *En åldrande befolkning och konsekvenserna för svensk ekonomi,* Apendix 9, (1999/2000); Thomas Lindh & Bo Malmberg, *40-talisternas uttåg. En ESO-rapport om 2000-talets demografiska utmaningar, (Stockholm, 2000).*

In recent years, researchers have devoted a great deal of literature to this problem. For the most part, it makes depressing reading. While politicians of various hues fight to curb rising costs, citizens are deprived of the chance to influence the direction in which society is moving. Welfare systems have quite simply proved more difficult to reduce, adapt and restructure than to build up and extend. Whereas the politicians of yesterday battled for the honour of introducing popular reforms, those who are active today seek to escape responsibility for painful cutbacks. The problem is intimately linked to the fact that the welfare state and the benefits that accompany it tend to be self-justifying. A government that wishes to retain power, therefore, has a powerful incentive either to avoid rocking the boat or to push through change as discreetly as possible.[4]

What opportunities are available in this respect partly depends on a country's democratic infrastructure in its broadest sense. A key issue here is the extent to which the constitutional order incorporates so-called institutional *veto points*. This term refers to stages in a decision-making process at which a player is able to delay or prevent the adoption of new legislation. There is an important difference here between parliamentary systems and systems that involve power sharing. In parliamentary systems, the legislative and executive bodies cannot be at variance since – unlike in a power-sharing system – a situation can never arise in which these bodies are controlled by different parties.

Veto points may also be built into the electoral system: is it based on proportional representation or single-member constituencies? Or they may be built into the parliamentary structure: are there one or two chambers? Or into the role of the head of state: is it ceremonial or substantial, as in the case of France or the US. The crucial question here is what level of *power concentration* a government can rely on when embarking on a controversial reform programme. Electoral systems with single-member constituencies, such as that of the UK, for instance, tend to throw up strong majority governments with a high level of power concentration, while for instance federal bicameral systems such as that of Germany spread the decision-making process across several power centres. Thus the amount of influence that external groups and opposition parties are able to exert

---

4 Paul Pierson, *Dismantling the Welfare State. Reagan, Thatcher, and the Politics of Retrenchment*, (Cambridge MA, 1994); Christoffer Green-Pedersen, *The Politics of Justification. Party Competition and Welfare State Retrenchment in Denmark and the Netherlands from 1982 to 1998*, (Amsterdam, 2002); Paul Pierson, 'The New Politics of the Welfare State', *World Politics*, 2, (1996); Stein Kuhnle, 'The Scandinavian Welfare State in the 1990s. Challenged but Viable', *West European Politics*, 2, (2000); Kees van Kersbergen, 'The Declining Resistance of Welfare States to Change', Stein Kuhnle (ed.), *The Survival of the European Welfare State*, (London, 2000).

on policy content is to some extent already determined by the formal structure of the system.[5]

Emphasising democratic infrastructures has proved a fruitful approach when seeking to analyse the reform process that is currently sweeping the Western world. In country after country, governments of widely differing types are developing strategies for overcoming recalcitrant voters and organised interests. Some are having more success than others. Both reforms that have been implemented and those that have not gained acceptance can be discussed in terms of the extent to which political institutions establish frameworks for government action. This is not to say that the pattern is the same everywhere. A high level of power concentration is not necessarily an advantage for a government wishing to reform an established welfare programme. The absence of veto points may give a government greater freedom of action, but it also means that the government must accept greater responsibility for the decisions it takes.[6] The greater the concentration of power, the greater the danger of being punished by the voters at the next election.[7] Research does, however, confirm the importance of political institutions for the content of reform policies. Countries with institutions where political power is concentrated tend to adopt one-sided strategies and make outright budget cuts, while governments in countries with a rich array of veto points often combine austerity policies with expansive measures and improvements in existing programmes.[8]

The Swedish Constitution is distinguished by few veto points and a high level of power concentration. This is because the unicameral system of parliament (the Riksdag) puts governments in a strong position. Constitutionally, there is nothing to prevent a government with a parliamentary majority behind it from pushing through a radical reform programme since such a move cannot be blocked in any

---

5 Ellen Immergut, *Health Politics.Interests and Institutions in Western Europe, (Cambridge, 1992)*; Guiliano Bonoli, *The Politics of Pension Reform. Institutions and Policy Change in Western Europe, (Cambridge, 2000)*; R. Kent Weaver & Bert A. Rockman, 'When and How Do Institutions Matter?', R. Kent Weaver & Bert A. Rockman (eds.), *Do Institutions Matter?*, (Washington DC, 1991).

6 Guiliano Bonoli, 'Political Institutions, Veto Points and the Process of Welfare State Adaptation', Paul Pierson (ed.), *The New Politics of the Welfare State*, (New York, 2001).

7 R. Kent Weaver, 'The Politics of Blame Avoidance', *Journal of Public Policy*, 6, (1986).

8 Bonoli, Guiliano, 'Political Institutions, Veto Points and the Process of Welfare State Adaptation', Paul Pierson (ed.), *The New Politics of the Welfare State*, (New York, 2001); Evelyne Huber & John D. Stephens, *Development and Crisis of the Welfare States. Parties and Policies in Global Markets*, (Chicago, 2001).

other arena.[9] Moreover, Swedish governments can count on a relatively high degree of party loyalty. In Sweden, as opposed to a country like France, for instance, individual members of parliament rarely defy their own party executive – at least not over issues where government power is at stake.[10]

But the Swedish Constitution also has features that point in a different direction. The concentration of power is eroded by a proportional electoral system that tends to produce weak minority or coalition governments.[11] During their 65 years in power between 1932 and 2006, the Social Democrats only had a majority of their own on two occasions. Otherwise, they either ruled in coalition with the Agrarian Party (now the Centre Party) or in a minority cabinet with the Communist Party (later with the Left Party and the Green Party) as their ultimate source of support.[12] The centre-right governments of 1976-1982 and 1991-1994 suffered from the fact that they were composed of several parties with fundamentally different views on a number of key issues.[13] Instead, the standard text book argues that the Swedish system has favoured the emergence of a class-based political culture in which the political parties – perceived as legitimate social interests – act as checks and balances on one another's parliamentary actions. To this, researchers have added the significant degree of influence that external interests wield over decision-making, i.e. the renowned Swedish corporativism, and the fact that conflicts in Sweden are frequently resolved outside the legislative assembly via central government committees and the system whereby proposals are widely referred for consideration by relevant bodies.[14]

9 Erik Holmberg & Nils Stjernquist, *Vår författning, 12th ed. (Stockholm, 2000)*; Sven Steinmo, *Taxation and Democracy. Swedish, British and American Approaches to Financing the Modern Welfare State*, (New Haven, 1991).

10 Ellen Immergut, *Health Politics. Interests and Institutions in Western Europe*, (Cambridge, 1992).

11 Maurice Duverger, *Political Parties. Their Organization and Acitivity in the Modern State, (London, 1964)*.

12 The first period lasted four years and occurred during the Second World War when Sweden nevertheless was governed by a cross-benched coalition that involved all parties represented in Parliament except for the Communist Party. The second period at the end of the 1960s lasted for only two years. See Göran Therborn, 'Swedish Social Democracy and the Transition from Industrial to Postindustrial Politics', Frances Fox Piven (ed.), *Labor Parties in Postindustrial Societies*, (Cambridge UK, 1991).

13 Hans Bergström, *Rivstart? Från opposition till regering,* (Stockholm, 1987); Sven-Erik Larsson, *Regera i koalition. Den borgerliga trepartiregeringen 1976-1978*, (Stockholm, 1986); Torbjörn Nilsson, *Mellan arv och utopi. Moderata vägval under 100 år, 1904-2004,* (Stockholm, 2004).

14 Olof Petersson, *Svensk politik, 6th edn, (Stockholm, 2005)*; Ellen Immergut, *Health Politics. Interests and Institutions in Western Europe*, (Cambridge, 1992); Steinmo, Sven, *Taxation and Democracy. Swedish, British and American Approaches to Fi-*

The Swedish pension reform – politicians and experts

On the surface, the major pension reform of 1994 fits into this pattern. It stemmed from a cross-bench compromise between five parties in the Riksdag who decided after a decade of wearisome conflict to make common cause. Following their election victory in 1991, the centre-right minority government appointed a public inquiry with representatives from all the parliamentary parties. Just two and a half years later, the 'Working Group on Pensions' presented guidelines for a new national pension system, and the scheme was adopted a short while later by a near-unanimous Riksdag.[15]

The promise of a cross-party and cross-bench compromise in the Riksdag meant there was every chance of overcoming the institutional inertia of the old pension scheme. The Working Group was thus free to develop an original and comparatively radical solution to the financing problems inherent in the national supplementary pension scheme (ATP) as described by the experts.[16] The reform meant moving from defined-benefit to defined-contribution pensions and from a fixed to a flexible retirement age. It also meant a partial transition from employer's contributions to personal contributions by employees, and the introduction of a new benefit formula known as the lifetime earnings principle. Along with these fundamental shifts in the national scheme towards a notional defined-contribution model, a decision was taken to set aside a small share of the pension contribution for a special premium pension that was not to be paid out to those

---

nancing the Modern Welfare State, (New Haven, 1991). However, according to many studies, in recent decades political decision making in Sweden has been subject to a process of decorporatization, see Jörgen Hermansson ea., *Avkorporativisering och lobbyism*, (Stockholm, 1999). This tendency is apparent also in the pension reform of the 1990s. Major stakeholders were excluded from the crucial committees in order to facilitate the political parties' work to crate a lasting compromise.

15 Karen Anderson & Traute Meyer, 'The Third Way in Welfare State Reform? Social Democratic Pension Politics in Germany and Sweden', Guiliano Bonoli & Martin Powell (eds.), *Social Democratic Party Policies in Contemporary Europe*, (London, 2004).

16 For introductions to the new Swedish pension system, see, Joakim Palme, 'Pension Reform in Sweden and the Changing Boundaries between Public and Private', Gordon L. Clark & Noel Whiteside (eds.), *Pension Security in the 21st Century. Redrawing the Public-Private Debate*, (New York, 2003); Karen M. Anderson & Ellen Immergut, 'Sweden: After Social Democratic Hegemony', Karen M. Anderson, Ellen Immergut & Isabelle Schulze (eds.), *Handbook of West European Pension Politics*, (Oxford UK, 2007); Edward Palmer, *'The Swedish Pension Reform Model. Framework and Issues'*, *Social Protection Discussion Paper/World Bank*, 12, (2000).

already in retirement but would be set aside for the benefit of the contributor.[17] By comparison with the ATP scheme launched in 1950, the new Swedish system is designed to reward wage-earners who delay their retirement for as long as possible.[18]

Both the Social Democrats and the centre-right parties were forced to make painful concessions. The Social Democrats gave their backing to an extensive reform of their 'jewel in the crown', the ATP scheme. The centre-right parties agreed to preserve a universal, mandatory pension system which, in the words of one of its chief architects, Bo Könberg of the Liberal Party, is to remain in place 'until the next ice age'.[19] From a planning viewpoint, the Swedish pension reform has been acclaimed a success. In contrast to many other western countries, Sweden has acquired a pension scheme that is both flexible and rational in relation to socioeconomic development, and which takes into account both the coming dependency ratio (which is deemed foreseeable) and the state of the economy (which is impossible to foresee). The idea is for the system to be both self-regulatory and externally adaptive. If this goal is to be achieved, however, the stability of the system must take precedence over the pension benefits of the individual.[20]

---

17 Besides Sweden variants of this model have been established by countries such as Poland, Italy, Latvia, the Kyrgyz Republic and Mongolia. There's already an abundance of research on this particular policy model, see John B. Williamson & Matthew Williams, 'The Notional Defined Contribution Model. An Assessment of the Strengths and Limitations of a New Approach to the Provision of Old Age Security', *Working Paper/CRR* (2003); Michael Cichon, 'Notional Defined Contribution Schemes. Old Wine in New Bottles?', *International Social Security Review*, 4, (1999); Salvador Valdés-Prieto, 'The Financial Stability of Notional Account Pensions', *Scandinavian Journal of Economics*, 3, (2000).

18 Lennart Flood, 'Vilka pensioner får framtidens pensionärer?', *Ekonomisk debatt*, 3, (2004); Edward Palmer, 'The Swedish Pension Reform Model. Framework and Issues', *Social Protection Discussion Paper/World Bank*, 12, (2000). It's hard to give a well informed opinion on the generosity of the new Swedish pension system. In the end it depends on both structural factors such as demography and economic growth as well as individual factors such as life time earnings and retirement age.

19 Urban Lundberg, *Juvelen i kronan. Socialdemokraterna och den allmänna pensionen*, (Stockholm, 2003).

20 The Swedish reform is a standard case in comparative studies on pension reform, see John Myles & Paul Pierson, 'The Comparative Politics of Pension Reform', Paul Pierson (ed.) *The New Politics of the Welfare State*, (New York, 2001); Karl Hinrich, 'Elephants on the Move. Patterns of Public Pension Reform in OECD-Countries', Stephan Liebfried (ed.), *Welfare State Futures*, (Cambridge UK, 2001); R. Kent Weaver, 'The Politics of Public Pension Reform', *Working Paper/CRR*, 6, (2003).

A democratic perspective – the citizens[21]

How does the new pension scheme appear when analysed from a democratic viewpoint? Its parliamentary roots should not necessarily be taken to mean that the reform had unusually wide democratic endorsement. Rather, it was the outcome of what could be described as a *loophole* in the Swedish Constitution that enables political parties to join together in removing sensitive issues from the democratic decision-making process. At the time, the general feeling was that none of the parties involved had anything to gain from further political squabbling over the future design of the national pension scheme.

The reform was never tested in conjunction with a parliamentary election. The voters never had the opportunity to adopt a position on the principles of the new system. The centre-right government's first move after its 1991 election victory was to invite the opposition to join a new inquiry into pensions. The last thing that the Social Democrats did prior to the 1994 election campaign was to support the government's proposals for new pension-scheme guidelines. As we watched, a relatively autonomous political formation began to emerge that was accountable neither to voters nor interest groups, only to the party leaderships themselves. This neatly removed the political obstacles to reform. Decision-making power was confined to a parliamentary majority that needed to worry neither about critical opposition nor about veto points. Responsibility for the reform was spread across a constellation that ran no risk of being taught a lesson by the electorate. The centre-right government was able to hide behind the strong Social Democratic opposition and the Social Democratic opposition could seek the protection of the weak centre-right government.

Another aspect of the pension reform of the 1990s was that the parties managed to exclude relevant stakeholders such as trade unions, pensioners and employer organisations from the process. This may be explained partly by what happened in the 1980s, when stakeholders played an obstructive role and hampered attempts by both Social Democratic and centre-right governments to curb cost rises in the retirement pension system, and partly by the economic crisis of the 1990s, which sent a shockwave through the entire political establishment. This 'crisis awareness' was particularly in evidence, perhaps, at the Swedish Trade Union Confederation (LO), whose executive abandoned their traditional defence of the ATP system and concurred with the government's overall assess-

21 This section is based on Urban Lundberg, *Juvelen i kronan. Socialdemokraterna och den allmänna pensionen*, (Stockholm, 2003).

ment of economic imperatives.[22] Also, the reform was circulated in the referral process (remiss) and dealt with in committee in record time. The aim was to arrive at a decision before the 1994 election campaign. The Working Group on Pensions feared that the fragile parliamentary consensus would be lost if the parties made pensions an election issue.[23]

Consensus and political cartels

It is important not to confuse cross-bench reforms with uncontroversial reforms. When faced with contentious and unpopular decisions, the parties may well be tempted – like businesses in a private market – to establish *political cartels* that eliminate the need to compete for voters. The cartel as a solution to political problems differs from the theory of *cartel parties*, which focuses primarily on how the parties, as their memberships decline, begin to secure their long-term funding through alternative channels, such as central government party subsidies or changes in the electoral system that impede the entry of new parties.[24] The concepts are, however, clearly related. Both involve the parties strengthening their autonomy in relation to voters and members. This interpretation is not indisputable, however, and has been fiercely criticised. Some researchers, for instance, see it as conspiratorial, and argue that objectively speaking there is nothing to suggest that competition between the parties will cease in the future. Furthermore, they lack control of the media.[25]

Such criticism is well founded, and it is perhaps something of an exaggeration to talk about a specific new *type of party*. But this is not to say that the financing problems of the welfare state do not give the parties – both those in government and those in opposition – an incentive to establish cartels in *certain policy areas* that could cause problems in future terms of office. As democracy researcher Ian

---

22 Karen Anderson & Traute Meyer, 'The Third Way in Welfare State Reform? Social Democratic Pension Politics in Germany and Sweden', Guiliano Bonoli & Martin Powell (eds.), *Social Democratic Party Policies in Contemporary Europe*, (London, 2004); Lundberg, Urban, *Juvelen i kronan. Socialdemokraterna och den allmänna pensionen*, (Stockholm, 2003).

23 Lundberg, Urban, *Juvelen i kronan. Socialdemokraterna och den allmänna pensionen*, (Stockholm, 2003).

24 Richard S. Katz & Peter Mair, 'Changing Models of Party Organisation and Party Democracy. The Emergence of the Cartel Party', *Party Politics*, 1, (1995).

25 See Herbert Kitschelt, 'Citizens, Politicians, and Party Cartellization. Political Representation and State Failure in Post-Industrial Democracies', *European Journal of Political Research*, 2, (2000); Knut Heidar & Jo Saglie, 'Predestined Parties? Organizational Change in Norwegian Political Parties', *Party Politics*, 2, (2003).

Shapiro points out in a critical comment on the US political system, there is an imminent risk that broad cross-party compromises in actual fact conceal narrow party self-interest.[26]

Consensus is not necessarily a 'bad thing', but nor is it automatically a 'good thing' expressing the will of the majority.[27] Even if the pension reform was constitutionally endorsed – it was, after all, no *coup d'état* – it is correct to say that it marked a departure both from the textbook description of the norms said to govern Swedish political culture and from the opposition's traditional role as watchdog in a parliamentary system. Voters, organised interests and relevant referral bodies were all set aside and the remarkably brief parliamentary debate on the subject was little more than symbolic in character.[28] Similar patterns – involving consensus or cartels outside accepted democratic procedures – were previously seen in Sweden in defence and foreign policy matters. What is striking in this particular instance is that we are dealing with a welfare issue that has defined the Swedish political landscape throughout the post-war period.

Good solutions and ill-functioning public spheres

In seeking to explain the remarkable nature of the Swedish pension reform of the 1990s, we would do well to contrast it with what is popularly known as the ATP reform of the 1950s. The latter was preceded by a long and sometimes bitter political conflict over the question of what a national supplementary pension scheme should look like. The ATP reform could be said to have involved handing over an issue that the parties were unable to settle among themselves to be settled publicly by the voters. The pension reform of the 1990s, on the other

26 Ian Shapiro, *The State of Democratic Theory,* (Princeton & New York, 2003), p. 62.

27 As once proclaimed by the grand father of Swedish political science, Fredrik Lagerroth, the conflict between the government and the opposition does not necessarily lead to discord and dissolution: 'it only generate the mutual competition that is the precondition for everything perfect. In the normal course of events political consensus within a population is rather an unfailing sign of death.' Fredrik Lagerroth, *Frihetstidens författning*, (Stockholm, 1915). But also contemporary scholars have questioned the merits of political consensus, see Richard A. Posner, *Law, Pragmatism and Democracy,* (Cambridge MA, 2003), for an argument derived from Joseph Schumpeters theory of democracy. Also Ian Shapiro, *The State of Democratic Theory,* (Princeton & New York, 2003).

28 Only thirteen Members of Parliament participated in the parliamentary debate and none of the party leaders were present in the chamber when the guidelines for the new system were finally decided. Parliament of Sweden, *Swedish Parliamentary Publications. RD-series for the 1993-94 session*, vol. 120, (Stockholm, 1993-94), p. 25.

hand, involved settling by means of internal, cross-party negotiation an issue that could not be resolved in the public arena – in sight of the electorate. Democratic participation in the process was extremely limited.[29]

The ATP conflict was the result of a lengthy democratic process. Voters had the opportunity to choose between clear alternatives. It was only after a couple of general elections, numerous inquiries by experts, a national referendum, a cabinet crisis and the longest debate in the history of the Swedish Riksdag that the Social Democrats managed to marshal enough parliamentary support to push through this comprehensive reform.[30]As the Social Democratic prime minister of the day, Tage Erlander, put it in his memoirs, it was 'the most savage conflict we have witnessed since the onset of democracy'. He added:

> Among the young, the struggle over the pension issue spawned a faith in the future the like of which we had never previously seen. They wanted to help build up a Sweden in which class barriers had been torn down. And above all, (the centre-right parties and private enterprise) had not reckoned with a conflict over pensions that welded together the unions and the political labour movement to such an unprecedented extent. It was incredible to see the enthusiasm and determination to win that informed the efforts of the union movement all over the country. The pension battle was the unions' own.[31]

The process that ushered in the new pension scheme forty years later stands in sharp contrast to the democratic manifestations of the 1950s. Open, public debate was scarcely on the agenda. Neither citizens nor party members were given a chance to take part in the process or to influence the outcome. The issue was never given any real public exposure. The reform did not draw on democracy for its legitimacy but on ideas about what is just for the individual and rational for society. Insofar as this is the case, the new pensions reflect a depoliticised hypothetical scenario. The politicians' job is primarily to develop abiding principles that encourage equal individuals to behave in such a way that socially desirable goals are achieved. Where the ATP system sought fair outcomes, the new pensions are designed to guarantee fair procedures. Any social gaps that arise are an expression of a just order, not of a circumvention of justice.[32]

---

29 Urban Lundberg, *Juvelen i kronan. Socialdemokraterna och den allmänna pensionen*, (Stockholm, 2003).

30 Björn Molin, *Tjänstepensionsfrågan. En studie i svensk partipolitik*, (Lund, 1967); Bo Stråth, *Mellan två fonder. LO och den svenska modellen*, (Stockholm, 1998); Hugh Heclo, *Modern Social Politics in Britain and Sweden. From Relief to Income Maintenance,* (New Haven, London, 1974); Torsten Svensson, *Socialdemokratins dominans. En studie av svenska socialdemokratins partistrategi*, (Uppsala, 1994).

31 Tage Erlander, *1955-1960*, (Stockholm, 1976), p. 261.

32 Urban Lundberg, 'Social Democracy Lost. The Social Democratic Party in Sweden and the Politics of Pension Reform, 1978-1998', Eero Carroll & Lena Eriksson (eds.),

It is worth deliberating further on the lack of public debate on this issue. There are usually two reasons for wanting to avoid public exposure. Either you are faced with a bad or unpopular decision that you need to hide from a well-informed public or you believe yourself possessed of a sound or necessary solution that a misguided public would wreck. The pension reform of the 1990s falls into the latter category. The politicians assumed that their proposals would never survive open debate, and they doubted the quality of public scrutiny. The same scepticism about the ability of citizens to cope with complicated future issues was not in evidence at the time of the ATP reform in the 1950s. But on that occasion the aim was different and would seem to have been more laudable: to lift pensioners out of poverty and to assure the broad majority of wage-earners a decent standard of living in old age.

These departures from political practice in the 1990s are also reflected in the desire of the political parties to establish an autonomous, self-regulating system that would live on 'without continual legislative intervention'. The foremost expression of this aim is the 'law of automatic age-balancing', which at times of financial embarrassment regulates the system's expenditure side (i.e. pension levels) without the politicians having to expose themselves to the political risks that in the old system were associated with the adjustment of citizens' pensions to economic fluctuations.[33] But elsewhere, too, the new Swedish pension scheme is full of examples of what welfare researchers call 'automatic politics', i.e. the responsibility for controversial decisions is either transferred to independent institutions that are not exposed to the whims of the voters or they are regulated by law through rules applied automatically.[34] Thus it was not a case of a temporary compromise between incompatible positions but of a long-term agreement to depoliticise the pension issue for the foreseeable future.[35]

Welfare Politics Cross-Examined. Eclecticist Analytical Perspectives on Sweden and the Developed Countries, (Amsterdam, 2005).

33 Sarah M. Brooks & R. Kent Weaver, 'Lashed to the Mast? The Politics of NDC Pension Reform', Robert Holzmann & Edward Palmer (eds.), *Pension Reform. Issues and Prospects for non-financial defined contribution (NDC) schemes*, (Washington DC, 2006).

34 For theoretical reasoning about so-called pre-commitment strategies, see Jon Elster, *Ulysses and the Sirens. Studies in Rationality and Irrationality,* (Cambridge, 1979); Thomas C. Schelling, *Choice and Consequence,* (Cambridge, 1984). For 'automatic politics' in modern pension reform, see Sarah M. Brooks & R. Kent Weaver, 'Lashed to the Mast? The Politics of NDC Pension Reform', Robert Holzmann & Edward Palmer (eds.), *Pension Reform. Issues and Prospects for non-financial defined contribution (NDC) schemes*, (Washington DC, 2006).

35 Urban Lundberg, 'Social Democracy Lost. The Social Democratic Party in Sweden and the Politics of Pension Reform, 1978-1998', Eero Caroll & Lena Eriksson (eds.),

To sum up, the pension scheme could be described as a response to the threat scenarios offered by the academic community, but one that lacks a democratic basis. In purely technical terms, it is an impressive innovation. Politically, it demonstrates the parties' willingness to exploit the absence of veto points in the Swedish political system. This in turn raises some critical questions about the status and legitimacy of the system: if pensions are not codified by *the people*, who will guarantee their introduction and their existence in the future? The ice age of the reformers, it seems, may arrive sooner than expected. Another absolutely vital question is who decides what is a good system – the experts who created it or the people who will be required to live under it? As Aristotle said: 'the diner – not the cook – will be the best judge of a feast'[36]

An internal party perspective – the members

It is also possible to analyse the Swedish pension reform on the basis of the parties' internal decision-making. Horizontal agreements at central level tend to develop into vertical conflicts between the executive and the rank and file.[37] Thus formally speaking, situations could arise in which party executives lock decisions in political cartels and exploit constitutional loopholes but where their party organisations assume the form of an institutional veto point. In such situations, the executives may feel that breaking free from their organisations is the only alternative. Also, in the case of the Social Democratic party elite, there is reason to suppose that they felt it would be it easier to establish a cartel with the centre-right parties than to convince their own members that the ATP system needed reforming. The ATP scheme with its universalism and security standard was more than just a sophisticated social policy instrument for ensuring that the elderly would not have to face poverty and poorer circumstances. It was also an important part of the Social Democrats' historical identity as a progressive party of reform and a key element in what both they themselves and the research community are fond of describing as the hegemony of social democracy over Swedish society.[38]

Welfare Politics Cross-Examined. Eclecticist Analytical Perspectives on Sweden and the Developed Countries, (Amsterdam, 2005)

36 Aristotle, *Politics*, transl. Ernest Barker, (Cambridge, 1961), p. 126.

37 Albert O. Hirschman, *Exit, voice, and loyalty. Responses to Decline in Firms, Organizations and States*, (Cambridge, 1970); Gunnar Sjöblom, *Party Strategies in a Multiparty System*, (Lund, 1968).

38 Svensson, Torsten, *Socialdemokratins dominans. En studie av svenska socialdemokratins partistrategi*, (Uppsala, 1994).

The Social Democrats did indeed encounter severe problems with their own supporters. Altogether, three party congresses, three internal consultations and an outright threat from the party executive were needed before the representatives at the congress held in Sundsvall in 1997 finally gave way and endorsed the new system.[39] By that time, almost four years had passed since the parties agreed on pensions in the Riksdag in 1994.

The members took a harsh view of the executive's actions. At the concluding debate in Sundsvall, one representative commented: 'When you change a system that is as widely accepted and endorsed as the great ATP reform of 1959 was, you must have the support of the party members. You have to involve them. You can't come to them afterwards, which is what happened in 1994.'[40] Another representative saw the new reform as an abuse of party democracy: 'Find out first what the members think, and then seek agreement. That's the last time we should allow something like this to happen. Everyone must learn from what took place.'[41] There were further examples of such censure. A common theme of the speeches at the congress was the executive's inability to speak plainly about what was in the offing.[42]

There were deeply-felt historical reasons for the Social Democrats' hesitation in this matter. In contrast to the centre-right parties, who could declare the reform to be a step in the right direction based on their own principles (e.g. in relation to the premium reserve system and opportunities for private pension saving), the Social Democrats hid behind a vague, contradictory line of reasoning that emphasised continuity with the past.[43] To borrow an expression from historian Gerassimos Moschonas, they were prepared to go to any lengths to avoid a situation in which the new pension scheme resulted in a 'loss of radical identity'.[44]

The democracy problem outlined above, then, needs to be understood in two separate dimensions: on the one hand, how the parties – faced by globalisation and demography – develop common interests as *parties* vis-à-vis the citizens, and on the other how the political party executives react by establishing an oligarchic relationship with their own members.[45] Having said this, it should be emphasised

---

39 Urban Lundberg, *Juvelen i kronan. Socialdemokraterna och den allmänna pensionen*, (Stockholm, 2003).

40 SAP, *Minutes*, Party Congress of 1996, (Stockholm), p. 155.

41 Op. Cit., p. 156.

42 Lundberg, Urban, *Juvelen i kronan. Socialdemokraterna och den allmänna pensionen*, (Stockholm, 2003).

43 Op. Cit.

44 Gerassimos Moschonas, *In the Name of Social Democracy. The Great Transformation, 1945 to the Present*, (London, 2002), p. 3.

45 Urban Lundberg, 'Social Democracy Lost. The Social Democratic Party in Sweden and the Politics of Pension Reform, 1978-1998', *Welfare Politics Cross-Examined.*

that a general assessment of the Social Democratic party organisation's strength and its influence on executive policies is not easily performed. This has probably varied over time and between policy issues.[46] The hierarchical decision-making structure has always been there. The image of a real, authentic grassroots party run by the masses is and always has been a myth.[47] Nevertheless, there is reason to consider the pattern that informs the way senior party members handled the pension reform internally. Pensions were a key issue for the Social Democrats.

Swedish Social Democrats like to talk about 'the party', 'the movement' or 'the people' as the source of power. But do they mean what they say? Such rhetoric could be described as the background noise of politics. In the foreground, we perceive other themes that better reflect the process leading up to the new pension scheme: opinions that must be restrained, ministers who must display leadership, stakeholders who must be kept out, and widespread citizen concern that must be allayed. In the foreground, there are concerns about the frail and therefore vulnerable policies that must be defended against the narrow outlook of ordinary people.[48] This ironic tone is applicable not only to the principles underlying the new pension system. The dissonance between the foreground and background noise in Swedish politics was equally in evidence in the way the Social Democratic elite handled the national referendum on EMU.

What effect are the parties' cartelisation, oligarchic tendencies and growing disregard for citizen participation in the democratic process having? In this respect, simple cause and effect is not easily proven. It is clear, however, that participation is in decline in Sweden. Numerous studies have shown that popular support for both the political institutions and the established parties is diminishing. General distrust of politicians – which in Swedish has its own term, *politikerförakt* – remains at a high level. Party identification, i.e. loyalty towards the policies of a given party, is also on the decline – as are party memberships. Levels of

---

Eclecticist Analytical Perspectives on Sweden and the Developed Countries, (Amsterdam, 2005).

46 Nicholas Aylott, 'After the Divorce. Intra-Party Power and Organisational Change in Swedish Social Democracy', *Working Paper/Keele European Parties Research Unit*, 1, (2001). See also, Jo Saglie & Knut Heidar, 'Democracy within Norwegian Parties. Complacency or Pressure for Change?', *Party Politics*, 4, (2004).

47 See: Jon Pierre, *Partikongresser och regeringspolitik. En studie av den socialdemokratiska partikongressens beslutsfattande och inflytande, 1948-1978*, (Lund, 1986); Jan Teorell, *Demokrati eller fåtalsvälde? Om beslutsfattande i partiorganisationer*, (Uppsala, 1998). Also Gullan Gidlund & Tommy Möller, *Demokratins trotjänare*, (Stockholm, 1999).

48 The distinction between the background noise and the foreground noise in constitutional discourse is taken from Richard D. Parker, *Here, the People Rule*, (Cambridge, 1994).

activity in party organisations, too – including participation at meetings, electioneering and the acceptance and completion of political terms of office – has been on the decline in recent decades.[49] Party subsidies and the number of political advisers both in government ministries and in the parliamentary party groups, on the other hand, are on the increase.[50] At a time when major changes are being planned, and when the need for democracy and public debate is growing, the citizens themselves are becoming increasingly convinced that there is no longer any point in taking part in the democratic process.

Not just pension reform

The tendency to avoid both public and internal debate and to transfer decision-making to experts, cartels and automatic rules is not unique to the pension reform of the 1990s. Rather, this has become the principal method of dealing both with problems involving economic or discretionary decisions in general and with problems specifically related to the need to limit rises in public expenditure. Monetary policy, for example, once the responsibility of the politicians, has been delegated to an independent central bank. Budget policy, once a subject of general debate, is now regulated by expenditure ceilings that all parliamentary parties have agreed to uphold.[51]

Study of the pension reform of the 1990s confirms this shift towards a narrower form of democracy and a situation in which due democratic process is not considered appropriate when dealing with important issues. All the evidence suggests that the politicians chose to act on the experts' analyses of the long-term consequences of demographic change and globalisation – the new system is flexible and robust in budget terms – but was unable to do so without manipulating the democratic process. This was admitted by former prime minister Göran Persson himself at a meeting with the press in Australia, where he said he was 'sure that what we've done will not be popular in twenty years' time when those who retire see what it is'.[52]

Nor is this challenge to democracy likely to disappear of its own accord. As the ageing process in the population intensifies and new reforms are needed, the

---

49 Olof Petersson et al., *Demokrati utan partier? Demokratirådets rapport 2000*, (Stockholm, 2000).
50 Op. Cit.
51 Lars Jonung, *Med backspegeln som kompass. Stabiliseringspolitiken som läroprocess*, (Stockholm, 1999).
52 Quotation from Prime Minister Göran Persson in Björn Elmbrant, *Dansen kring guldkalven. Så förändrades Sverige av börsbubblan*, (Stockholm, 2005).

political system will face difficult decisions time and again. These will concern social insurance (where a political process explicitly modelled on the pension reform is already under way), regional distribution and public services.[53] Governments that challenge the established order in these areas face an uncertain future. The temptation to exploit constitutional loopholes, to set up political cartels or to transfer power of decision to experts, independent institutions or automatic regulation is hardly likely to diminish in the years to come. But this would deprive the public discourse of crucial issues – and reduce democracy to a ceremonial facade.

Popular rule or government by politicians

How concerned should we be about a development in which democracy – like the monarchy before it – assumes ceremonial garb? In a sense, the answer depends on how we view democracy as a concept. Throughout its existence, it has been exposed to powerful criticism and powerful critics.[54] And even if the concept as such is not negotiable, there are still many influential theoreticians who doubt its ability to deliver what it promises. It would be too simplistic, however, to dismiss such contentions as anti-democratic or as examples of authoritarian reasoning.[55]

A fairer dividing line that better captures the ambiguities associated with the pension reform of the 1990s is the one between parliamentarians and constitutionalists. Here, it is a case of two qualitatively different views of democracy. The former is based on the sovereignty of the people and the immediate reflection of popular will in parliamentary action, the latter on distrust of both power concentration and majority rule.[56] Not that the constitutionalists are opposed to popular rule. But they sound warnings about parliamentary failings. As constitutionalist advocates in the economic and legal debate see it, society should be governed by means of neutral regulations rather than through political authorities

53 That this problem is recognized by the political establishment is evident from how instructions to commissions of inquiry were formulated on areas such as social insurances and public sector responsibilities, see Instructions for the Commission of Inquiry (Direktiv), *Översyn av* socialförsäkringarna (2004:129); Instructions for the Commission of Inquiry (Direktiv), *Översyn av strukturen och uppgiftsfördelningen inom samhällsorganisationen*, 10 (2003).

54 Robert A. Dahl, *Democracy and its Critics*, (New Haven, 1989); Ian Shapiro, *The State of Democratic Theory*, (Princeton & New York, 2003).

55 Ian Shapiro, *The State of Democratic Theory*, (Princeton & New York, 2003).

56 Urban Lundberg & Mattias Tydén, 'State versus Individual: Dimensions of Individual Rights and Citizenship in Sweden', *New Perspectives on the History and Future of the Swedish Model*, (forthcoming).

with the power to decide collective matters. Parliamentary majorities should be constrained by social contracts and legally established individual rights. Democracy, they claim, can not be automatically equated with majority rule. A frequent argument from this quarter is that growth and stability require written constitutions and courts that monitor legislative assemblies, so called judicial review. Such arrangements strengthen economic actors' confidence and their will to invest, and thus work to the general good.[57]

How deeply rooted has this kind of thinking become in the Swedish discourse? Here, too, foreground and background static are at variance. When democracy presents itself in statements of government policy and government commissions on democracy, it continues to assert the absolute power of the people. In the background, however, the constitutionalists' scepticism towards parliament is developing as a tendency for our age; it is discernable not least in the politicians' readiness to submit to constraints of their own making, such as budget ceilings, inflation targets, an independent central bank, or for that matter, the automatic balancing of the pension system.[58]

A common perception underlying these institutional control mechanisms is that the manifestation of popular will in the Riksdag would disrupt social harmony and cause the quality of public decision-making to deteriorate.[59] People in general do not know what is best for them, and political parties do not feel capable of dealing with emotional outbursts from ordinary citizens.[60] To some extent, it is this self-critical analysis that explains the politicians' attempts in connection with the pension reform to avoid or influence the processes through which public decisions normally acquire democratic legitimacy in the Swedish political culture: general elections, debates, the circulation of government proposals to relevant bodies, committee deliberations etc.[61]

This in turn brings to the fore another type of criticism that is often levelled at parliamentarism, namely that it leads to *government by politicians* and not *rule*

57 Ran Hirschl, *Towards Juristocracy. The Origins and Consequenses of the New Constitutionalism*, (Cambridge, 2004).

58 For arguments in favour of a constitutionalisation of the Swedish political system, see Olof Petersson ea., *Demokratins grundlag. Demokratirådets rapport 2004*, (Stockholm, 2004); Niclas Berggren, Nils Karlson & Joakim Nergelius (eds.), *Makt utan motvikt. Om demokrati och konstitutionalism*, (Stockholm, 1999).

59 Assar Lindbeck ea., *Ekonomirådets rapport 2000. Politisk makt med oklart ansvar*, (Stockholm, 2000).

60 Richard D. Parker, *Here, the People Rule*, (Cambridge, 1994).

61 Sarah M. Brooks & Kent R. Weaver, 'Lashed to the Mast? The Politics of NDC Pension Reform', Robert Holzmann & Edward Palmer (eds.), *Pension Reform. Issues and Prospects for non-financial defined contribution (NDC) schemes*, (Washington DC, 2006).

by the people. This objection, too, is rooted in a constitutional mindset and draws attention to the perils of concentrating all public power in one and the same institution and in a limited group of powerholders. In this connection, it makes no difference that the powerholders in a parliamentary democracy are many and that they are in possession of a popular mandate. Rather, this is a part of the problem.[62] In contrast to the tyrant who rules his hereditary kingdom by divine right, and for whom the people represent something specific that he or she can rule *over*, there is a very real danger that the members of the popularly elected Riksdag are beginning to imagine that they literally *are* the people – a case of what might be termed 'misunderstood' or 'misplaced' representation.[63] 'The concentration of [all power] in the same hands', in the words of Thomas Jefferson, 'is precisely the definition of despotic government.' He adds:

> It will be no alleviation that these powers will be exercised by a plurality of hands, and not by a single one. One hundred and seventy three despots would surely be as oppressive as one [...]. As little will it avail us that they are chosen by ourselves. An *elective despotism* was not the government we fought for [...].[64]

Inherent in parliamentarism, as Jefferson describes it, is the dangerous belief that by gathering together a few hundred people to represent the nation, we imagine we can emulate the direct democracy of antique times.[65] But this is an illusion, which is why he argues that power without a counterweight can be harmful.

What does all this have to do with the Swedish pension reform of the 1990s? At first glance, it would appear to invalidate the constitutionalists' critique rather than support it. What we meet in the present case is a set of parliamentarians who sought to avoid being confronted by short-term opinions, who actively tried to overcome political and social conflicts for the purpose of pushing through, at a critical moment, a controversial reform that was rooted in a rational analysis of society. At the same time, it is precisely this readiness to accommodate the constitutionalists in their critique that betokens the democratic deficit. Instead of a

62 Scott Gordon, *Controlling the State. Constitutionalism from Ancient Athens to today*, (Cambridge, 1999).

63 Bruce Ackerman, *We the People. Foundations*, (Cambridge, 1991).

64 *The Federalist Papers [1788]*, no. 48, (London, 1987), *p. 310. Madison quoting Jefferson.*

65 We don't have to step over the Atlantic in order to find eloquent explications about the vices of parliamentary absolutism. In the Swedish tradition, the so-called Age of Liberty (1719-1772), an early experiment in parliamentarism, used to be described in this light: a period which illustrated that 'also the dictatorship of parliaments is something evil', Rudolf Kjellén, *Om den svenska grundlagens anda. Rättspsykologisk undersökning*, (Göteborg, 1897), p. 25.

constitutional democracy – sceptical towards popular sovereignty, majority rule and the concentration of power – the politicians create a space for themselves that is not constitutionally regulated where they assume the right to act outside the well-trodden paths to popular legitimacy that democratic infrastructures provide them with.

The question we have to ask ourselves, then, is whose interests are served by the absence of veto points in the Swedish political system. By way of example we might consider the distinctive role of the Supreme Court in the US system – an almost emblematic veto point. From a parliamentary viewpoint it appears deeply undemocratic, marred by what is commonly referred to as 'the countermajoritarian difficulty'.[66] How can nine judges have the right to set aside the popular will as expressed in the decisions of popularly elected assemblies? The answer is that the court – within the bounds set by the constitution – acts as a defender of the people against elected politicians who misunderstand or abuse their positions. In the United States, too, all public power proceeds from the people. The difference is simply that there it is much harder to assume the role of their mouthpiece.[67]

Another point in favour of the US system is the fact that those reforms principle importance which are nevertheless adopted are more robust and possess greater legitimacy. US politics may be a quagmire but where matters of fundamental importance are concerned it is impossible to make decisions in secret. The most entrenched political cartels possessing rational solutions to crucial problems are forced into the light sooner or later. There they have to account for their actions not only to suspicious voters but also to powerful interests and skilled lawyers.[68] On the negative side, as parliamentarians are quick to point out, this makes it difficult to achieve anything at all.[69] Crucial reforms fail to materialise, and much-needed reforms of existing systems never come about.[70] Consequently, the national pension scheme in the US is still facing considerable financial problems and there are no lasting solutions in sight.[71]

---

66 Alexander Bickel, *The Least Dangerous Branch*, (Indianapolis, 1962).

67 Ackerman, Bruce, *We the People. Foundations*, (Cambridge, 1991).

68 Op. Cit.

69 Ian Shapiro, *The State of Democratic Theory*, (Princeton & New York, 2003), pp. 109-110.

70 Michael B. Katz, *The Price of Citizenship. Redefining the American Welfare State*, (New York, 2001); Daniel Lazare, *The Frozen Republic. How the Constitution is Paralyzing Democracy*, (New York, 1996).

71 Leslie Pal & R. Kent Weaver (eds.), *The Government Taketh Away. The Politics of Pain in the United States and Canada*, (Washington DC, 2003).

A democracy worthy of the name

The pension reform of the 1990s raises a number of questions about the way democracy works in modern Sweden. One of the prime ambiguities is its many favourable aspects – the fact that it has succeeded and has elicited international admiration, and that it has thereby established a model for the continuing reform of the public sector.[72] In other words, there is reason to believe that the parties will exploit the absence of veto points in the Swedish Constitution in the future as well, and that new cartels will be established for important policy areas. This in turn will create mounting discord between the political foreground noise and background noise, between the ritual references to the absolute power of the people and the parties' concrete attempts to deal with the double pressure of globalisation and demography outside the customary infrastructures of democracy.

As the case of the pension reform shows, there is a very real danger that democracy will fall by the wayside when the politicians are faced with genuinely important matters. The national pension scheme, remember, is both the largest and the costliest part of the Swedish welfare system. It is also a long-term project that transcends generational barriers. The parliamentary decision taken in 1994 applies not only to the generations active today but to an even greater extent to coming generations and to those still unborn.[73] In this respect, the pension reform bears out the time-honoured critique levelled by parliamentarism to the effect that democracy can easily and imperceptibly metamorphose into party rule or government by politicians. An important explanation for this is the fundamental lack of veto points in Swedish politics. Their *democratic* function in a political system is quite simply that they stop politicians from misinterpreting their popular mandates. A parliamentary seat is not necessarily the same thing as authorisation from the people to remodel key principles.

According to the US professor of law and political science Bruce Ackerman, any democratic decision-making process worth the name must go through four distinct phases. Firstly, a *signalling phase* in which a movement earns the authority to claim that its reform proposals deserve a central place in the public debate on the direction society is to take. Secondly, the *proposal phase* in which the political system urges the movement in question to be specific in its rhetoric and to propose a number of achievable and sustainable reforms. Thirdly, the *popular deliberation phase* in which the reform proposals are considered and reviewed

---

72 See for example the final report from the Social insurance committee, SOU, *Mera försäkring och mera arbete*, (2006:86), in which the pension reform is presented as a role model for the continuing reform of the social insurance systems.

73 Thomas Lindh & Urban Lundberg, 'Predicaments in the futures of ageing democracies', *Futures*, 40 (2008).

time and again by the formal political institutions. This phase may very well prove a disappointment to many activists. Their initial success during the signalling phase may, for instance, result in a backlash in which a previously silent majority organises its defence of the traditional order. If, however, the reform survives this careful scrutiny with its popular support intact, the decision-making process enters a final phase, that of *legal codification*. In this phase, the earlier proposals are translated into concrete legal wording. Clear principles are established that will guide practical policies in the years to come.[74]

Not until it has passed through these four phases, says Ackerman, can a reform be described as democratically approved and endorsed, as something that represents the true will of the people. Göran Persson would not have to have any qualms about what future pensioners might say. On the contrary, the pension statements dispatched annually to all Swedish wage-earners would reflect awareness among both committed voters and responsible politicians that public action has its limitations, and would also constitute a response to the need for solidarity between generations in an era of ageing populations and growing dependence on the outside world.

As may now be evident, the new national pension scheme in Sweden did not come about in this way. It was not carried along by a movement. The warnings sounded by the experts were never heard outside the corridors of the Riksdag and the Government Offices. The reform was never a subject of open discussion or in-depth analysis. The negotiations took place behind closed doors. The 'silent majority' never had a chance to organise its defence of the old order. Codification took the form of decrees from on high rather than of transparent agreements. As a result, confusion continues to reign among both citizens and politicians as to what the guiding principles will be in future political reforms.[75]

Also, it is far from clear whether the Swedish pension reform would have survived Ackerman's democratic embrace. We will never know. The parties dared not put it to the test. Instead of recognising the opportunities afforded by parliamentarism, they sought to constrain and restrict them. Thus the status of the new pension scheme is patently unclear. This applies both to its democratic legitimacy and to its long-term significance for income distribution in society, to pensioners' living standards and to social security in general. And who knows, perhaps another model for future pensions would have stood a better chance of success. A model that was naturally no worse than this one, that was put in place after thor-

74 Bruce Ackerman, *We the People. Foundations*, (Cambridge, 1991).

75 Claes Belfrage, 'Den villige, den tveksamme, den hopplöse. En svensk massinvesteringskultur?', Urban Lundberg (ed.), *Mellan folkbildning och fondrådgivning. Nya perspektiv på pensionssystemet*, (Stockholm, 2007).

ough institutional consideration and an open battle for citizen support, that had paid due attention both to the experts' 'insider wisdom' and analyses of ageing and globalisation. And most importantly, a model that rested on the well-founded approval of the people.

Bibliography

Ackerman, Bruce, *We the People. Foundations*, (Cambridge, 1991)

Adema, Willem & Ladaique, Maxime, 'Net Social Expenditure, 2005 Edition', *OECD Social, Employment and Migration Working Papers*, 29 (Paris, 2005)

Andersen, Torben M., 'Increasing longevity and social security reforms', *Journal of Public Economics* (2007)

Andersen, Torben. M, 'Ageing and globalisation in the Scandinavian welfare model', *Ageing Horizons*, 4 (6th November, 2006)

Andersen, Torben. M, *Social security and longevity,* Working Paper, (Aarhus, 2006)

Anderson, Karen M., 'The Europeanization of Pension Arrangements: Convergence or Divergence?' Caroline de la Porte & Philippe Pochet (eds.), *Building Social Europe through the Open Method of Co-ordination*, (Brussels, 2002)

Anderson, Karen M. & Immergut, Ellen, 'Sweden: After Social Democratic Hegemony', Karen M. Anderson, Ellen Immergut & Isabelle Schulze (eds.), *Handbook of West European Pension Politics*, (Oxford, 2007)

Anderson, Karen & Meyer, Traute, 'The Third Way in Welfare State Reform? Social Democratic Pension Politics in Germany and Sweden', Guiliano Bonoli & Martin Powell (eds.), *Social Democratic Party Policies in Contemporary Europe*, (London, 2004)

Auerbach, Walter, ''Modell' eines Sozialplanes – Eine Skizze', *Die Krankenversicherung*, 4 (1952)

Augusztinovics, Mária, 'Mit reformáljon a nyugdíjreform?', *Népszabadság*, (16th September, 2006)

Augusztinovics, Mária (ed.), *Körkép reform után. Tanulmányok a nyugdíjrendszerről*, (Budapest, 2000)

Augusztinovics, Mária & Köllő, János, 'Munkapiaci pálya és nyugdíj, 1970-2020', *Közgazdasági Szemle*, LIV (2007)

Augusztinovics, Mária ea., *The Hungarian Pension System Before and After the 1998 Reform. Strengthening Social Security in Central and Eastern Europe through Research and Technical Cooperation*, RER/OO/MO/FRA, (Budapest, 2001)

Augusztinovics, Mária, Mit reformáljon a nyugdíjreform? [What should be reformed by the pension-reform?] *Népszabadság*, (undated)

Aylott, Nicholas, 'After the Divorce. Intra-Party Power and Organisational Change in Swedish Social Democracy, *Working Paper/Keele European Parties Research Unit*, 1 (2001)

Baldwin, Peter, *The Politics of Social Solidarity. Class Bases of the European Welfare State 1870-1970*, (Cambridge, 1990)

Belfrage, Claes, 'Den villige, den tveksamme, den hopplöse. En svensk massinvesteringskultur?', Urban Lundberg (ed.), *Mellan folkbildning och fondrådgivning. Nya perspektiv på pensionssystemet*, (Stockholm, 2007)

Bennett, Colin J., 'Review Article: What Is Policy Convergence and What Causes It?', *British Journal of Political Science*, 21 (1991)

Berggren, Niclas, Karlson, Nils & Nergelius, Joakim (eds.), *Makt utan motvikt. Om demokrati och konstitutionalism*, (Stockholm, 1999)

Bergström, Hans *Rivstart? Från opposition till regering*, (Stockholm, 1987)

Betænkning om almindelig folkepension afgivet af folkepensionskommissionen af 1961, Betænkning nr. 324, (København, 1963)

Betænkning om Folkepension, Betænkning nr. 123, (København, 1955)

Beveridge, William, *Social Insurance and Allied Services, Report by Sir William Beveridge*, (London, 1942)

Bickel, Alexander, *The Least Dangerous Branch*, (Indianapolis, 1962)

Blake, David, 'Contracting Out of the State Pension System: The British Experience of Carrots and Sticks', Martin Rein & Winfried Schmähl (eds.), *Rethinking the Welfare State: The Political Economy of Pension Reform*, (Cheltenham, 2004)

Bonoli, Giuliano, 'The Two Worlds of Pension Reform in Western Europe', *Comparative Politics*, 35, (2003)

Bonoli, Guiliano, 'Political Institutions, Veto Points and the Process of Welfare State Adaptation', Paul Pierson (ed.), *The New Politics of the Welfare State*, (New York, 2001)

Bonoli, Guiliano, *The Politics of Pension Reform. Institutions and Policy Change in Western Europe*, (Cambridge, 2000)

Bonoli, Guiliano, George, Vic & Taylor-Gooby, Peter, *European Welfare State Futures. Towards a Theory of Retrenchment*, (Cambridge, 2000)

Brennan, Geoffrey & Buchanan, James M., *The power to tax*, (Cambridge, 1980)

Bridgen, Paul & Meyer, Traute, 'When Do Benevolent Capitalists Change Their Mind? Explaining the Retrenchment of Defined-benefit Pensions in Britain', *Social Policy and Administration*, 39 (2005)

Brittan, Samuel, 'The economic contradictions of democracy', *British Journal of Politcal Science*, 5:2 (1975)

Brooks, Sarah M. & Weaver, R. Kent, 'Lashed to the Mast? The Politics of NDC Pension Reform', Robert Holzmann & Edward Palmer (eds.), *Pension Re-*

form. Issues and Prospects for non-financial defined contribution (NDC) schemes, (Washington DC, 2006)
Browning, Edgar K., 'Why the social insurance budget is too large in a democracy', *Economic Inquiry*, 13 (1975)
Brussig, Martin, *Vier von zehn Zugängen in Altersrente erfolgen mit Abschlägen*, Altersübergangs-Report, (January 2007).
Bundesregierung, 'Nationaler Strategiebericht Alterssicherung 2005', *Deutscher Bundestag*, Drucksache 15/5571, (Berlin v. 27.05. 2005)
Bönker, Frank, 'Changing Ideas on Pensions: Accounting for Differences in the Spread of the Multipillar Paradigm in Five EU Social Insurance Countries', Peter Taylor-Gooby (ed.), *Ideas and Welfare State Reform in Western Europe*, (Houndmills, Basigstoke, 2005)
Börsch-Supan, Axel, 'From traditional DB to notional DC systems: The Pension Reform Process in Sweden, Italy and Germany', *Journal of the European Economic Association*, 2-3 (2005)
Börsch-Supan, Axel & Wilke, Christina, 'The German Public Pension System: How It Will Become an NDC System Look-Alike', Robert Holzmann & Edward Palmer (eds.), *Pension Reform: Issues and Prospects for Non-Financial Defined Contribution (NDC) Schemes*, (Washington, D.C., 2005)
Castles, Francis, *The future of the welfare state. Crisis myths and crisis realities*, (Oxford, 2004)
Chand, Sheetal K. & Jaeger, Albert, 'Reform Options for Pay-as-you-go Public Pension Systems, World Bank, Social Protection', *Discussion Paper no. 9927*, (Washington, D.C, 1999)
Chong, Dennis, 'Creating common frames of reference on political issues', Diana C. Mutz, Paul M. Sniderman & Richard A. Brody (eds.): *Political persuasion and attitude change*, (Ann Arbor, 1996)
Christensen, Jacob, *Socialpolitiske strategier 1945-1972*, (Odense, 1998)
Christiansen, Niels Finn & Petersen, Klaus, 'The Dynamics of Social Solidarity. The Danish Welfare State 1900-2000', *Scandinavian Journal of History*, 26:3 (2001)
Cichon, Michael, 'Notional Defined Contribution Schemes. Old Wine in New Bottles?', *International Social Security Review*, 4 (1999)
Clark, Gordon, 'The UK Occupational pension System in Crisis' , H. Pemberton, P. Thane & N.Whiteside (eds.), *Britain's Pensions Crisis. History and Policy*, (Oxford, 2006)
Converse, Philip E., 'Public opinion and voting behavior', Greenstein, Fred I. & Polsby, Nelson W. (eds.): *Handbook of Political Science vol 4: Nongovernemental politics*, (Reading-Massachusetts, 1975)
Dahl, Robert A., *Democracy and its Critics*, (New Haven, 1989)

De Nederlandsche Bank, 'Dutch Pension Sector: Sustainability Under Pressure', *Quarterly Bulletin*, (December, 2004)
deMayo, T. 'Social desirability and survey measurement. A review', Charles F. Turner & Elizabeth Martin (eds.): *Surveying subjective phenomena*, (New York, 1984)
de Swaan, Abram, *In Care of the State. Health Care, Education and Welfare in Europe and the USA in the Modern Era*, (Cambridge, 1988)
Dent, Kevin & Sloss, David, 'The global outlook for defined contribution and defined benefit plans', *Benefits Quarterly*, 23 (1996)
Department for Work and Pensions, *Security in Retirement: Towards a New Pensions System*, Cm 6841, (Norwich, 2006)
Department for Work and Pensions, *Personal Accounts: A New Way to Save*, (Norwich, 2006)
Department for Work and Pensions, *Simplicity, Security and Choice: Informed Choices for Working and Saving*, Cm 6111, (London, 2004)
Department of Social and Family Affairs, *Green Paper on Pensions*, (Dublin, 2007)
Deutsche Bundesbank, 'Gesetzliche Rentenversicherung', *Monatsberichte der Deutschen Bundesbank 19*, 8 (1967)
Dich, Jørgen, 'Udviklingen af skatte og tilskudspolitikken siden 1939', *Økonomi og Politik* (1965)
Downs, Anthony, *An Economic Theory of Democracy*, (New York, 1957)
DREAM, *Befolkningsprognose*, (København, 2006)
DREAM, *Langsigtet økonomisk fremskrivning 2006 – med vurdering af velfærdsreform*, (København, 2006)
Duverger, Maurice, *Political Parties. Their Organization and Acitivity in the Modern State*, (London, 1964)
Eckardt, Martina, 'The Open Method of Coordination on Pensions: An Economic Analysis of Its Effects on Pension Reforms', *Journal of European Social Policy*, 15 (2005)
Elmbrant, Björn, *Dansen kring guldkalven. Så förändrades Sverige av börsbubblan*, (Stockholm, 2005)
Elster, Jon, *Ulysses and the Sirens. Studies in Rationality and Irrationality*, (Cambridge, 1979)
Engels, Wolfram ea., *Reform der Alterssicherung*, (Bad Homburg, 1987)
Erlander, Tage, *1955-1960*, (Stockholm, 1976)
Eschtruth, Andrew D. & Gemus, Jonathan, 'Are Older Workers Responding to the Bear Market?', *Just the Facts on Retirement Issues*, 5 (September, 2002)
Esping-Andersen, Gøsta, *The Three Worlds of Welfare Capitalism*, (Princeton, 1990)

Esping-Andersen, Gøsta, *Politics against Markets. The Social Democratic Road to Power*, (Princeton, 1985)
European Commission (Social Protection Committee), *Promoting Longer Working Lives Through Pension Reforms. First Part: Flexibility in Retirement Age Provision*, (Brussels, 2007)
European Commission, *Adequate and Sustainable Pensions: Synthesis Report 2006*, (Luxembourg, 2006)
Eurostat, *Social protection expenditure and receipts. Data 1980-1997*, (1999)
Fehr, Hans & Jokisch, Sabine, 'Demographischer Wandel und internationale Finanzmärkte', *Perspektiven der Wirtschaftspolitik* 7 (2006)
Feldman, David, *Englishmen and Jews: Social Relations and Political Culture, 1840-1914*, (New Haven, 1994)
Ferge, Zsuzsa, 'Is there a specific East Central European welfare culture?', Wim van Oorschot, Michael Opielka & Birgit Pfau-Effinger (eds.), *Culture and Welfare State, Values of Social Policy from a Comparative Perspective*, (Cheltenham,Camberley & Northampton, 2007)
Ferge, Zsuzsa, 'The Politics of the Hungarian Pension Reform', Müller, K., Ryll, A. & Wagener, J. (eds.), *Transformation of Social Security: Pensions in Central-Eastern Europe*, (Heidelberg, New York, 1999)
Ferge, Zsuzsa, *Fejezetek a magyar szegénypolitika történetéből*, (Budapest, 1986)
Ferrera, Maurizio & Gualmini, Elisabetta, 'Reforms Guided by Consensus: The Welfare State in the Italian Transition', *West European Politics*, 23 (2000)
Flodén, Martin, 'Public saving and policy coordination in aging economies', *Scandinavian Journal of Economics*, 105 (2003)
Flood, Lennart, 'Vilka pensioner får framtidens pensionärer?', *Ekonomisk debatt*, 3 (2004)
Flora, Peter & Jens Alber, 'Modernization, Democratization, and the Development of Welfare States in Western Europe', Peter Flora & Arnold J. Heidenheimer (eds.), *The Development of Welfare States in Europe and America*, (New Brunswick, 1981)
Flora, Peter & Heidenheimer, Arnold J. (Eds.), *The Development of Welfare States in Europe and America*, (New Brunswick, 1981)
Fong, Monika & Paull, Gillian, *Women's Economic Status in the Restructuring of Eastern Europe. Democratic Reform and the Position of Women in Transitional Economies*, (Oxford, 1993)
Frederiksen, Dennis, Heide, Kim M., Holmøy, Erling & Solli, Ingeborg F., *Makroøkonomiske virkninger av pensjonsreformer – Beregninger baseret på forslag fra Pensjonskommisjonen, Working Papers Statistics Norway*, (Oslo, 2005)

Galasso, Vincenzo & Profeta, Paola, 'The political economy of social security: a survey', *European Journal of Political Economy*, 18 (2002).
George, Vic; Stathopoulos, Peter & Garces, Jorge, 'Squaring the welfare circle and government ideology: Greece and Spain in the 1990s', *International Social Security Review*, 52:4 (1999)
Gidlund, Gullan & Möller, Tommy, *Demokratins trotjänare*, (Stockholm, 1999)
Gilbert, Neil, *Transformation of the welfare state*, (Oxford, 2002)
Gillion, Colin, *Social security pensions. Development and reform*, (Geneva, 2000)
Ginn, Jay; Fachinger, Uwe & Schmähl, Winfried, 'Pension reform and the socio-economic status of older people', Naegele, Gerhard & Walker, Alan (eds.), *Ageing and Social Policy for Seniors in Germany and in the United Kingdom – a Comparative Overview of Policy Approaches and Research Perspectives*, (London, in print)
Ginn, Jay,'Gender Inequalities: Sidelines in British Pension Policy', Hugh Pemberton, Pat Thane & Noel Whiteside (eds.), *Britain's Pensions Crisis. History and Policy*, (Oxford, 2006)
Gjedrem, Svein E., *Økonomiske perspektiver. Foredrag på Norges Banks representantskapsmøte 17 februar*, (Oslo, 2005)
Gordon, Scott, *Controlling the State. Constitutionalism from Ancient Athens to today*, (Cambridge, 1999)
Green-Pedersen, Christoffer, *The Politics of Justification. Party Competition and Welfare State Retrenchment in Denmark and the Netherlands from 1982 to 1998*, (Amsterdam, 2002)
Greve, Bent, 'Indications of Social Policy Convergence in Europe', *Social Policy and Administration*, 30 (1996)
Gutowski, Armin & Merklein, Renate, 'Arbeit und Soziales im Rahmen einer marktwirtschaftlichen Ordnung', *Hamburger Jahrbuch für Wirtschafts- und Gesellschaftspolitik*, 30 (1985)
Hall, Peter A., 'Policy Paradigms, Social Learning, and the State: The Case of Economic Policymaking in Britain', *Comparative Politics*, 25 (1993)
Haney, Lynne, *Inventing the Needy: Gender and the Politics of Welfare in Hungary*, (Berkley, 2002)
Hannah, Leslie, *Inventing Retirement. The Development of Occupational Pensions in Britain*, (Cambridge, 1986)
Harris, Jose, *William Beveridge*, (Oxford, 1997)
Haverland, Markus, 'When the Welfare State Meets the Regulatory State: EU Occupational Pension Policy', *Journal of European Public Policy*, 14 (2007)
Heclo, Hugh, *Modern Social Politics in Britain and Sweden. From Relief to Income Maintenance*, (New Haven & London, 1974)

Heidar, Knut & Saglie, Jo, 'Predestined Parties? Organizational Change in Norwegian Political Parties', *Party Politics*, 2 (2003)
Hennock, E.P., *The Origins of the Welfare State in England and Germany, 1850-1914*, (Cambridge, 2007)
Hermansson, Jörgen ea., *Avkorporativisering och lobbyism*, (Stockholm, 1999)
Hinrichs, Karl, 'Enlarging Freedom of Choice: Pension Reforms in the Nordic Countries and Germany', Björn Hvinden & Håkon Johansson (eds.), *Citizenship in Nordic Welfare States: Dynamics of Choice, Duties and Participation in a Changing Europe*, (London/New York, 2007)
Hinrichs, Karl, 'New Century – New Paradigm: Pension Reforms in Germany' Giuliano Bonoli and Toshimitsu Shinkawa (eds.), *Ageing and Pension Reform Around the World*, (Cheltenham, 2005)
Hinrichs, Karl, 'Active Citizens and Retirement Planning: Enlarging Freedom of Choice in the Course of Pension Reforms in Nordic Countries and Germany', *ZeS-Arbeitspapier* 11 (Bremen, 2004)
Hinrichs, Karl, 'Alterssicherungspolitik in Deutschland: Zwischen Kontinuität und Paradigmenwechsel', Jürgen Beyer and Petra Stykow (eds.), *Gesellschaft mit beschränkter Hoffnung. Reformfähigkeit und die Möglichkeit rationaler Politik*, (Wiesbaden, 2004)
Hinrichs, Karl, 'Elephants on the Move. Patterns of Public Pension Reform in OECD-Countries', Stephan Liebfried (ed.), *Welfare State Futures*, (Cambridge, 2001)
Hinrichs, Karl, 'Elephants on the Move: Patterns of Public Pension Reform in OECD Countries', *European Review*, 8 (2000)
Hinrichs, Karl & Aleksandrowicz, Paula, 'Reforming European Pension Systems for Active Ageing', *International Social Science Journal*, 190 (2008)
Hinrichs, Karl & Kangas, Olli, 'When Is a Change Big Enough to Be a System Shift? Small System-Shifting Changes in German and Finnish Pension Policies', *Social Policy and Administration*, 37 (2003)
Hirschl, Ran, *Towards Juristocracy. The Origins and Consequenses of the New Constitutionalism*, (Cambridge, 2004)
Hirschman, Albert O., *Exit, voice, and loyalty. Responses to Decline in Firms, Organizations and States*, (Cambridge, 1970)
Hockerts, Hans Günther, 'Die Rentenversicherung 1957', Ruland, Franz (ed.), *Handbuch der gesetzlichen Rentenversicherung*, (Neuwied, 1990)
Hockerts, Hans Günther, 'Sicherung im Alter: Kontinuität und Wandel der gesetzlichen Rentenversicherung 1889-1979', Conze, Werner & Lepsius, Reiner (eds.), *Sozialgeschichte der Bundesrepublik*, (Stuttgart, 1982)

Hockerts, Hans Günther, *Sozialpolitische Entscheidungen im Nachkriegs-Deutschland – Alliierte und deutsche Sozialversicherungspolitik 1945-1957*, (Stuttgart, 1980)

Holmberg, Erik & Stjernquist, Nils, *Vår författning*, 12th edn., (Stockholm, 2000)

Holzinger, Katharina & Knill, Christoph, 'Causes and Conditions of Cross-National Policy Convergence', *Journal of European Public Policy*, 12, (2005)

Huber, Evelyne & Stephens, John D., *Development and Crisis of the Welfare States. Parties and Policies in Global Markets*, (Chicago, 2001)

IMF, *Global Financial Stability Report: Market Developments and Issues. April 2005*, (Washington, 2005)

IMF, *World Economic Outlook – The Global Demographic Transition*, (Washington, 2004)

Immergut, Ellen, *Health Politics. Interests and Institutions in Western Europe*, (Cambridge, 1992)

Inglot, Tomasz, *'Emergency' Welfare States in East Central Europe, 1919-1999: A Comparative-Historical Analysis*. Paper presented at the ESPAnet Conference, (Vienna, Austria, 20-22 September 2007)

International Monetary Fund, *Global Financial Stability Report: Market Developments and Issues. April 2005*, (Washington, D.C., 2005)

Iyengar, Shanto, 'Framing responsibility for political issues: The case of poverty', *Political Behaviour*, 22:1 (1990)

Janos, Andrew C. & Slottman, William (eds.), *Revolution in perspective : essays on the Hungarian Soviet Republic of 1919*, (Berkeley, California, 1971)

Jespersen, Knud J.V., *A History of Denmark*, (Basingstoke, 2004)

Johnson, Kazuko Fukasawa, *Voluntary provision for old age by trade unions in Britain before the coming of the welfare state*, (unpublished PhD thesis, University of London, 1996)

Johnson, Paul, *Saving and Spending. The Working-Class Economy in Britain, 1870-1939*, (Oxford, 1985)

Jonung, Lars, *Med backspegeln som kompass. Stabiliseringspolitiken som läroprocess*, (Stockholm, 1999)

Jurth, Rudolf, 'A társadalombiztosítási ellátások alakulása 1950-1982 között', *Szociálpolitkai Értesítő*, (Budapest, 1987)

Jørgensen, Jørgen, *Jørgen Jørgensens Erindringer*, (København, 1970)

Katz, Michael B., *The Price of Citizenship. Redefining the American Welfare State*, (New York, 2001)

Katz, Richard S. & Mair, Peter, 'Changing Models of Party Organisation and Party Democracy. The Emergence of the Cartel Party', *Party Politics*, 1 (1995)

Kaufmann, Franz-Xaver, *Sozialpolitik und Sozialstaat. Soziologische Analysen*, (Opladen, 2002)
Kitschelt, Herbert, 'Citizens, Politicians, and Party Cartellization. Political Representation and State Failure in Post-Industrial Democracies', *European Journal of Political Research*, 2 (2000)
Kjellén, Rudolf, *Om den svenska grundlagens anda. Rättspsykologisk undersökning*, (Göteborg, 1897)
Klein, Rudolf and Millar, Jane,'Do-It-Yourself Social Policy', *Social Policy and Administration*, 29 (1995)
Klein, Viola, *Britain's Married Women Workers*, (London, 1965)
Knill, Christoph, 'Introduction: Cross-National Policy Convergence: Concepts, Approaches and Explanatory Factors', *Journal of European Public Policy*, 12 (2005)
Kolstrup, Søren, *Velfærdsstatens rødder. Fra kommunesocialisme til folkepension*, (København, 1996)
Korpi, Walter, *The Democratic Class Struggle*, (London, 1983)
Kovrig, Béla, Frisch, Ferenc & Dréhr Imre, *Öregségi és rokkantsági biztosítás. A Lex Vass II. előkészítése*, (Budapest, 1928)
Krug, Leopold, *Die Armenassekuranz, das einzige Mittel zur Verbannung der Armuth aus unserer Kommune*, (Berlin, 1810)
Krupp, Hans-Jürgen, 'Ein Vorschlag zur voll eigenständigen Sicherung der Frau', Krupp, Hans-Jürgen ea. (eds.), *Alternativen der Rentenreform '84*, (Frankfurt & New York, 1980)
Krupp, Hans-Jürgen & Weeber, Joachim, 'Volkswirtschaftliche Aspekte eines Grundrentensystems', Opielka, Michael (ed.), *Grundrente in Deutschland*, (Wiesbaden, 2004)
Kuhnle, Stein, 'The Scandinavian Welfare State in the 1990s. Challenged but Viable', *West European Politics*, 2, (2000)
Kuklinski, James H. & Hurley, Norman L., 'It's all a matter of interpretation', Diana C. Mutz, Paul M. Sniderman & Richard A. Brody (eds.), *Political persuasion and attitude change*, (Ann Arbor, 1996)
Lagerroth, Fredrik, *Frihetstidens författning*, (Stockholm, 1915)
Larsson, Sven-Erik, *Regera i koalition. Den borgerliga trepartiregeringen 1976-1978*, (Stockholm, 1986)
Lazare, Daniel, *The Frozen Republic. How the Constitution is Paralyzing Democracy*, (New York, 1996)
Lewis, Jane, *The End of Marriage?*, (Cheltenham 2001)
Lindbeck, Assar ea., *Ekonomirådets rapport 2000. Politisk makt med oklart ansvar*, (Stockholm, 2000)

Lindh, Thomas, 'Offentlig sektor och åldersfördelningen', Bo Malmberg & Lena Sommestad (eds.), *Befolkning och välfärd. Perspektiv på framtidens välfärdspolitik*, (Stockholm, 2002)
Lindh, Thomas & Lundberg, Urban, 'Predicaments in the futures of ageing democracies', *Futures*, 40 (2008)
Lindh, Thomas & Malmberg, Bo, *40-talisternas uttåg. En ESO-rapport om 2000-talets demografiska utmaningar*, (Stockholm, 2000)
Lowe, Rodney, *The Welfare State in Britain since 1945*, (London, 2004)
Lundberg, Urban, 'Social Democracy Lost. The Social Democratic Party in Sweden and the Politics of Pension Reform, 1978-1998', Eero Carroll & Lena Eriksson (eds.), *Welfare Politics Cross-Examined. Eclecticist Analytical Perspectives on Sweden and the Developed Countries*, (Amsterdam, 2005)
Lundberg, Urban, *Juvelen i kronan. Socialdemokraterna och den allmänna pensionen*, (Stockholm, 2003)
Lundberg, Urban, 'Socialdemokratin och 1990-talets pensionsreform', Joakim Palme (ed.), *Hur blev den stora kompromissen möjlig?*, (Stockholm, 2001)
Lundberg, Urban & Tydén, Mattias, 'State versus Individual: Dimensions of Individual Rights and Citizenship in Sweden', Joakim Palme & Torbjörn Lundqvist eds, *New Perspectives on the History and Future of the Swedish Model*, (forthcoming)
Långtidsutredningen, *Alternativ finansiering av offentliga tjänster*, Apendix 7, (2003)
Långtidsutredningen, *En åldrande befolkning och konsekvenserna för svensk ekonomi,* Apendix 9, (1999/2000)
Mandin, Christelle & Palier, Bruno , 'The Politics of Pension Reform in France: The End of Exceptionalism?' Giuliano Bonoli & Toshimitsu Shinkawa (eds.), *Ageing and Pension Reform Around the World*, (Cheltenham, 2005)
Marshall, Thomas Humphrey, 'Class, Citizenship and Social Development', *Essays by T.H.Marshall,* (Chicago, London, 1964)
Marshall, Thomas Humphrey, *Citizenship and social class*, (Cambridge, 1950)
Meißner, Matthias, 'Familienarbeit in der Alterssicherung in Europa', *Deutsche Rentenversicherung* 61 (2006)
Mesa-Lago, Carmelo & Müller, Katharina, 'The politics of pension reform in Latin America', *Journal of Latin American Studies*, 34 (2002)
Mitchell, Brian R. & Deane, Phyllis, *Abstract of British Historical Statistics,* (Cambridge, 1962)
Mieck, Ilja, 'Zielsetzung und Ertrag der preußischen Reformen', Schlenker, Manfred (ed.), *Preußen – Beiträge zu einer politischen Kultur*, (Reinbek bei Hamburg, 1981)

Miegel, Meinhard, *Sicherheit im Alter – Plädoyer für die Weiterentwicklung des Rentensystems*, (Stuttgart, 1981)
Miegel, Meinhard & Wahl, Stefanie, *Gesetzliche Grundsicherung. Private Vorsorge – der Weg aus der Rentenkrise*, (Stuttgart, 1985)
Mihelics, Vid, *A Beveridge Terv*, (Budapest, 1943)
Mischnick, Wolfgang, 'Gedanken zur Neugestaltung der Alterssicherung', *Betriebliche Altersversorgung*, 18 (1963)
Molin, Björn, *Tjänstepensionsfrågan. En studie i svensk partipolitik*, (Göteborg, 1965)
Molin, Björn, *Tjänstepensionsfrågan. En studie i svensk partipolitik*, (Lund, 1967)
Mortensen Erik, *Social leksikon 2003-2004*, (København, 2004)
Moschonas, Gerassimos, *In the Name of Social Democracy. The Great Transformation, 1945 to the Present*, (London, 2002)
Mulligan, Casey B. and Sala-i-Martin, Xavier 'Political and Economic Forces Sustaining Social Security', *Advances in Economic Analysis & Policy*, 4:1, Article 5 (2004)
Müller, Katharina, 'A magyar nyugdíjreform politikai gazdaságtana,' Augusztinovics, Mária (ed.), *Körkép reform után. Tanulmányok a nyugdíjrendszerről*, (Budapest, 2000)
Müller, Katharina, *The Political Economy of Pension Reform in Central-Eastern Europe*, (Chetelham, Northampton, 1999)
Müller, Katharina, Ryll, Andreas & Wagener, Jürgen (eds.), *Transformaiton of Social Security: Pensions in Central-Eastern Europe*, (Heidelberg, New York, 1999)
Munnell, Alicia H., 'Employer-Sponsored Plans: The Shift from Defined Benefit to Defined Contribution', Gordon L. Clarke; Alicia H. Munnell & J. Michael Orszag (eds.), *Oxford Handbook of Pensions and Retirement Income*, (Oxford, 2006)
Munnell, Alicia H. & Sundén, Annika, '401(k) Plans Are Still Coming Up Short', *Issues in Brief*, 43 (March, 2006)
Møller, Poul, *Gennembrudsår. Dansk politik i 1950'erne*, (København, 1977)
Myles, John & Pierson, Paul, 'The Comparative Politics of Pension Reform', Paul Pierson (ed.), *The New Politics of the Welfare State*, (New York, 2001)
Natali, David, 'The Hybridisation of Pension System Within the Enlarged EU: Recent Reforms in Old and New Members', *Belgisch Tijdschrift voor Social Zekerheid*, 46 (2004)
Natali, David & Rhodes, Martin, 'The Berlusconi pension reform and the emerging 'double cleavage' in distributive politics', James L. Newell & Carlo Guarnieri (eds.), *Politica in Italia/Italian Politics*, (Berghahn, 2005)

National Strategic Report on Social Protection and Social Inclusion, (2006-2009)
Nielsen, Niels Jul, *Mellem storpolitik og værkstedsgulv. Den danske arbejder – før, under og efter den kolde krig*, (København, 2004)
Nilsson, Torbjörn, *Mellan arv och utopi. Moderata vägval under 100 år, 1904-2004*, (Stockholm, 2004)
OECD, *Reforms for an Ageing Society*, (Paris, 2000)
OECD, *Economic Surveys – Sweden*, (Paris, 2005)
OECD, *Improving Financial Literacy: Analysis of Issues and Policies*, (Paris, 2005)
OECD, *Solving the Pensions Puzzle*, OECD Policy Brief, (Paris, March 2005)
OECD, *Pensions at a Glance: Public Policies across OECD Countries*, (Paris, 2005)
OECD, *Pensions at a Glance: Public Policies Across OECD Countries. 2007 Edition* (Paris, 2007)
Opielka, Michael (ed.), *Grundrente in Deutschland*, (Wiesbaden, 2004)
Opielka, Michael & Vobruba, Georg (eds.), *Das garantierte Grundeinkommen. Entwicklung und Perspektiven einer Forderung*, (Frankfurt/Main, 1986)
Orbán, Gábor & Palotai, Dániel, 'Gazdaságpolitikai és demográfiai kihívások a magyar nyugdíjrendszerben', *Közgazdasági Szemle,* LIII, (2006)
Orenstein, Mitchell. *Political and Institutional Impacts on Pension Reform in the Transition Countries*, (Unpublished manuscript, 1998)
Ostrop, Paul, Eggers, Ernst & Köhler, Günter, 'Neugestaltung der Alterssicherung. Drei-Stufen-Plan zur Altersvorsorge und -versorgung', Friedrich-Naumann-Stiftung (eds.), *Schriftenreihe des Instituts für politische Planung und Kybernetik (IPK)*, (Bonn undated [1969])
Overbye Einar, 'The redistributional impact of a World Bank 'pension regime'', Clasen, Jochen (ed.), *What future for social security?*, (Hague, 2001)
Overbye Einar, 'Mainstream pattern, deviant cases: The New Zealand and Danish pension systems in an international context', *Journal of European Social Policy*, 7:2 (1997)
Overbye, Einar, 'Making a Case for the Rational, Self-Regarding, 'Ethical' Voter...and solving the Paradox of Not Voting in the process', *European Journal of Political Research*, 27:3 (1995)
Pacolet, Jozef & Coudron, Veronique, 'De staat van den verzorgingsstaat in Belgie omstreeks 2005', *Belgisch Tijdschrift voor Sociale Zekerheid*, 48 (2006)
Pal, Leslie & Weaver, R. Kent (eds.), *The Government Taketh Away. The Politics of Pain in the United States and Canada*, (Washington DC, 2003)
Palier, Bruno, 'Tracking the Evolution of a Single Instrument Can Reveal Profound Changes: The Case of Funded Pensions in France', *Governance*, 20 (2007)

Palme, Joakim, 'Pension Reform in Sweden and the Changing Boundaries between Public and Private', Gordon L. Clark & Noel Whiteside (eds.), *Pension Security in the 21st Century. Redrawing the Public-Private Debate*, (New York, 2003)

Palmer, Edward, 'The Swedish Pension Reform Model. Framework and Issues', *Social Protection Discussion Paper/World Bank*, 12 (2000)

Parker, Richard D., *'Here, the People Rule'*, (Cambridge, 1994)

Parliament of Sweden, *Swedish Parliamentary Publications. RD-series for the 1993-94 session*, 120 (Stockholm, 1993-94)

Pemberton, Hugh, 'Politics and Pensions in Post-War Britain', Hugh Pemberton, Pat Thane & Noel Whiteside (eds.), *Britain's Pensions Crisis. History and Policy,* (Oxford, 2006)

Penkert, Annette, *Arbeit oder Rente?*, (Göttingen, 1998)

Pensions Commission, *Implementing an Integrated Package of Pension Reforms: The Final Report of the Pensions Commission*, (Norwich, 2006)

Pensjonskommissjonen, *Moderniseret Folketrygd – Bærekraftig Pensjobn for Fremtida*, NOU (Norges Offentlige Udredninger), (Oslo, 2004:1).

Pers, Henrik, *Velfærdsstatens gennembrud i Danmark. Den politiske debat omkring folkepensionens gennemførelse*, (København, 1981)

Pestieau, Pierre (ed.), *Public Finance in a World of Transition, Proceedings of the 47th Congress of the International Institute of Public Finance*, (St. Petersburg, 1991),

Petersen, Jørn Henrik, *Den danske alderdomsforsørgelseslovgivnings udvikling vol. 1*, (Odense, 1985)

Petersen, Jørn Henrik, 'Altersversicherung und Altersversorgung. Ein dänischer Kommentar anläßlich des hundertjährigen jubiläums des deutschen invalitäts- und altersversicherugsgesetzes', *Deutsche Retenversicherung,* (1989)

Petersen, Jørn Henrik, 'The Danish 1891 Act on old age relief: A response to agrarian demand and pressure', *Journal of Social Policy,* 19 (1990)

Petersen, Jørn Henrik, *Den danske lovgivning om alderdomsforsørgelse II 1891-1933*, (Odense, 2006)

Petersen, Jørn Henrik & Petersen, Klaus, *Danish old age pensions with a focus on the Folkepension*, (unpublished manuscript)

Petersen, Jørn Henrik & Petersen, Klaus, 'Shake, Rattle and Roll! From Charity to Social Rights in the Danish Welfare State 1890-1933', Steven King & John Stewart (eds.), *Welfare Peripheries. The Development of Welfare States in Nineteenth and Twentieth Century Europe*, (Bern, 2007)

Petersen, Jørn Henrik & Petersen, Klaus, 'Folkepensionsreformen 1956', Jørn Henrik Petersen & Klaus Petersen (eds.), *13 reformer af den danske velfærdsstat,* (Odense, 2005)

Petersen, Klaus, 'Om formuleringen af velfærdsstaten som et politisk projekt. Et bidrag til den moderne velfærdsstats historie', *Arbejderhistorie*, 4 (1996)

Petersen, Klaus, *Legitimität und Krise. Die politische Geschichte des dänischen Wohlfahrtsstaates 1945-1973*, (Berlin, 1998)

Petersen, Klaus, 'Velfærdsstaten i dansk politisk retorik.' *Tidsskrift for velferdsforskning*, 4 (2001)

Petersen, Klaus, 'Fordelingspolitik, samfundsøkonomi og spørgsmålet om tillægspension 1963-1990', *Historisk Tidsskrift*, (2002)

Petersen, Klaus, 'Efterløn', Jørn Henrik Petersen & Klaus Petersen (eds.), *13 reformer af den danske velfærdsstat,* (Odense, 2005)

Petersen, Klaus, ' Constructing Nordic Welfare? Nordic Social Political Cooperation 1919-1955', Niels Finn Christiansen ea. (eds.), *The Nordic Model of Welfare. A Historical Reappraisal*, (Copenhagen, 2006)

Petersen, Klaus & Åmark, Klas, 'Old Age Pensions in the Nordic Countries, 1880-2000', Niels Finn Christiansen ea. (eds.), *The Nordic Model of Welfare. A Historical Reappraisal*, (København, 2006).

Petersson, Olof, *Svensk politik*, 6th edn, (Stockholm, 2005)

Petersson, Olof ea., *Demokratins grundlag. Demokratirådets rapport 2004*, (Stockholm, 2004)

Petersson, Olof ea., *Demokrati utan partier? Demokratirådets rapport 2000*, (Stockholm, 2000)

Pettersson, Thomas; Petersson Thomas och Westerberg, Anna, *Generationsanalyser – omfördelning mellan generationer i en växande välfärdsstat.* Expertgruppen för Studier i Samhällsekonomi (ESS), 6, (Stockholm, 2006)

Peyer, Károly, 'Az öregségi és rokkantsági biztosítás', *Szakszervezeti Mozgalom*, VII, (Budapest [1929])

Pierre, Jon, *Partikongresser och regeringspolitik. En studie av den socialdemokratiska partikongressens beslutsfattande och inflytande, 1948-1978*, (Lund 1986)

Pierson, Paul, *Dismantling the welfare state? Reagan, Thatcher and the Politics of Retrenchment*, (Cambridge, 1994)

Pierson, Paul, 'The New Politics of the Welfare State', *World Politics*, 2 (1996)

Pierson, Paul 'Increasing returns, path dependence, and the study of politics'. *American Political Science Review*, 94:2 (2000)

Pierson, Paul, 'Coping with Permanent Austerity. Welfare Restructuring in Affluent Democracies', Paul Pierson (ed.), *The New Politics of the Welfare State*, (New York, 2001)

Ponds, Eduard H.M. & van Riel, Bart, 'Sharing Risk: The Netherlands' New Approach to Pensions', *Issues in Brief*, 7-5 (2007)

Posner, Richard A., *Law, Pragmatism and Democracy*, (Cambridge, 2003)

Preller, Ludwig, 'Unsere Forderung auf Soziale Sicherung. Rede auf dem Parteitag der SPD in Dortmund am 26. September 1952', *SPD*, (1952)

Preller, Ludwig & Lünendonk, Heinrich, 'Das englische Sicherungssystem und Deutschland. Ein Briefwechsel', *Sozialer Fortschritt*, 2 (1953)

Rasmussen, Hanne & Rüdiger, Mogens, *Danmark efter 1945*, (København, 1990)

Recker, Marie Luise, *Nationalsozialistische Sozialpolitik im Zweiten Weltkrieg*, (München, 1985)

Remsperger, Hermann & Stöß, Elmar, 'Spar- und Anlageverhalten in Deutschland: Trends und Perspektiven', *Deutsche Bundesbank. Auszüge aus Presseartikeln*, 44 (19th October, 2005)

Report of the Committee on Pensions for Unmarried Women, (CMD 5991, 1939)

Rieger, Elmar & Liebfried, Stephan, *Limits to Globalization*, (Cambridge, 2003)

Ritter, Gerhard A., *Sozialversicherung in Deutschland und England – Entstehung und Grundzüge im Vergleich*, (München, 1983)

Rodgers, Daniel T., *Atlantic Crossings. Social Politics in a Progressive Age*, (Cambridge, 1998)

Roebroek, Joop & Nelissen, Jan H. M., 'Die 'heimliche Revolution'. Struktur, Entwicklung und Zukunft des holländischen Rentensystems', Opielka, Michael (ed.), *Grundrente in Deutschland, Wiesbaden*, (2004)

Saglie, Jo & Heidar, Knut, 'Democracy within Norwegian Parties. Complacency or Pressure for Change?', *Party Politics*, 4 (2004)

Schelling, Thomas C., *Choice and Consequence*, (Cambridge, 1984)

Schieber, Sylvester J. & Shoven, John B., 'The Consequences of Population Aging for Private Pension Fund Saving and Asset Markets', Michael D. Hurd & Naohiro Yashiro (eds.), *The Economic Effects of Aging in the United States and Japan*, (Chicago/London, 1997)

Schludi, Martin, 'Chances and Limitations of 'Benchmarking' in the Reform of Welfare State Structures – the Case of Pension Policy', Paper presented at the Amsterdam Instituut voor Arbeidsstudies, (Amsterdam, 8th May 2003)

Schmähl, Winfried, *Systemänderung in der Altersvorsorge – Von der einkommensabhängigen Altersrente zur Staatsbürger-Grundrente*, (Opladen, 1974)

Schmähl, Winfried, 'Übergang zu Staatsbürger-Grundrenten. Ein Beitrag zur Deregulierung der Alterssicherung?', Theo Thiemeyer (ed.), *Regulierung und Deregulierung im Bereich der Sozialpolitik, (Schriften des Vereins für Socialpolitik, Band 177)*, (Berlin, 1988)

Schmähl, Winfried, 'Beitragsfinanzierte Mindestsicherung im Alter', *Hamburger Jahrbuch für Wirtschafts- und Gesellschaftspolitik*, 35 (1990)

Schmähl, Winfried, 'Reformen der Rentenversicherung: Gründe, Strategien und Wirkungen – Das Beispiel der 'Rentenreform 1992'', Bernhard Gahlen ea. (eds.), *Theorie und Politik der Sozialversicherung*, (Tübingen, 1990)
Schmähl, Winfried, Alterssicherung in der DDR und ihre Umgestaltung im Zuge des deutschen Einigungsprozesses – Einige verteilungspolitische Aspekte –', Gerhard Kleinhenz (ed.), *Sozialpolitik im vereinten Deutschland I,(Schriften des Vereins für Socialpolitik, Neue Folge, Bd. 208/I)*, (Berlin, 1991)
Schmähl, Winfried, 'Vermeidung von Armut im Alter durch eine obligatorische beitragsfinanzierte Mindestversicherung – Leopold Krugs Plan einer 'Armen-assekuranz' von 1810', *Jahrbücher für Nationalökonomie und Statistik*, 209 (1992)
Schmähl, Winfried, 'Transformation and Integration of Public Pension Schemes – Lessons from the Process of the German Unification', *Public Finance*, 47 (1992)
Schmähl, Winfried, 'Proposals for flat-rate public pensions in the German debate', Jos Berghman, Bea Cantillon (eds.), *The European Face of Social Security*, (Aldershot, 1993)
Schmähl, Winfried, 'The 1992 Reform of Public Pensions in Germany: Main Elements and some Effects', *Journal of European Social Policy*, 3 (1993)
Schmähl, Winfried (ed.), *Mindestsicherung im Alter*, (Frankfurt/Main, New York, 1993)
Schmähl, Winfried, 'Avoiding Poverty in Old Age by an Obligatory Contribution-Financed Minimum Insurance – Leopold Krug's 'Poor Man's Insurance' of 1810 in the Light of Present Day Discussions,' Jürgen Backhaus (ed.), *Essays on Social Security and Taxation*, (Marburg, 1997)
Schmähl, Winfried, 'Sicherung bei Alter, Invalidität und für Hinterbliebene', Bundesministerium für Arbeit und Sozialordnung und Bundesarchiv (eds.), *Geschichte der Sozialpolitik in Deutschland seit 1945. Band 2/1: 1945-1949 Die Zeit der Besatzungszonen – Sozialpolitik zwischen Kriegsende und der Gründung zweier deutscher Staaten,* (Baden-Baden, 2001)
Schmähl, Winfried, 'Umlagefinanzierte Rentenversicherung in Deutschland, Optionen und Konzepte sowie politische Entscheidungen als Einstieg in einen grundlegenden Transformationsprozeß', Schmähl, Winfried & Ulrich, Volker (eds.), *Soziale Sicherungssysteme und demographische Herausforderungen*, (Tübingen, 2001)
Schmähl, Winfried, 'Übergang zu einem Grundrentensystem: Vom radikalen Systemwechsel zur schleichenden Systemtransformation', Opielka, Michael (ed.), *Grundrente in Deutschland, Wiesbaden*, (2004)
Schmähl, Winfried, 'Sicherung bei Alter, Invalidität und für Hinterbliebene', Bundesministerium für Gesundheit und Soziale Sicherung und Bundesarchiv

(eds.), *Geschichte der Sozialpolitik in Deutschland seit 1945. Band 7: 1982-1989 Bundesrepublik Deutschland – Finanzielle Konsolidierung und institutionelle Reform*, (Baden-Baden, 2005)

Schmähl, Winfried, 'Sicherung bei Alter, Invalidität und für Hinterbliebene', Bundesministerium für Arbeit und Soziales und Bundesarchiv (eds.), *Geschichte der Sozialpolitik in Deutschland seit 1945. Band 3: 1949-1957 Bundesrepublik Deutschland – Bewältigung der Kriegsfolgen, Rückkehr zur sozialpolitischen Normalität*, (Baden-Baden, 2005)

Schmähl, Winfried, 'Sicherung bei Alter, Invalidität und für Hinterbliebene', Bundesministerium für Arbeit und Soziales und Bundesarchiv (eds.), *Geschichte der Sozialpolitik in Deutschland seit 1945. Band 5: 1966-1974 Bundesrepublik Deutschland – Eine Zeit vielfältigen Aufbruchs*, (Baden-Baden, 2006)

Schmähl, Winfried, 'Dismantling an Earnings-Related Social Pension Scheme: Germany's New Pension Policy', *Journal of Social Policy*, 36:2 (2007)

Schmähl, Winfried, 'Die Einführung der Dynamischen Rente im Jahr 1957: Gründe, Ziele und Maßnahmen – zugleich Versuch einer Bilanz nach 50 Jahren', Deutsche Rentenversicherung Bund (ed.), *Die gesetzliche Rente in Deutschland – 50 Jahre Sicherheit durch Anpassungen, DRV-Schriften, Bd. 73*, (Bad Homburg, 2007)

Schmähl, Winfried & Oelschläger, Angelika, 'Abgabenfreie Entgeltumwandlung in sozial- und verteilungspolitischer Perspektive', (Berlin, 2007)

Schuman, Howard & Presser, Stanley, 'Public opinion and public ignorance: The fine line between attitudes and nonattitudes', *American Journal of Sociology*, 85:5 (1980)

Schumpeter, Joseph A., *Capitalism, socialism and democracy*, (New York, 1996 [1942])

Shapiro, Ian, *The State of Democratic Theory*, (Princeton & New York, 2003)

'Situation analysis to chapter 1', *the National Strategy Report on Social Protection and Social Inclusion*, (2006-2008)

Sjöblom, Gunnar, *Party Strategies in a Multiparty System*, (Lund, 1968)

Skocpol, Theda, *Protecting Soldiers and Mothers: the Political Origins of Social Policy in the United States*, (Cambridge,1992)

Smith, Tom W., 'Nonattitudes: A review and evaluation', Charles F. Turner & Elizabeth Martin (eds.): *Surveying subjective phenomena*, (New York, 1984)

Social Insurance and Allied Services, Command 6404, (1942)

Steiger, Joseph & Nussbaum, Hans, 'Pensionskassen in Unterdeckung – die wichtigsten Ergebnisse der Erhebung BSV 2005', *Soziale Sicherheit (CHSS)*, 1, (2006)

Steincke, Karl Kristian, *Fremtidens Forsørgelsesvæsen i Danmark*, (København, 1920)
Steinmo, Sven, *Taxation and Democracy. Swedish, British and American Approaches to Financing the Modern Welfare State*, (New Haven, 1991)
Streeck, Wolfgang & Thelen, Kathleen, 'Introduction: Institutional Change in Advanced Political Economies', Wolfang Streeck & Kathleen Thelen (eds.), *Beyond Continuity*, (Oxford, 2005)
Stråth, Bo, *Mellan två fonder. LO och den svenska modellen*, (Stockholm, 1998)
Svensson, Torsten, *Socialdemokratins dominans. En studie av svenska socialdemokratins partistrategi*, (Uppsala, 1994)
Swank, Duane, *Global Capital, Political Institutions and Policy Change in Developed Welfare States*, (Cambridge, 2002)
Szabó, Sándorné, *A társadalombiztosítási nyugdíjrendszer története Magyarországon. II/B Rész. Változások, viták és nyugdíjrendszerek 1945 után*, (manuscript) (2000)
Szalai, Júlia, 'A társadalombiztosítás érdekviszonyairól. Történeti vázlat a hazai társadalombiztosítás funkcióinak változásairól,' *Szociológiai Szemle*, 2 (1992)
Szikra, Dorottya, 'The Thorny Path to Implementation. Bismarckian Social Insurance in Hungary in the late 19th Century', *European Journal of Social Security*, 6:3 (2004)
Szikra, Dorottya, 'Family and Child Support in a Postcommunist Society: Origins of the Mixed Hungarian Welfare Capitalism,' Cain, Michael, Gelazis, Nida & Inglot, Tomasz: *Fighting Poverty and Reforming Social Security. What Can Post-Soviet States Learn from the New Democracies of Central Europe?*, (Washington, 2006)
Tennstedt, Florian & Winter, Heidi, 'Quellensammlung zur Geschichte der deutschen Sozialpolitik 1867 bis 1914', Born, Karl Erich ea. (eds.), *Grundfragen staatlicher Sozialpolitik*, 1 (Stuttgart, Jena, New York, 1994)
Teorell, Jan, *Demokrati eller fåtalsvälde? Om beslutsfattande i partiorganisationer*, (Uppsala, 1998)
Thane, Pat, 'What Difference did the Vote Make?', Amanda Vickery (ed.) *Women, Privilege and Power. British Politics, 1750 to the Present*, (Stanford, 2001)
Thane, Pat, *Old Age in English History*, (Oxford, 2000)
Thane, Pat, 'The British Imperial State and the Construction of National Identities', Billie Melman ed. *Borderlines. Gender and Identities in War and Peace, 1870-1930*, (London, 1998)
Thane, Pat, 'The debate on the declining birth-rate in Britain: the 'menace' of an ageing population, 1920s-1950s', *Continuity and Change*, 5:2 (1990)

Thane, Pat, 'Non-Contributory versus insurance Pensions 1878-1908', Thane, Pat (ed.), *The Origins of British Social Policy*, (London, 1978)

Therborn, Göran, 'Swedish Social Democracy and the Transition from Industrial to Postindustrial Politics', Frances Fox Piven (ed.), *Labor Parties in Postindustrial Societies*, (Cambridge UK, 1991)

Titmuss, Richard, *'Essays on the Welfare State'*, 1st edn., (London, 1958)

Tomka, Béla, 'The Politics of Institutionalized Volatility. Lessons from East Central European Welfare Reforms', Cain, Michael, Gelazis, Nida & Inglot, Tomasz: *Fighting Poverty and Reforming Social Security. What Can Post-Soviet States Learn from the New Democracies of Central Europe?*, (Washington, 2006)

Tomka, Béla, *Welfare East and West. Hungarian Social Security in an International Comparison 1918-1990,* (Berlin, 2004)

Trovik, Tørres & Vikøren, Birger, 'Anvendte analyser i aksjemarkedet: Hvilke verktøy har vi?' *Norsk Økonomisk Tidsskrift*, 117, (2003)

UK Pensions Commission, *A New Pension Settlement for the Twenty-First Century. The Second Report of the Pensions Commission*, (London, 2005)

UK Pensions Commission, *Pensions: Challenges and Choices. The First Report of the Pensions Commission*, (London, 2004)

UK Department of Work and Pensions, *Pensions Report shows 'historical divide' faced by women*, Press Release, (3rd November, 2005)

United Nations, *World Population in 2300*, (New York, 2004)

Valdés-Prieto, Salvador, 'The Financial Stability of Notional Account Pensions', *Scandinavian Journal of Economics*, 3 (2000)

van Kersbergen, Kees, 'The Declining Resistance of Welfare States to Change', Stein Kuhnle (ed.), *The Survival of the European Welfare State*, (London, 2000)

Velfærdskommissionen, *Fremtidens velfærd kommer ikke af sig selv, Analyserapport*, (København, 2004).

Velfærdskommissionen, *Fremtidens velfærd – vores valg, analyserapport*, (København, 2006).

Vidlund, Mika, *Old-Age Pension Reforms in the EU-15 Countries at a Time of Retrenchment. Finnish Centre for Pensions,* Working Paper 2006:1, (Helsinki, 2006)

Wagner, Gert, 'Bedarfs- oder beitragsorientierte Grundsicherung in der Rentenversicherung?', Klanberg, Frank & Prinz, Aloys (eds.), *Perspektiven sozialer Mindestsicherung*, (Berlin, 1988)

Weaver, R. Kent, 'The Politics of Public Pension Reform', *Working Paper/CRR*, 6 (2003)

Weaver, R. Kent, 'The Politics of Blame Avoidance', *Journal of Public Policy*, 6 (1986)
Weaver, R. Kent & Rockman, Bert A., 'When and How Do Institutions Matter?', R. Kent Weaver & Bert A. Rockman (eds.), *Do Institutions Matter?*, (Washington DC, 1991)
Wechselmann, Sigurd., *The Danish National Insurance Act*, (København, 1936)
Werding, Martin, Hofmann, Herbert & Reinhard, Hans-Joachim, *Das Rentenmodell der katholischen Verbände*, (München, 2007)
Wilensky, Harold, *Rich Democracies*, (Berkeley, 2002)
Wilensky, Harold, *The Welfare State and Equality*, (Berkeley, 1975)
Wilensky, Harold & Lebeaux, Charles N., *Industrial Society and Social Welfare*, (New York, 1965)
Williamson, John B. & Williams, Matthew, 'The Notional Defined Contribution Model. An Assessment of the Strengths and Limitations of a New Approach to the Provision of Old Age Security', *Working Paper/CRR*, (2003)
World Bank. *Averting the old age crisis*, (Oxford, 1994)
Yoo, Kwang-Yeol & de Serres, Alain, 'Tax Treatment of Private Pension Savings in OECD Countries', *OECD Economic Studies*, 39 (2004)
Zaller, John 'The myth of massive media impact revived: new support for a discredited idea', Diana C. Mutz, Paul M. Sniderman & Richard A. Brody (eds.), *Political persuasion and attitude change*, (Ann Arbor, 1996)
Åmark, Klas, 'Inkomsttryghet i Norge och Sverige. Klass, arbetarrörelse och välfärdspolitik 1930-1970' *Arkiv för studier i arbetarrörelsens historia*, 77-78 (1999)

Notes on Contributors

Torben M. Andersen is a professor at the School of Economics and Management, University of Aarhus. Main research interests: The economics of the welfare state, labour economics, public economics and business cycle theory. Recent publications include ′Increasing longevity and social security reforms – a legislative procedure approach′ in *Journal of Public Economics* (forthcoming) and ′The Scandinavian model – prospects and challenges′ in *International Tax and Public Finance* (Special Issue) 2008, 15: 45-66. Current research includes projects on the Scandinavian welfare model, globalization, and labour market policy as well as ageing and fiscal sustainability.

Karl Hinrichs is a professor of political science at the Centre for Social Policy Research, University of Bremen. Main research interests: Old age pensions and pension reform, labour market policy, comparative social policy. Recent publications include ′Forming European Pension Systems for Active Ageing′ in *International Social Science Journal* No. 190, 2008, 585-599 (with Paula Aleksandrowicz) and ′Forming Labour Market Policy in Germany′ in *Benefits. The Journal of Poverty and Social Justice* 15, 2007, No. 3: 221-231. His current research projects focus on pension reforms in Europe and the interplay between pension systems and labour market flexibility.

Urban Lundberg is a senior researcher at the Institute for Futures Studies, Stockholm. He writes on welfare state development, individual rights, and the Scandinavian labour movement generally, as well as on the politics of pensions. Recent publications include *Juvelen i kronan: Socialdemokraterna och den allmänna pensionen*, Hjalmarson & Högberg 2003 and ′Social Democracy Lost: The Social Democratic Party in Sweden and the Politics of Pension Reform′ in Carroll & Eriksson (eds.) *Welfare Politics Cross-Examined*, Aksel Atland 2005. Current research includes projects on *State versus Individual: Dimensions of Individual Rights and Citizenship in Sweden.*

Einar Overbye is a professor of political science at Oslo University College. Main research interests: Various aspects of social policy. Publications include: E. Overbye & P. Kemp (eds.), *Pensions: Challenges and reforms*, Ashgate 2004 and ′Extending social security in developing countries: A review of three main strategies', in *International Journal of Social Welfare* 2005 no 4, 305-14. Present research includes an eight-country study on the rescaling of European social assistance and old-age services, and studies on the growth of disability benefits.

Jørn Henrik Petersen is Professor of social policy at Centre for Welfare State Research, University of Southern Denmark. Main research interests: Social policy history, pensions in historical and contemporary perspective, normative foundations of the welfare state. Publications include: *Den danske lovgivning om alderdomsforsørgelse 1891-1933, Fra skøn til ret*, Syddansk Universitetsforlag, 2007, and (with Klaus Petersen) 'Shake, rattle and roll! From charity to social rights in the Danish welfare state 1890-1933', in Steven King & John Stewart (eds.), *Welfare Peripheries*, Peter Lang 2007. Current research includes a project (with Klaus Petersen) on The History of Danish Social Policy (2008-2014).

Klaus Petersen is Professor of Welfare State History at Centre for Welfare State Research, University of Southern Denmark. Main research interests: The historical development of the Danish and Nordic Welfare State, the history of the Danish labour movement, Americanisation, and transnational history. Publications include: Niels Finn Christiansen, Klaus Petersen ea. (eds.), *The Nordic Model of Welfare. A historical Re-Appraisal*, Copenhagen 2006; Niels Finn Christiansen & Klaus Petersen, 'The Dynamics of Social Solidarity: The Danish Welfare State, 1900-2000', in *Scandinavian Journal of History*, Vol. 26, No. 3, 2001, s. 177-196. Current research: Participation in the Nordic Centre of Excellence Nordwel (see: *http://blogs.helsinki.fi/nord-wel/*) and a project (with Jørn Henrik Petersen) on The History of Danish Social Policy (2008-2014).

Winfried Schmähl is a professor at the Centre for Social Policy Research, University of Bremen. Main research interests: Old age pensions in a historical and contemporary perspective, health policy, and welfare state financing. Recent publications include 'Ökonomische Grundlagen sozialer Sicherung', in B. Baron von Maydell, F. Ruland; U. Becker (eds.), *Sozialrechtshandbuch*, Nomos-Verlag 2008, 148-195 and 'Sicherung bei Alter, Invalidität und für Hinterbliebene', in Gerhard Ritter (eds.), *Geschichte der Sozialpolitik in Deutschland seit 1945*. Vol. 11: 1989-1994, Nomos-Verlag 2007, 541-648. Current research includes a project on income security in old age in Germany during the Kohl Era (1982-1994).

Dorottya Szikra is an associate professor at the Institute of Sociology, Eötvös University, Budapest. Main research interest: Social work, social policy, gender and welfare state, welfare state history. Publications include 'Tradition Matters: Child Care Policy in Pre- and Post-Socialist Hungary', in K. Hagemann e.a (eds.), *Child Care and Primary Education in Post-War Europe*, Berghahn Books 2008 (forthcoming) and 'Social Policy and Anti-Semitic Exclusion before and during World War II in Hungary. The Case of the Productive Social Policy', in Gisella Hauss e.a. (eds.). *The Dual Mandate. Social Work between Serving the State and Serving the Client*, Barbara Budrich Publishers 2008 (forthcoming). Current research includes the history of social work, comparative welfare state history.

Pat Thane is Leverhulme Professor of Contemporary British History of the Institute for Historical Research in London. Main research interests: Gender and women studies, social and economic policy, and history of the labour party. Publications include: (ed.) *The Long History of Old Age*, Thames & Hudson 2005 and *Old Age in English History: Past Experiences, Present Issues*, Oxford University Press 2000. Current research includes a study of unmarried motherhood in England, 1918 to the present.

Peter Lang · Internationaler Verlag der Wissenschaften

Kenneth Harttgen

Empirical Analysis of Determinants, Distribution and Dynamics of Poverty

Frankfurt am Main, Berlin, Bern, Bruxelles, New York, Oxford, Wien, 2007.
XX, 184 pp., num. fig. and tab.
Göttingen Studies in Development Economics.
Edited by Hermann Sautter and Stephan Klasen. Vol. 19
ISBN 978-3-631-57398-3 · pb. € 41.10*

Poverty and inequality persist in many dimensions in the developing world. In order to understand the determinants of poverty and its distribution between and within countries, it is necessary to know its dimensions and the channels through which poverty and inequality affect human well-being. This book analyzes the spatial disparities of the outcomes and determinants of poverty, the interdependencies of dimensions of poverty, the distribution of progress in human development over the population and the dynamics of poverty risk over time. The study takes into account the global spread of poverty. Based on cross-country comparisons of countries from Africa, Latin America, and South Asia, this study does not only consider on average outcomes and determinants of different indicators of human well-being, but also examines their distribution between and within countries.

Contents: A Regional Puzzle of Child Mortality and Undernutrition · The Impact of HIV on Childrens' Welfare · Measuring Pro Poor Growth in Non-Income Dimensions · Estimating Vulnerability to Covariate and Idiosyncratic Shocks

Frankfurt am Main · Berlin · Bern · Bruxelles · New York · Oxford · Wien
Distribution: Verlag Peter Lang AG
Moosstr. 1, CH-2542 Pieterlen
Telefax 00 41 (0) 32 / 376 17 27

*The €-price includes German tax rate
Prices are subject to change without notice

Homepage http://www.peterlang.de

www.ingramcontent.com/pod-product-compliance
Ingram Content Group UK Ltd.
Pitfield, Milton Keynes, MK11 3LW, UK
UKHW021014120926
8556IPUK00040B/1133

9 783631 581919